CW00417874

1 MONTH OF
FREE
READING

at

www.ForgottenBooks.com

By purchasing this book you are eligible for one month membership to ForgottenBooks.com, giving you unlimited access to our entire collection of over 1,000,000 titles via our web site and mobile apps.

To claim your free month visit:
www.forgottenbooks.com/free49173

ISBN 978-1-5282-5490-8
PIBN 10049173

EUTHANASY;

OR

HAPPY TALK

TOWARDS THE END OF LIFE.

By WILLIAM MOUNTFORD,

AUTHOR OF "MARTYRIA," "CHRISTIANITY THE DELIVERANCE OF THE
SOUL AND ITS LIFE," &c., &c.

SECOND EDITION, WITH ADDITIONS.

BOSTON:
WM. CROSBY AND H. P. NICHOLS,
111 WASHINGTON STREET.
1850.

GIFT

MAY 1 5 1914

CAMBRIDGE:

STEREOTYPED AND PRINTED BY

METCALF AND COMPANY,

PRINTERS TO THE UNIVERSITY.

PREFACE.

THIS is not meant to be a work for the conversion of persons who do not believe in a world to come, but rather it is intended to originate in the reader that atmosphere of thought in which faith can live.

There are pious men who find their faith failing them in some strange way, which they cannot account for. They are serious persons; they live honorably and righteously; they keep all the commandments; their path is that of the just; and yet somehow to their eyes it shines less and less, and evermore it gets darker and darker, as though unto perfect night.

There are Christians who worship ouᵗ
of the same book of prayers which their
fathers used; who keep the same solemn
seasons of humiliation and joy which they
wondered at as children; and who repeat
the same creeds which they learned in their
youth. And yet, in the anguish of their,
souls, they say every Sabbath, more and
more bitterly, " Lord, I believe more and
more feebly; help thou mine unbelief."

There are men who are now of little
faith, and yet who once believed themselves to be in a state of grace. They sing
the same hymns they used to, but not with
their old fervor. Their seasons of religious
joy are rarer and shorter than they used
to be. And their belief in immortality is
becoming only a fitful persuasion, a Sunday feeling, a transient mood.

The world is another world than what
these persons first learned to be pious in.

There are men who cannot read a scientific work, or peruse history as it is commonly written, or acquaint themselves with modern literature in some of its more popular volumes, or feel what the spirit of the age is, without being conscious of a weakening of their faith.

Certainly there are some few men as pure in heart as most saints have been, who long to see, and yet cannot see, in the world that now is, any signs of there being a world which is to come. They would be willing to sell all that they have and give to the poor, if they could be told of a way, by following which they could find themselves within hearing of Christ, and persuaded of there being treasure possible for them in heaven.

This present age is an epoch in the Christian Church; — very important, and perhaps what may yet be very sad.

The purpose of this book is to aid persons to discern the religiousness of life, and to suggest to them that Christian faith cannot only live, but strengthen, in the world as it now is, though it is becoming light with science, and is altered in many a domain of thought, and has sounding in it voices which ought to be religious, but which unfortunately are not.

CONTENTS.

—◆—

CHAPTER I.

On Old Age — The State of Religion. — On Affliction   PAGE 1

CHAPTER II.

Trust in the Mysteriousness of Life   19

CHAPTER III.

The Hopefulness of Spring-time. — The Death of Birds
and Flowers. — On Prayer. — The Hope of Immortality   28

CHAPTER IV.

The Dread of becoming afraid of Death. — Death as Natural as Life   37

CHAPTER V.

On Faith in a Future Life, and how to increase it   .   47

CHAPTER VI.

On Resignation   57

CHAPTER VII.

A Dream 62

CHAPTER VIII.

On living in the Thought of Mortality. —Death a New
    Birth 70

CHAPTER IX.

On some Unfinished Works of Genius . . . 77

CHAPTER X.

On Despondency 90

CHAPTER XI.

The Soul consciously Immortal 95

CHAPTER XII.

Recollections and Thoughts on a Birthday . . . 101

CHAPTER XIII.

Death to be waited for in Faith 118

CHAPTER XIV.

On Remembrances of Youth, Pain, Pleasure, and Depart-
    ed Friends. — On Old Age. — Anticipations of Heaven.
    — Listening to the Past 122

CHAPTER XV.

Misfortune a Test of Character. — Uses of Old Age . 135

CHAPTER XVI.

A Sermon 143

CHAPTER XVII.

On Poverty. — Posthumous Influence. — Life after Death 164

CHAPTER XVIII.

On Knowledge of Human Nature. — Shakspeare. — Everlastingness of Truth. — Heirship of the Past . . 176

CHAPTER XIX.

On Flowers and on Beauty. — York Minster. — God in
Nature. — The Witness of the Spirit. — The Feeling of
Infinity 195

CHAPTER XX.

The Swiftness of Time. — On Heaven. — The Vastness
of the Universe. — Knowledge proportioned to Duty. —
The Wisdom of Humility. — The Will of God. — On
George Herbert 209

CHAPTER XXI.

The Uncertainty of Life 226

CHAPTER XXII.

On the Feeling of Beauty 229

CHAPTER XXIII.

Plotinus. — George Fox. — Henry More. — The Song of
the Soul. — Gratitude to Great Authors . . . 240

CHAPTER XXIV.

Human Greatness. — Humility. — God in the Soul. — Nature and the Soul. — Faith in Christ. — Religious Melancholy 262

CHAPTER XXV.

The World full of Promise. — Man made for Happiness.
— On Sympathy with Others. — What Heaven will be 281

CHAPTER XXVI.

One Spirit in Men. — One Meaning of Heroic Lives. —
On Art. — On Civilized Life. — The Human Hand. —
The Present Life suggestive of the Next .   .   .   291

CHAPTER XXVII.

On Action. — The Way of Providence in Life   .   .   307

CHAPTER XXVIII.

On Creation. — The Law of Progression. — Man the Infinity of God's Purpose in the World   .   .   .   317

CHAPTER XXIX.

The End of Summer. — Perfect Love. — Hope of Immortality. — On Spiritual Longing   332

CHAPTER XXX.

Dying daily. — Changes of Feeling. — Old Age. — On
Affliction   342

CHAPTER XXXI.

Patience. — Readiness for Heaven. — Immortality   .   358

CHAPTER XXXII.

The Effects of Prayer. — How to grow in Faith. — En-
durance and Forgiveness. — Righteous Failures. — The
Good of Affliction. — On Sincerity. — On Troubles. —
On Music. — The Thought of God. — The Instinct of
Prayer. — The Wonder of this Present Life   .   .   365

CHAPTER XXXIII.

On Embalming. — Right Thoughts about the Dead. — On
Bodily Changes. — Spirit its own Evidence. — How the
Body lives. — On Burial 389

CHAPTER XXXIV.

On Epitaphs. — How some Men have wished to die . 398

CHAPTER XXXV.

The Last Vision of Tasso 408

CHAPTER XXXVI.

Nature in Autumn. — A City renewing its Population. —
Thoughts of Ancient Times. — Another Life in Justice
to this. — The Witness of the Spirit. — Faith in God.
— Expectation of Death 431

CHAPTER XXXVII.

On Nature and Man. — On Memory 449

CHAPTER XXXVIII.

Human Evanescence. — The Stars. — Mysteriousness of
Life. — God in Nature 463

CHAPTER XXXIX.

A Scene revisited. — A fine Day. — On Old Age . 475

CHAPTER XL.

On the Love of Life. — On Virtue and Vice . . 484

CHAPTER XLI.

Seven Conclusions from a Week of Sad Evenings . 491

CHAPTER XLII.

Thoughts while in Pain 494

CHAPTER XLIII.

The Manifold World. — On Fitness for Heaven. — The Recognition of Friends hereafter. — Kindred to the Blessed Great 501

EUTHANASY.

CHAPTER I.

A soul by force of sorrows high
Uplifted to the purest sky
Of undisturbed humanity. — WORDSWORTH.

There never lived a mortal, who bent
His appetite beyond his natural sphere,
But starved and died. — KEATS.

May you never
Regret those hours which make the mind, if they
Unmake the body; for the sooner we
Are fit to be all mind, the better. Blest
Is he whose heart is the home of the great dead,
And their great thoughts. — BAILEY.

MARHAM.

Now, Oliver, you are settled with me, to live with me as long as I live myself. And that is your side of the fireplace, and that is your chair. And a comfortable room this library is; is it not? There shall be a sofa brought into it, and every thing else that will be for your comfort shall be got. And here will we wait till our change come, for many, many pleasant hours, I

hope.   For me, Oliver, it is a happiness to see
you so resigned.   And to hear you talk does me
good.   But it is of little use my company can
be to you.   I am old, and I am older than my
years, I think.   I am not the man I was once.
Still, I am not declining into second childhood
yet, I hope.

AUBIN.

No, uncle, you are not, and never are to be, I
hope ; though, if you were, it would not be a
thing to be mourned for, dear uncle, would it ?
For the second childhood of a saint is the early
infancy of a happy immortality, as we believe.

MARHAM.

What you say does cheer me so, Oliver !
But, indeed, I am often distressed at being so
useless in my old age.

AUBIN.

Useless ! You are of great use, uncle Stephen, you really are. How are you useful ? By
being a man that is old. Your old age is a public good. It is, indeed. For out of all the boys
and girls, and young men and women of this
neighbourhood, probably not ten, and perhaps not
even one, will ever be as old as you. But something of the good of old age they may all get,
through sympathy with you. No child ever listens to your talk without having a good done it
that no schooling could do. When you are walk-

ing, no one ever opens a gate for you to pass through, and no one ever honors you with any kind of help, without being himself the better for what he does ; for fellow-feeling with you ripens his soul for him. At the longest, I cannot have long to live ; and I shall never be old. But through living with you, uncle, and loving you, I hope to understand, and feel, and make my own, those changes which come over the soul with length of life.

MARHAM.

When the powers of the body fail, the feelings do alter much ; and with me they grow melancholy, which, perhaps, they should not do. But they are sad experiences, when sight and hearing and motion fail.

AUBIN.

Not sad, uncle Stephen, but serious ; and not so serious as solemn. Is your eyesight dimmer ? Then the world is seen by you in a cathedral light. Is your hearing duller ? Then it is just as though you were always where loud voices and footsteps ought not to be heard. Is your temper not as merry as it was once ? Then it is more solemn ; so that round you the common atmosphere feels like that of the house of the Lord. Yes, for twilight and silence and solemnity, old age makes us like daily dwellers in the house of the Lord ; and a mortal sickness does

this, sometimes, as well as old age.   But it is our
own thoughts that have to supply the service,
and our own hearts that have to make the music
triumphant, or else like a dirge.   And the sermon is preached to us by conscience from some
text taken out of the book of our remembrance.
While to it all, Amen has to be said by ourselves ; and when it is said gladly, then there
is an echo to it in heaven, and joy among the
angels.

MARHAM.

You are so at home in religion, Oliver !   And
that is why your talk pleases me so much, I think.
For with most persons, it is as though they had
forced themselves to be religious.

AUBIN.

At present, in men's minds, religion is not as
spontaneous as poetry is ;   and, indeed, is not
genial at all.

MARHAM.

And in this room are books which are weary
reading to us, but which, a hundred years ago,
our forefathers wept over, and prayed upon, and
thanked God for.

AUBIN.

We cannot feel as they did, because we do
not think as they thought.   Once, men thought
themselves to be the only creatures in a state of
probation ;   and this little earth was fancied to be

almost the only spot, excepting hell, that was not heaven. From astronomy, we know this to have been an error. And many, very many things which our forefathers were sure of one way, in science and philosophy, we are sure of otherwise. And so, under these errors, what they said and wrote religiously is either lower than our feeling, or else beside it. But some time religion will be familiar to men again, although we have got among different circumstances from what our fathers worshipped. in ; for there is religion in all things, just as there is poetry, though as yet it is waiting to be discovered ; but when once it has been found, all persons will see it at last, and it will be natural to them. Immortality is not now believed in, commonly, in the manner it ought to be. The doctrine of it wants to be familiarized into feeling ; and especially, I think, there want to be developed such corroborations of the great truth as are latent in science, history, philosophy, and in the fresh experiences which, as human beings, we are always passing through. The Greek Gospels require to be made English, for common use ; and for daily, homely feeling, the great doctrine of immortality wants familiarizing.

MARHAM.

You are hinting at what would be as great as a new Reformation in the Church.

AUBIN.

And greater, I think.

MARHAM.

There is no chance of it, I am afraid.

AUBIN.

There was none of Luther, till he was born. Religion will be natural to men again ; and he that is merry will sing psalms yet. And even the soul is growing, perhaps, that is to bless the world this way.

MARHAM.

And it will be soon, we will hope, and with a welcome.

AUBIN.

That will not be ; for to bless the world implies being above it, and to be above the world is to have few or no friends in it. For the first of the earnest believers that are to be, we will wish some likely thing, and what they will want ; we will wish them courage to speak on, though it seem to be to the winds, and courage enough to think of dying in a garret at last, without being frightened.

MARHAM.

I must hope the world is better than you think it, Oliver. Though your experience of it has been very disheartening.

AUBIN.

Nay, dear uncle, I was not thinking of myself at all.

MARHAM.

But, Oliver, I have been thinking of you, and what you had to bear.

AUBIN.

And which I am the better for. Yes, when I remember what I was, I am sure of my misfortunes having been messengers to me from God; for they were so exactly suited to do for my character what it wanted.

MARHAM.

And perhaps the greatest grace that came to you from God was willingness to know those messengers.

AUBIN.

Poverty came to me, and she said, "I must dwell with thee." And while I held the door of my room half open, she was hideous and ragged, and her voice was hoarse. But when I said to her, "Thou art my sister," her face looked divincly thoughtful, and there was that in her voice which went to my heart, and she was ragged no longer, nor yet gay, but like the angels, whom God so clothes. And through looking into her eyes, my sight was cleared. And so I first saw the majesty of duty, and that beauty in virtue which is the reflection of the countenance of God. For, before this, my eyes could see only what coarse worth there is in medals, and stars, and crowns, and in such character as gets itself talked of and apparelled in purple and fine linen.

MARHAM.

O Oliver !

AUBIN.

I was ambitious, uncle, once ; very greatly so
I was.   And from my own knowledge, I know
that pride is a fearful peril.   I was a student, and
truth was my business ; but now it seems to me
that I must have loved it basely, and for the fame
of stamping it with my own name.

MARHAM.

Hardly so, Oliver.   I am sure you judge yourself not justly.   For the love of fame is not always lust of flattery, but something not unwise
nor unhealthy.   For fame is a great thing for a
man ; it is silence for him, when he wants to
speak ; it is a pulpit to preach from, more au-
thoritative than an archbishop's throne ; and it is
affectionate attention from a multitude of hearers.
Badly ambitious I do not think you could have
been.

AUBIN.

My ardor was too much of a worldly fever, as
I know by this ; that when, time after time, Disappointment stepped between me and my object,
he was like ice to my heart.   But now I can
embrace him as a friend ; and I do hold him as a
dear friend ; and I bless God for his having found
me.   Though latterly I have known him by another than the mournful name by which he is called
on earth.

MARHAM.

You have been afflicted, and it is a happy thing for you to feel that it has been good for you. As human creatures, we have all of us to suffer, and to have some of our dearest plans spoiled.

AUBIN.

And it is well; for if we could be half sufficient to ourselves, we should soon lose the secret sense of dependence upon God. We build our plans up about us, and so we shut out the sight of heaven, and very soon the thought of it, and we say to ourselves that we will be merry with the goods we shall have stored up with us. But some earthquake of Providence shakes our building, and overhead it is unroofed, and the walls of it give way. And then there is heaven to be seen again, and infinity is open round us, and the dews of the Divine grace can fall on us again, and again we feel ourselves at the mercy of God, to be spared from cold, and storms, and enemies. And so, among the ruins of our pride, we grow to be loving children of the Most High, instead of worldly creatures.

MARHAM.

And you have felt that. But now you will be able to tell me all your experiences; and you must, whenever they come into your mind.

AUBIN.

For some time I have wished to write a book

on the immortality of the soul, and if I had been well enough, I should have done it ; for I think on that subject I could write as not many have done. I have been without a friend in the world. And that is a state in which a man knows wheth- er he believes in God or not ; for if he does, his soul craves God, in such a way as that almost he is seen in the clouds, and felt in the air and in the coming of thoughts into the mind. I have known the want of food, and, one whole winter, the want of warm clothing ; and I have known what it is to need medical help, and not to have it, because unable to pay for it.

MARHAM.

Have you ?

AUBIN.

Yes, I have. And in such circumstances, I know that life looks quite another thing to what it does to a man at ease.

MARHAM.

Poor Oliver ! life must have looked stern to you, very stern.

AUBIN.

For a while it did, and then it grew sublime ; for I saw God in it all. And, besides, there is in the soul an instinct of her having been made for a foreordained end, of her having been cre- ated for a special purpose, which only she her- self can answer, and not any one other out of a hundred million other souls. So the more lonely I was, and the poorer, and the more the pain in my forehead grew like the pressure of a crown of thorns, and the more I was an exception among men, so much the more I was persuaded of having a destiny of my own, and a peculiar one. And I said to myself, " What I am to be, I can suffer for, and I will." So as my lot in life grew strange, I had a trembling joy in it for the sake of what I thought must spiritually come of it. But, dear uncle! those tears, — I cannot bear them. Besides, I am happy now. And now our souls, yours and mine, have found one another.

MARHAM.

But to have suffered as you have, and been alone ——

AUBIN.

Lonely I never was ; indeed I was not.

MARHAM.

For God was with you. And I do believe he was.

AUBIN.

And so were the souls of many saints, and heroes, and noble thinkers, — men of like sufferings with my own.

MARHAM.

True saints and true heroes. But now, Oliver, tell me, were you never tempted to forego your scruples, and enter ——

AUBIN.

No, uncle, not for a moment.

MARHAM.

If you had flattered a little, or been less nobly scrupulous, your genius would have been acknowledged and well paid very soon. No doubt you felt this ; and was not it ever a temptation ?

AUBIN.

No, uncle.

MARHAM.

My noble boy ! And you sat down so long to poor food, and scanty, perhaps.

AUBIN.

But I ate it, like the sacrament, in a high communion of soul. For sometimes I felt as though there stood about me Tasso, and others like him. And I thought of one who was so holy, that priests could not understand him, and who was therefore so poor and unfriended, that he had not where to lay his head ; I thought of Christ in the wilderness, hungry and alone.

MARHAM.

And in that way you held faithful to your convictions.

AUBIN.

Yes.

MARHAM.

And yet, — am I right, Oliver ? Surely I must be, for you are young still. And was not a home sometimes a hope with you ?

AUBIN.

And so a temptation ?   No, uncle.

MARHAM.

But with such prospects as I found you with, you must have been in dread of starvation, as not an unlikely thing for you some time.

AUBIN.

One while I had that. fear ; but I made an Ode to the Poor-house, and then I was not afraid of poverty any more.

MARHAM.

What do you mean ?

AUBIN.

And I was the better man, besides.   I mean, that I made up my mind to die in rags and want, and then I was not afraid of doing so.   And as soon as there was nothing in this world that could frighten me, at once, with ease of mind, goodness grew easier with me.

MARHAM.

Ease of mind !   But I think I can guess at what you mean. God became every thing to you, as the world grew nothing.

AUBIN.

But the world never did become nothing to me ; for always, even from the middle of a city, it felt great and wonderful about me ; but when no temporal good could come of it to me, then the eternal meaning of it entered my soul freshly

every day.   The more I felt the world was not
mine at all, and could not be, the more blessedly
I felt it was God's ; and so, another way, it was
mine again, gloriously.

MARHAM.

And so the world was yours through not being
yours, was it ?   Your experience was like St.
Paul's, — as having nothing, and possessing all
things.   Have you the Ode to the Poor-house
which you wrote ?   I should like to see it.

AUBIN.

I have not it, uncle.   You think the writing of
it a curious cure for poverty.

MARHAM.

But before writing it, your feeling of misery
must have been abating.

AUBIN.

Yes.   As soon as my poverty felt poetical, it
ceased to be only wretched.   But always I have
found, that any thing bad is most bearable by
knowing the worst of it, — by thinking, and feeling, and living it all over.

MARHAM.

. And so draining the cup of sorrow at a manly
draught.

AUBIN.

Many years ago, when my mother died, I was
in an agony of grief till I saw her body and held
her dead hand, and then I was calmed.   I sup-

pose the reason of it was this, that what we see with our eyes is seen at once to be finite ; and finite evil but serves by its endurance to quicken into intensity that presentiment of infinite good which has been made instinctive in us.

MARHAM.

To some persons, it is a satisfaction to know the worst, because it is never so bad as their fears ; and others, I think, like to know it, because they are uneasy at any thing that is uncertain ; and others like to know it for other reasons, perhaps.

AUBIN.

Perhaps so. But I would rather think that all these reasons have one source, and from it I would draw this truth, or, at least, some confirmation of it, that the inner is the more real and the intenser world. While we have only heard of misfortune, we only know it as though spiritually ; and the unrestrained grief of the spirit, like the spirit itself, partakes of the infinite. But as soon as with our bodily eyes we see an evil, we see that it is finite, measurable, little. And then against this littleness the soul measures her own almost infinite power of endurance. And from this comes that complacency, that almost joy in misfortune, which some sufferers have felt, when once they have learned the worst of it.

MARHAM.

O Oliver ! I am proud of what you are, but over what you have been as a sufferer I could cry ; and yet I think I am proud of that too, for you are my sister's son. Oliver, you are not well, you look ——

AUBIN.

Uncle, one thing I have to ask of you, and that is, that you will not for a while ask me any thing about my past life. I can think it over on my knees, and be thankful to God for it ; but your pitying it is too much for me. For I have not been as manful as you think, or else my courage was only just enough. For now that I am out of my troubles, I could cry for hours sometimes, though a month ago I could have said that I had not had a tear in my eyes for years.

MARHAM.

And now you are ill. O, very sorry I am that, — that ——

AUBIN.

That I should only have been helped out of my wretchedness just against my death. But better men than I will die in worse miseries than mine were.

MARHAM.

I do not think so, Oliver, and I should be very sorry to believe it. For I have never heard of another instance like yours in all my life. For

opportunity to help a good man and a man of genius is a treasure ——

AUBIN.

Which not many men are good enough to value. But this is a thing which it is better not to
say, even if quite true. And so I will not say it.
For the soul gets embittered with saying bitter
things. And then even good men may not find
one another out, as I ought to remember from
the way in which even you and I did not know
one another for so long, and never should have
done but for an accident, — no, a providential
event ; for so it was for me.

MARHAM.

And for me, too, Oliver. But you suffered so
strangely ! Why, O, why did not I know of it,
or guess it ? And why did I let my foolish prej-
udices, — foolish and worse ——

AUBIN.

No, dear uncle, uncle Stephen ; do not talk so.
But let our not knowing one another be among
the strange things of the world, and they are very
many. Why they are allowed, we cannot tell
always. But they are wisely allowed, no doubt.
Why, why is this ? But for any of us asking
so, there is no special answer vouchsafed. The
wheels of the universe do not stop for us to examine their mechanism ; for if they did, there
would be no progress ; because, at every moment,

2

the self-will of some creature or other is in collision with that Divine will which is the mainspring of creation.

MARHAM.

It does my heart good, and it does my soul good, to see you so happy, Oliver, and so at peace with the world, after having been so hardly used in it.

AUBIN.

It would be a shame if I were not so ; and the more I have suffered, the greater shame. Because, with a Christian, at the end of a grievous trial, and when the soreness of it is abating, there is a strange and sublime experience. There is the feeling of sorrow, and there is that of infinite goodness ; and the two blend into a consciousness like that of having been just about to be spoken to by God. And this is not a deceptive feeling, though God is silent towards us all our lives ; for with him a thousand years are as one day ; and when he will justify himself to us, it will not be our fleshly impatience which he will address, but the calm estate of spirits everlasting like himself.

CHÀPTER II.

The very spirits of a man prey upon the daily portion of bread and flesh; and every meal is a rescue from one death, and lays up for another; and the clock strikes, and reckons on our portion of eternity: we form our words with the breath of our nostrils, — we have the less to live upon for every word we speak. — JEREMY TAYLOR.

All death in nature is birth, and in death appears visibly the advancement of life. There is no killing principle in nature, for nature throughout is life; it is not death which kills, but the higher life, which, concealed behind the other, begins to develop itself. Death and birth are but the struggle of life with itself to attain a higher form. — J. G. FICHTE.

MARHAM.

OUT of our hearts, and out of our reasons, many things are said to us about our immortality; but they would not be listened to believingly, if it were not for our Christian courage. Christ said, that because he lives we shall live also. This is what emboldens our faith.

AUBIN.

Twice did Christ enter this world, and twice did he depart from it, and so the other world and this were made to feel the nigher.

MARHAM.

Twice, did you say, that Jesus came into this life?

AUBIN.

Once through his mother's womb and his mother's cares, and once from withinside the grave of the Arimathean. To and fro, between this and the other world, Christ passed. So that to us believers this earth feels like the fore-court of heaven, and death like the door into eternity.

MARHAM.

At that door, threescore years and ten make a loud knocking for me ; and old age is like an anxious waiting for the door to open. And awful waiting it would be, were it not for Christ inside. But for him, it would be dreadful leaving this known for the unknown world.

AUBIN.

This known world, you say. But now, uncle, is it known ? No, it is not. It feels known, because we feel foolishly. For every grain of sand is a mystery ; so is every daisy in summer, and so is every snow-flake in winter. Both upwards and downwards, and all round us, science and speculation pass into mystery at last.

MARHAM.

We will say, then, that this world is little known, and the other still less.

AUBIN.

Perhaps it is so.

MARHAM.

Why, Oliver, how can you say perhaps, as though you were not sure ?

AUBIN.

Nay, but, uncle, how can I be sure ?

MARHAM.

Very easily, I should think ; as you have lived thirty years in this world, and into the other have never had one glance.

AUBIN.

But, dear uncle, I think I may have had. For I am of two worlds, matter and spirit. With these gray eyes I have never known the world of spirit, but known it I have through certain feelings, very faintly, and yet plainly, as I think.

MARHAM.

But still, as you say, very faintly.

AUBIN.

And very little, too, is my knowledge of this world. It is not unlikely, I think, on my dying, that the other world will feel as familiar to me as this does. For body and breathing, table, chair, and house, are unfelt, and are nothing to me, while I am in thought ; so that when I am in spirit they will not be much missed, perhaps. And then there are states of mind which will be as common to me hereafter as here, and more so ; so that with them, at once, I shall be familiar. In prayer, the furniture of my room is forgotten, and praying hereafter in our Father's house, the fresh splendor of it will be forgotten. And I shall feel and be what I am now at times, but more purely, — a worshipper only. And other states of mind there will be, in which, at once, I shall feel as native to the world of spirits as I do to this world of earth.

MARHAM.

Still, death is a leaving of one world for another.

AUBIN.

So it is. And life is an outliving of world after world. Where is now what the world was to you at ten years old ? It is gone, gone for ever. And where is the world which you saw and felt, and which you hoped in, at twenty ? You are not in it now, and you never will be again, —never again.

MARHAM.

To my eyes it is the same world.

AUBIN.

But it is a very different world to your judgment and to your imagination, and to your heart. While sight is but one of our faculties, and in this instance the least sufficient one. For though the world looks to be in the same place which it was in fifty years ago, yet it is widely away from it, having gone along with the sun towards the constellation Hercules.

MARHAM.

O the depth of the wisdom of God, and his ways past finding out !

AUBIN.

Yes, dear uncle. And that is the right mood for waiting death in. I mean, a trustful consciousness of the mystery of the universe.

MARHAM.

The world of my boyhood, and that of my youth, and this of my old age, have been quite different from one another, and would have felt quite distinct, only that it was by little and little that the first changed into the second, and the second into the third. A third world am I living in ? Then the fourth, which waits me, is in a quite natural course. But it will be more sudden than the others. One moment, the soul is in this life, and the next, in another.

AUBIN.

So it is. But very often the soul outgrows this world before the other world opens above it. And in a last long sickness, many a Christian soul grows more akin to the great family in heaven than it ever was to fellow-creatures in this earth. And with an old man, shorter and shorter are his walks round home, and the cunning of his hand grows less and less ; dimmer and dimmer grow his eyes, and more and more dull his ears, and less and less of this earth he becomes, till at last he is not of this earth at all.

MARHAM.

I was young, but now I am old. This change I have lived through, and my next great change will be death.

AUBIN.

From manhood of thirty to old age of eighty

seems a great change ; but in this present life, there is a change which is greater and more sudden, and it is at the time when a youth first makes out what it is to be a man, and, instead of a dreamer, he has suddenly to be a doer and a sufferer. Often let a youth know himself to be a man, and then he will not shrink much from the thought of being an old man and a dying man. For he has known and outlived the greatest vicissitude, when of a youth he became a man. Because the world to come is not stranger than the reality of this world is to a young man, sometimes ; and for him to feel the strangeness of it, and part with his hopes and old feelings, is not less painful, nay, is worse, than parting with the flesh. One way or another, we most of us have changes come over us that frighten us more than death, and at the first feeling of which we have every one of us said, perhaps, " Would God that I might die ! " These seasons it is well for us to remember and live over again. And we will do it. We shall have tears in our eyes the while, and a choking in our throats, perhaps. But our minds will be the better for such recollections, and our hearts will open the more earnestly into prayer. And when we feel how God was in our sorrows, we shall trust the more blessedly that he will be in our deaths.

MARHAM.

And so he will be, and blessedly so, we will hope. For we cannot die without him, any more than be born. And now that we must die, we will think of the times when we would have died if we could. And I will think of them to make me the more resigned when I remember that I am old ; for old age is only a slow dying.

AUBIN.

Growing old is like bodily existence refining away into spiritual life. True, the ripeness of the soul is hidden in the decay of the body; but so is many a ripe fruit in its husk.

MARHAM.

So strangely old age does alter us, Oliver.

AUBIN.

A man vain of his person may be dismayed by looking thoughtfully on the face of old age ; but, rightly looked at, there is to be read in every line of it the exhortation, " Be of good cheer." Only let us love God, and then all things of God's doing look lovely, and promise us good. To a good old man, his gray hair is a crown ; and it may be worn, and it ought to be, like what has been given as an earnest of the crown of immortality.

MARHAM.

Our hearts keep beating not by our wills, and our looks change by a will not our own, but one to be trusted in infinitely.

AUBIN.

A trustful heart never breaks ; it strengthens •
to the last.   And to the last we will trust.   God
is almighty ; then all things are his mightiness,
and all life is his will.   With us, spring and summer and autumn and winter. shall be the will of
God ; and the will of God shall be the wisdom of
the starry courses.   The vital nature of the air
about us shall be the will of God ; and it shall be
the will of God that we breathe without thinking.
And to us joys shall be the will of God, and so
shall pains and sorrows be.   Providence is in all
things, so that whatever we do not understand
shall be to us nothing to be frightened about, but
it shall be mystery and the will of God.   And so,
no less than birth, death shall be to us the will of
God ; and in it we will rejoice always, though
sometimes, perhaps, not without trembling.

MARHAM.

We neither live nor die to ourselves, and when
we die, we die unto the Lord.   This we will remember, Oliver, and rejoice in.

AUBIN.

Yes, uncle.   In joy and sorrow I will remember what I am ; that I am more than flesh and
blood, more than the weight of one hundred and
ten pounds of earth ; that I am a creature of God,
with the wisdom of God in my shape, and the
goodness of God in my senses, and the provi-

dence of God in my life, from hour to hour. Yes, and more than a creature of God I am. I am a child of God. Some share in the Divine nature I have, and a larger share I am destined to. A little while, and then I shall be immortal. And what I am to be soon, cannot I almost feel as though I were? Yes, I can. I will think more, then, of what I am to be, and less of what I am to be saved from.

MARHAM.

You mean ——

AUBIN.

Day by day I am watched over by the loving eye of God. What unchangeableness there is in that Divine eye I will think of, and not so much of what change there grows in my own looks. Night by night I will lie down and sleep in the thought of God, and in the thought, too, that my waking may be in the bosom of the Father; and some time it will be; so I trust.

CHAPTER III.

All that God owns, he constantly is healing,
Quietly, gently, softly, but most surely; —
He helps the lowliest herb, with wounded stalk,
To rise again. See! from the heavens fly down
All gentle powers to cure the blinded lamb!
Deep in the treasure-house of wealthy Nature,
A ready instinct wakes and moves
To clothe the naked sparrow in the nest,
Or trim the plumage of an aged raven; —
Yea, in the slow decaying of a rose,
God works as well as in the unfolding bud;
He works with gentleness unspeakable
In death itself; a thousand times more careful
Than even the mother, by her sick child watching.
                              LEOPOLD SCHEFER.

AUBIN.

I COULD wish to die on a day like this.

MARHAM.

Oliver, you surprise me.   You wish to die!

AUBIN.

No, dear uncle.   But when I do die, I hope it
will be on a day like this.

MARHAM.

Most others would think their feelings would
be best composed for death in autumn.   For
then all things are dying round us, or are in harmony with death, — flowers blackening to the
ground, leaves falling from the trees, nights length-

ening, and days less bright ; and in the air a mist, feeling like the presence of a pall. But why would you rather die in the spring ?

AUBIN.

On the first day of spring ? Because, at this time, the instinct of immortality feels strongest in me. Only a fortnight since, there was snow on the ground ; and it was still a time of great-coats, and neckerchiefs, and cautiousness, and numb-ness, and thick breathing. So suddenly out of winter, to-day does feel like newness of life.

MARHAM.

So it does. There is not a cloud in the sky ; and how warm it is, and how soft the air is ! I feel quite young again.

AUBIN.

You must feel more than that, uncle. For no young man, while he is well, ever feels as though he could die. But you, in your decay, have the feeling of youth ; therefore it is that of the youth of your immortality. It is the youth of the soul that one feels, on such a day as this.

MARHAM.

On such a day as this, then, the body —

AUBIN.

With me, feels like a garment outgrown by the spirit.

MARHAM.

So, then, Oliver, you would rather die in the spring ?

AUBIN.

Yes, in hope, and in the season of hope. Now let us go into the garden, uncle. Shall we ? — See here, how fast these daffodils have grown. They will be in blossom next week, and the snowdrop not be out of flower.

MARHAM.

So they will be, and they will soon be out again. Oliver, do you know Herrick's address to the daffodils ?

> We have short time to stay as you,
> We have as short a spring ;
> As quick a growth to meet decay
> As you or any thing.
>   We die
> As your hours do, and dry
>   Away,
> Like to the summer's rain,
> Or as the pearls of morning's dew,
> Ne'er to be found again.

They are pretty lines, though rather pensive ; are they not, Oliver ?

AUBIN.

Yes, uncle. But I do not like flowers being made to smell of the grave. Besides, we do not die like daffodils ; or, if we do, it is in a way that Herrick did not mean. I shall die as the daffodils did last year. But see, here they are, the very same flowers, alive and growing again ! And I, — I shall live again, and everlastingly.

MARHAM.

Tulips, lilies, tiger-lilies, violets, blue-bells, hyacinths, — all are coming up. And here are primroses quite yellow with blossoms. Ay, how all the flowers are pushing themselves through what was as hard as ice a few days since !

AUBIN.

It is as though the dead earth were blossoming.

MARHAM.

Yes, but these stems, and leaves, and flowers have sprung out of roots.

AUBIN.

Well, so they have. But then those roots were formed out of the earth. And there is not a fibre of any one of them but was mould a little while since. Look at the honeysuckle ; it is in leaf ; and so is the lilac, almost ; and the gooseberry bushes are very nearly. The flowers draw nourishment out of the ground for themselves, and encouragement for us ; and in sight of a thinker, when they blossom, it is not only into beautiful colors, but into suggestions of immortal hope. O, no, no, no ! There is not all this abounding, teeming life in nature for us to see, and think of, and trust in, and then fail of.

MARHAM.

O these birds ! how joyously they do sing ! the blackbird, the lark, the hedge-sparrow, ay, and the bulfinch, and the robin. I remember,

when I was a boy, a robin used to build in the
garden gate-post.   Three or four years he did ;
and I suppose he died then.   Birds, our English
birds, most of them, and I suppose most birds,
are very short-lived.   Well, it is something to
think of, that none of all these birds were what I
listened to when I was a boy.

AUBIN.

Nor any of them birds that God fed at that
time, and made a delight of in the world.

MARHAM.

Well, Oliver.

AUBIN.

I mean, that you ought to listen to the songs
of these birds like a child of God, and not like
one without hope.   You said that the birds now
are not what you listened to in your youth.   And
you said this mournfully ; — yes, uncle, you did ;
— and so you well might, if you thought yourself
made altogether as they are ; which you are not.

MARHAM.

No ; all flesh is not the same flesh, St. Paul
says ; but there is one kind of flesh of men, and
another of birds.

AUBIN.

And so you are not to feel, along with these
birds, in such a way as though, like a bird, you
were yourself only a little clay made alive.   Birds
do not live long ; but they do sing with rapture ——

MARHAM.

So they do. But an old man cannot but think how they will all be dead in a year or two, and he himself as well.

AUBIN.

One star differs from another star in glory, and one world from another world in character, most likely. And so it is not unlikely that into this world of mortality angels may be admitted by God as visitors; and if so, no doubt it is to them a joy to see how in decay, and through it, the world renews itself, — how the dead leaves of autumn and the perishing trees of the forest do but deepen the mould, and make it productive of new and sometimes better trees, — and to hear how fresh and joyful the chorus of the woods always is. In the hearing of God, an undying song kept up by dying things. And we, — we will hear it like children of God, with our souls as well as with our mortal ears. Thoughts of mortality may be too much with us. And the birds were never meant to sing them to us. Rather it ought to be a joy to us, that God perfects for man such delight, and for himself such endless thanksgiving, out of the throats of such frail things as birds.

MARHAM.

Thank you, Oliver, thank you. You will have your wish, as to your dying-time, I am almost sure. For you have years to live yet, I hope.

3

And a few Aprils lived like the last half-hour will make it be spring-time in your soul always.

God grant it !

All that is good for our souls, God does grant ; and to have it, we have only to ask it.

An undevout soul is like a tree in rich earth, but with perished roots. Such a tree may have the sun to warm it, and the dews to moisten its bark, and the breezes to blow through its branches ; and so it may maintain a show of life, but only a show. And the soul of a man may receive into itself, through his eyes, all the objects of the world, and through his ears, the knowledge of all that has ever happened, and his mind become, at the best, not much better than a dictionary of words, and a growing catalogue of things. Because, for knowledge to become wisdom, and for the soul to grow, the soul must be rooted in God ; and it is through prayer that there comes to us that which is the strength of our strength, and the virtue of our virtue, the Holy Spirit.

And so we will pray often and heartily while we can ; for soon we shall be cut down. But we shall live again like these flowers. Yes ! I shall blossom again into beauty, withered as I look.

AUBIN.

Yes, uncle ; within your shrunk form there is what will spread itself into an angel, winged, and free of the heavens. And there is in you a swiftness, that may some time make of worlds mere resting-places on a journey into infinity. But there is in you more than this ; for there is hidden in you a likeness to the everlasting youth of the Son of God.

MARHAM.

Can these bones live ? Or can there be in them what will quicken into an immortal ? Lord God, thou knowest !

AUBIN.

See this vine. It is merely dry sticks and ragged bark, to look at. Yet inside there is what will be, in August, gracefulness, and thick leaves, and a hundred bunches of grapes. Do I know this of the vine, and cannot I be sure that I know something like it of myself?

MARHAM.

God makes these flowers what they are, and he will not forget us, nor fail us ; and we ought to feel this the more, the more we consider the flowers.

AUBIN.

From all God's works, the spirit of God is to be caught, if they are but looked at religiously. And by our dwelling devoutly in the world, our

souls will have in them the full meaning of the
world. And then, die when we may, in foggy
November, or in January and the middle of winter, there will be spring within our souls ; feelings
of hope, caught from budding trees, and from the
smell of the first violet, and the opening of the
first rose, and from the March song of the lark,
and the April return of the swallow from beyond
the sea. And this hopefulness of nature we cannot give into too believingly. And in all things
that we hope humbly, we shall be more than justified by that "great hope which maketh not
ashamed."

CHAPTER IV.

There is no danger to a man that knows
What Life and Death is; there 's not any law
Exceeds his knowledge; neither is it lawful
That he should stoop to any other law.
He goes before them, and commands them all,
That to himself is a law rational. — GEORGE CHAPMAN.

MARHAM.

SOMETIMES I shrink from expecting death; but for long I do not. But, Oliver, as I grow older, I am afraid I may get to dread death.

AUBIN.

Uncle, you must not be afraid at all; neither of death, nor of the fear of death. For if you are afraid of fearing death, you will fear it.

MARHAM.

And after all, perhaps, death was not meant to be altogether pleasant to us.

AUBIN.

No; a skeleton is a skeleton. And a death's head is a death's head, ugly in itself, and without eyes; but then through the eye-sockets there shines the light of God; and that light the children of God know, and it gladdens them.

MARHAM.

You mean, that, the more godlike we become,

the more godlike death will feel ; and that is true.
But, Oliver, one day I am quite resigned to death,
and perhaps the next day I am not so submissive.
This ought not to be.

AUBIN.

And why not ?   Is there any thing toward
which you always feel the same ?   Do pictures
always please you the same ?   Does not music
please you less some days than others ?   There
was an acquaintance whom you would have been
very glad to have seen yesterday, but not to-day.
Are there any of your friends who are always the
same to you ?   Then why do you think death
ought to be ?   Man is a creature of many moods,
and the thought of death does not, and cannot,
agree with them all alike.

MARHAM.

Well, I hope my last day will not happen to be
one of my fearful ones.

AUBIN.

Uncle, it will not.   In a Jewish house, at a
marriage feast, wedding garments were given the
guests at the beginning.   And when the Spirit and
the Bride say, "Come," death brings us mortals
a garment of willingness to put on.   For I have
known -several good men who were afraid of being
afraid at the last ; but none of them were.   Of
the fear of death we must not make a trouble, nor
must we try to reason ourselves out of it ; for it

will grow stronger so. There is no arguing with the fear of death ; for it is a ghost in a dark room, and vanishes only with a candle.

MARHAM.

In the eighteenth Psalm, David speaks of his having been compassed about by the sorrows of death and the grave. And then he blesses God for deliverance, and says, " Thou wilt light my candle ; the Lord my God will enlighten my darkness." In our fears we must pray, and so bring the light and the power of God over our souls.

AUBIN.

Yes, uncle.

MARHAM.

Prayer in the darkness of the night is the light of the heart. This was said by one whose meaning ought to be surpassed in experience by the weakest of us Christians.

AUBIN.

It is a beautiful saying. Who said it ? Some Jew ?

MARHAM.

A Mahometan. And I think he was a friend of Mahomet's.

AUBIN.

And a man that did not fear death, then ; though hardly a man, to be franticly persuaded, with Mahomet, that paradise is under the shadow

of swords. For an awe of death we were meant
to have ; and fears of it have their use. Down
the valley of the shadow of death do dreadful
mists arise ; then let the thought of God shine out
from my soul, and it will glorify the mists, and
make them golden with the light of heaven.

MARHAM.

Most of the reasons that frighten men at death
ought to make them afraid to live. And besides,
really, life is only a lengthened dying.

AUBIN.

Yes, our life is a dying daily, as Paul says ;
and at the longest, it is not such a very long death.
For a man may be ever so young and strong, yet
it is likely the wood is growing in which he will
be coffined ; and there is a divine dial-plate, on
which the hour of his death is pointed to ; and
what is to be his grave will be his grave ; and his
body is waited for.

MARHAM.

Yes, we were as much born to die as to live.
And if life is worth living, we ought to think that
death is worth dying. But then we were not
born sinners ; but sinners we shall die. Yes, but
there is Christ Jesus ; and if we are in him, there
is no condemnation for us. Martin Luther says,
the fear of death is merely death itself, and that
whoever utterly abolishes death out of the heart
neither tastes nor feels any death.

AUBIN.

Yes, uncle; but sometimes fear of death is a disease of the nerves, and no fault of the heart; and sometimes it is a restless fancy. Sir Walter Raleigh, the night before his execution, could snuff the candle and make this couplet : —

Cowards fear to die; but courage stout,
Rather than live in snuff, will be put out.

But Doctor Johnson dreaded death all his life. He believed in another world almost desperately. Doubt it he did not, and could not. Yet he would like to have seen a spirit. An apparition would have been a happiness to him, for it would have made him sure of an hereafter. I suppose he feared dying, because he would have to leave his body behind him, — the eyes he had been used to see through, and the ears he had been used to hear through. To many men, the next world is blank, because they do not know how they are to feel in it. Yet how they now hear, and see, and feel, they cannot at all tell. I touch this table with my hand, and now in my mind there is knowledge whether the table is hard or soft; but, up my fingers and arm, how did the sensation of touching the table pass into my brain? I do not know. Now, as I speak, the air between us vibrates; there are airy vibrations; this we know : but there is no knowing how the words of my mouth become instant ideas in your mind.

MARHAM.

It is the will of God.

AUBIN.

So it is ; and that is what we have to say of every function of our bodies and power of our minds, and of the whole world. How our souls will live hereafter is not a greater mystery, than how our bodies do live now. This world is not like a parlour, in which we know all the furniture, and every corner ; if it were, we might well shrink from death, and think it a door opening out of the familiarly known into the fearfully unknown. Birth, growth, health, and sickness, labor wearying the body, and sleep refreshing it, food supporting, and poisons hurting it, — of life in every way, we must say that we cannot tell how it is. And yet there are persons that shrink from the future life, and some that do not believe it, because they do not feel in what way it will be ; while what the way is of the very life they are in they cannot tell. For they cannot tell how sight gets into the brain through the humors of the eye, nor how movements of the air get through the ear to be thoughts in the soul. They do not like thinking of death, because it opens into mystery ; while they themselves live in mystery, and move in it, and have all their being in it. A man fears for his soul in a new world, while he cannot find a bird, or animal, or insect, not one, which its life does not exactly suit. Out of the body his soul will go into the man knows not what state, and so his mind misgives him ; while there is not a swallow comes out of its egg-shell into this great world unsuited to its manner of life ; and because the swallow wants it, there is an instinct of flight in it at a month old, which is wiser than geography and astronomy and meteorology.

MARHAM.

And yet we are afraid of what will go with our souls ; as though they could go anywhere else than to God !

AUBIN.

There is an awe of death which is right, but it is not common ; and it is what life would be the sublimer for. What are the common fears of death ? They are what we caught from the tones in which our nurses used to frighten us with the grave ; they are terrors which survive among us from cowardly ages. Weaker and weaker I shall grow, and perhaps my mind may get infected with the failing of my body. And there may come upon me the forms of old terrors, and my reason may not be strong enough to command them back, but my faith will sustain me, I hope. Fear, fear, why should I fear ? For is not this a world which Christ died in ?

MARHAM.

Yes. And this is what makes me dread being afraid of death.

AUBIN.

Is it anywhere written in the New Testament that you shall not fear death ? It is a privilege not to fear it ; but a duty it is not. Well, dear uncle, if your terrors cannot be borne with in faith, and if they do come upon you, then they may be laughed away, perhaps ; for dying men do laugh, sometimes.

MARHAM.

Laughed away, Oliver !

AUBIN.

Yes, uncle ; as being the perverse ingenuities of a soul frightening itself. But you will say, they will not seem perverse. Well, then, one way or another, in merriment or soberness, all things are to be denied which cannot be believed in the love of God. For it is no fancy, and it is the experience of our life, and it is Scripture, and it is the Gospel, that God is love.

MARHAM.

God is love. God is love itself.

AUBIN.

And this truth we will die in. Let what things will come into our thoughts. Wonderful is man's power of self-torture. And in some moods of our minds, we could fancy some most blessed truths ending in a frightful application to ourselves. Just as, in the Middle Ages, in a church built for the peace of the soul, a worshipper might get his eye fixed by some diabolical face carved on a corbel. Do not I live in God ? And shall I be afraid of dying in God ? Is it I that keep my heart going ? And ought I then to dread its stopping ? Rather what I ought to fear is the will which it does beat with, — the Divine will. And if I am wisely afraid of that, I have nothing else to fear. God is the life of my life, I know and feel. And so I will not fear dying. I am in God, and I shall be in him everlastingly. Die in him I cannot, except as a grain of seed dies in the ground, to spring up again into a cluster of wheat-ears waving to the wind on lofty stalks.

MARHAM.

Yes, Oliver, when we die, I hope it will be in full faith of a new and a hundred-fold greater life. The hour is getting late. I am afraid, Oliver, I have made you talk more than you ought to have done.

AUBIN.

O, no, uncle, no !

MARHAM.

Look at your watch, Oliver. It is getting late.

AUBIN.

So it is, uncle. And I ought to be readier for burial than I am.

MARHAM.

Why, Oliver, what do you mean ?

AUBIN.

That it is time I had my clothes off, and was getting into bed.

MARHAM.

I have known one or two instances of persons being found dead in their beds. The night before, they did not think when they went up stairs ——

AUBIN.

How much farther they were going.

MARHAM.

No.

AUBIN.

And so, sometimes, while I am undressing myself, I think that perhaps in an hour or two my soul may be unapparelled of my body. And then, through Christ within me, the hope of glory, my bedroom feels like the cave of the Arimathean, and full of a power that will not suffer my soul to see corruption. And then, as I lie down, I say a few lines out of what the knightly physician of Norwich used to call his dormitive to bedward.

> Sleep is a death; — O, make me try,
> By sleeping, what it is to die!
> And as gently lay my head
> On my grave, as now my bed.
> Howe'er I rest, great God, let me
> Awake again at last with thee!

CHAPTER V.

This life of mine
Must be lived out, and a grave thoroughly earned.

R. BROWNING.

The quantity of sorrow he has, does it not mean withal the quantity of sympathy he has, the quantity of faculty and victory he shall yet have? "Our sorrow is the inverted image of our nobleness." The depth of our despair measures what capability and height of claim we have to hope. Black smoke, as of Tophet, filling all our universe, it can yet by true heart-energy become flame and brilliancy of heaven. Courage!

T. CARLYLE.

MARHAM.

I AM not afraid of death, Oliver, but some time perhaps I may be; for better men than I have grown so in old age. Dr. Isaac Milner, — did you never read his life, Oliver? He was Dean of Carlisle. In one of his letters, written in tears, and with his door bolted, he said it seemed as though Almighty God had hidden his face from him; that his prayers were unanswered; that his heart failed him; and that it was no easy matter for him to look death and judgment in the face. Oliver, I do not dread death, but I may yet. For I think it is no clear view which I have of the next world; and I fear it is from this world's being too pleasant to my eyes.

AUBIN.

This world is more to you than the world to
come is. Well, uncle, so I think it ought to be.

MARHAM.

But my thoughts of an hereafter are so vague.

AUBIN.

How should they be otherwise ?. This ought
not to distress you. It is not littleness of faith.
You have no clear notions of a future world ; but
you are doubtful, not about its certainty, but only
about the place of it, and the look and the manner of it. Now, in these respects, nothing has
been shown us of the world to come. Our next
will be a spiritual state ; and so, much more than
the certainty of it could not be told us ; for the
things of a purely spiritual life could not be made
to be understood by us, whose language and ways
of thinking have come so largely from our bodily
experience. This world we breathe, and feel,
and see ; but the world to come we can only
have faith in.

MARHAM.

And so I am afraid, Oliver, that my faith in an
hereafter is weaker than it ought to be.

AUBIN.

It is not, uncle. From my knowledge of you,
I know it is not. Men are capable of faith in
another life ; some more, some less, than others.
And I might have all faith in it, and not be the

better for it, but be nothing st ll.   Our degree of
faith is not a thing for us to be torturing ourselves
about.   But, uncle, you do believe in a future life,
only not as strongly, perhaps, as you are conscious
of being alive.   Why, how should you ?   This
green, familiar earth ! — it is home to live in it.
And to this domestic feeling the other world may
well be foreign, sometimes.

MARHAM.

You think so, Oliver ?

AUBIN.

If your faith in the world to come were the
strongest possible, it could not possibly be of the
same nature as your faith in the existence of India,
or in your being able to get to

> Where the remote Bermudas ride
> In the ocean's bosom unespied.

We can say a hundred and a hundred thousand
things about the life we are living ; but about the
life we trust to live, we can say only one thing.
And so it feels as though we were saying almost
nothing, though the one thing we can say is the
greatest that can be said ; for we can say that a
world of spirit there is, there certainly is.   And
so, as I was saying, uncle, your belief in an hereafter is greater than you think it.   And if it feels
vague, it is because the world to come is vague as
yet to us all.

4

MARHAM.

What you say is a relief to me, Oliver.

AUBIN.

It is impossible that you could think of the future life in the same way as you think of to-morrow.　In regard to the manner of the life to come, you can only say that it will be a spiritual world, a world of spirits.　But of the way of the present life, a thousand things might be said.　It is sleeping and waking ; it is " Good night " on going to bed, and " Good morning " on getting up ; it is to wonder what the day will bring forth ; it is sunshine and gloominess ; it is rain on the window, as one sits by the fire ; it is to walk in the garden, and see the flowers open, and hear the birds sing ; it is to have the postman bring letters ; it is to have news from east, west, north, and south ; it is to read old books and new books ; it is to see pictures and hear music ; it is to have Sundays ; it is to pray with a family morning and evening ; it is to sit in the twilight and meditate ; it is to be well, and sometimes to be ill ; it is to have business to do, and to do it ; it is to have breakfast and dinner and tea ; it is to belong to a town, and to have neighbours, and to be one in a circle of acquaintance ; it is to have friends to love one ; it is to have sight of dear old faces ; and, with some men, it is to be kissed daily by the same loving lips for fifty years ; and it is to know themselves thought of many times a day, in many places, by children, and grandchildren, and many friends.

MARHAM.

You remind me, Oliver, of a passage in one of Hazlitt's works. I wish I could remember where ; but I cannot. But I have interrupted you, which I ought not to have done.

AUBIN.

No, uncle, you did not. All that I was going to say was, that, this life being so many happy things to some men, it is no wonder, and no fault, if they do not long for a change. They know what this world is ; it is all this happiness : the other world they do not know ; they know that it is happiness, all happiness, but they do not know what.

MARHAM.

But, Oliver, we are to long for the future life, for the sake of being with God.

AUBIN.

And have not we God with us now, uncle ? All I mean is this, that we ought not to distress ourselves about our piety, if this earth is so pleasant that we are not eager to be out of it. For did not God make the earth, as well as the heavens ?

MARHAM.

I think, Oliver, I cannot understand you.

AUBIN.

I mean to say, that I do not think God wishes to have us live in a transport about heaven. Many persons think it is a duty to be ecstatic about what their reward in heaven will be ; but this violent feeling they cannot keep up ; and if they could, then they would be the worse for it, for it would disgust them with their duties and work.

MARHAM.

That is so unlike your usual way of talking !

AUBIN.

No, dear uncle, it is not. What I have just said is in regard to heaven as a reward, and that is the only feeling about it which most persons have. There is another expectation of an hereafter, that is like a Jacob's ladder, reaching from our souls to heaven, and up and down which, for our help, ascend and descend thoughts, like angels. Selfishness, eager for a heaven of enjoyment, is quite a different thing in the soul from love, and purity, and truth, yearning together for what is their native element.

MARHAM.

So it is.

AUBIN.

Uncle, with you to love, and all these comforts about me, these many helps for improvement, these books to read, and all my time for myself, and with the green fields to walk in, and with you to think of me, and to talk to, and to be with, very, very pleasant is my life that now is. And pleasant, too, is my expectation of the life which is to come. My thought of heaven is this earth at its best, blossoming into infinity.

MARHAM.

Ay, now I understand you, not at all. But now, about what I interrupted you in, just now.

AUBIN.

About the world to come, it ought not to be as though we did not know surely, because we do not know much. From the nearest star, our earth, if it is seen, looks hardly any thing at all. It shines, or rather it twinkles, and that is all. To them afar off, this earth is only a shining point. But to us who live in it, it is wide and various; it is sea and land; it is Europe, Asia, Africa, and America; it is the lair of the lion, and the pasture of the ox, and the pathway of the worm, and the support of the robin; it is what has day and night in it; it is what customs and languages obtain in; it is many countries; it is the habitation of a thousand million men; and it is our home. All this the world is to us, though, looked at from one of the stars, it is only a something that twinkles in the distance.

MARHAM.

Twinkles; that is, it is seen one instant, and lost another.

AUBIN.

And seen only as a few intermittent rays of light ; though, to us who live in it, it is hill and valley, and land and water, and many thousands of miles wide. So that if the future world is a star of guidance for us, it is enough ; because it is not for us to know, but to believe, that it will prove our dear home.

MARHAM.

That is very well said, Oliver. A little while ago, you said you thought that all men could not, perhaps, hope alike for the next life.

AUBIN.

Not with the same warmth. And then there is this. To a man lying hopelessly ill, heaven is a comfort ; to a martyr just about to suffer, it was courage ; and to a man laboring on in poverty and neglect, it is holy strength. But a man who is not poor, nor ill, nor about to be stoned to death, must not distress himself, if he does not feel all through his life what faith Stephen had only in his last moments. Faith comes of virtue. What are the virtues, then, through which an increase of faith can come to us ? Kindness to all men, sympathy with goodness in God and man, and what is more peculiar for our way of living, thankfulness for the ease and the many delights we have. In this comfortable house, uncle, ours ought to be very largely what is so very rare in men, the faith which comes of gratitude.

MARHAM.

This faith we will seek through prayers and hymns. And as gratitude to God can be shown only through goodness to his creatures, Oliver, you shall think of some person for us to assist, — some one, I mean, whom we should not perhaps have helped, but for this conversation.

AUBIN.

And through sympathy with him, our souls shall be the better. And we will remember, besides, that for us faith can and ought to grow out of the love of friends, and nature, and art. For, in any right direction, our love can grow so strong and pure as to feel immortal.

MARHAM.

You mean ——

AUBIN.

That with a father of a family, if his is a wholesome hope in Providence, it has grown greatly out of what he has felt while embracing his children, and playing with them, and while thinking for them in the night, and hoping for good, and useful, and happy lives for them. And, of necessity, a child's feeling towards God is the infinity of what it feels for its parents. My faith is to be out of my own Christian heart, and not to be precisely what Stephen showed, or Paul felt, or Polycarp had. But let any one be of the Christian spirit, and he will feel himself of the

Christian heaven. Love, integrity, disinterested-
ness, — these, blending together, make a consciousness that crowns me with immortality ; I
do not say very brightly so, but certainly.

MARHAM.

Is not that, Oliver, — is not that pride, or
what may end in it ?

AUBIN.

No, uncle ; indeed it is not. For in this way,
when I feel myself immortal without thinking of
it, I clasp my hands, and sometimes I kneel and
lay my forehead to the ground, worshipping God,
because I am made to feel justly and holily and
lovingly. And because I love along with God,
along with God I am sure I shall live. And so
every man I love makes me feel myself immortal.
And something of the same experience is worked
in me by reading a good book, or hearing of a
right action, and by the sight of any thing beautiful or sublime in nature.

CHAPTER VI.

Blessed are they who see, and yet believe not!
Yea, blest are they who look on graves, and still
Believe none dead; who see proud tyrants ruling,
And yet believe not in the strength of Evil; —
Blessed are they who see the wandering poor,
And yet believe not that their God forsakes them;
Who see the blind worm creeping, yet believe not
That even that is left without a path. — LEOPOLD SCHEFER.

MARHAM.

You are not well this evening, Oliver.

AUBIN.

No, uncle, I am not.

MARHAM.

Not very unwell, I hope; though you do look so, Oliver. What have you seen, or heard, or been thinking? Dear Oliver, something has distressed you, I think.

AUBIN.

No, uncle. Only I have been thinking over my life before I knew you.

MARHAM.

Too painful for you, in your weak state, to think of. But it was for the best for you, we are sure. But I, — I ought not to be saying it, I know. That I ever lost sight of you is what I can never forgive myself.

AUBIN.

Now, uncle, I am distressed, or I shall be very soon.

MARHAM.

Good Oliver, O, if only I could —— But I cannot.

AUBIN.

Nay, dear uncle, now no more.

MARHAM.

Of all your many sufferings, I cannot retrieve one. What your lot in life has been, it has been. And what it is to be will not be as happy as I could wish, and as I would make it, only that your health —— But, indeed, had I found you earlier, things might have been different.

AUBIN.

Uncle, uncle, you have been very good to me, and you are. And believe me, uncle, that I am very happy. For this is only nervous weakness.

MARHAM.

But, O, Oliver, only to think ——

AUBIN.

Uncle, I quite agree with something of Jean Paul's which I have seen, somewhere.

MARHAM.

And what is it ?

AUBIN.

That if God were to show himself to us in the distribution of the suns, and in what makes our

tears fall, and in the abysses, of which he is the
fulness, and himself the bounds, we should not be
willing to say to him, " Be other than thou art."

MARHAM.

It is rightly and beautifully said, — very beautifully. But, Oliver, my dear Oliver, I am very
sorry for you. But it is such a pleasure to me
that I have never heard you murmur !

AUBIN.

I hope not to be impatient. I hope to be patient. God has done with me what is right ; and
so he will do with me.

MARHAM.

Yes, dear Oliver, so we trust, and so we will
believe.

AUBIN.

Yes, uncle, and so I do. God might inclose
me in himself, and let me look through the eyes
of his omnipresence ; and if he did, I should see,
in the infinite, the mystic order to which the
starry systems move ; and in a drop of water, I
should witness the roomy space there is for the
movements of a thousand lives ; I should know
the way in which the armies of heaven are placed,
and the wise purpose there is in the succession of
human generations, as they are born and die. I
should look into the mysteries of eternity, and
feel that in human suffering God's love is the
same as in the blessedness of the angels. I

should see, all round the wide earth, how good all things are in their relation to the everlasting whole. And then, looking up the heights of heaven, and down the depths of life, I should feel the goodness of the universe. And on seeing my own lot left empty amongst men, I should then long to return to it and fill it. Yes, if only for a moment I saw that look which always the universe has to God, I should pray the Father for ever, out of my whole heart and the joy of it, " Thy will be done ; thy will be done." I should be happy for one glimpse of what life really is. But I may be happier without it ; because through faith we may be more blessed than through our mere eyesight. For a man tó see, and so believe, is well ; but blessed are they who do not see, and yet believe. Sorrow and pain ! I will bear them. Lord ! I will bear them. Not yet, O, not yet, would I pray to be taken out of this world ! Awhile, awhile longer may this chastening last. Lord ! let it end, not when I will, but when thou wilt. O, there are fields in the universe, so wide, and on which God's glory shines brightly and for ever, and, O, so blessedly ! But I would not enter on them yet, — not yet. This valley of the shadow of death I will wait in ; and I could wish to have the shadow of death on me, till my soul has fully and rightly felt it. A spirit I am, and so is God. And like a spirit with a spirit, is all which he does with me. A soul, a living soul, I am ; and I will think this strongly, and so feel myself to be God's. And God's I am for ever. And bright and beautiful is what his eye looks on, as my place in heaven, that is to be.

CHAPTER VII.

My soul such pleasure oft in sleep receives,
 That death begins to seem a pleasant thing,
 Not to be armed, perchance, with such a sting,
 Or taste so bitter, as the world conceives.
For if the mind alone sees, hears, believes,
 While every limb is dead and languishing,
 And greatest pleasure to herself can bring
 When least the body feels, and least perceives,
Well may the hope be cherished, that, when quite
 Loosed from the burden of her earthly chain,
 She hears, and sees, and knows her true delight.
Rejoice, thou troubled spirit! though in pain.
 If thou canst take, even here, so sweet a flight,
 What wilt thou in thy native seats again?

SANNAZARO.

ONE weary evening in illness, I fell asleep, it having been just before a subject of prayer with me, that God would grant me a right frame of mind to die in. For, as I said to myself at the end of my prayer, "It would be dreadful in death if sight were to fail me, and I could see no friendly face, and hearing were to fail me, and I could hear no comforting voice, and in my soul there were to be doubts and an agony of doubt." And as I thought this, weakness overcame me, and I slept; and very soon I dreamed.

And in my dream I heard voices and footsteps. And it was as though many persons were going to and fro, in great gladness and in light. But I could not myself see at all, and I was like one blind. And I was persuaded that I had died in my sleep, and that I was at the gate of the city of God, and unable to enter in, on account of my darkness. And I was afraid to move ; for I did not know but that, in one step, I might fall head-long from the narrow way that leads into life. And I said in myself, "Unblessed art. thou, and not able to see God ; and thou must have died in impurity of heart ; and always, always thou wert fearful, and like one not quite believing." I was terrified. I felt, as it were, the pit of destruction yawning against me ; I was to be an example of the just judgment of God ; and in my end was to be seen how, without any great wandering, the path of the commandment may be kept up to the last step, and that last step be perdition, through weakness of faith. O the dread I was in, and the terror !

I listened, and there was silence. It was as though all things were hushed by the awfulness of what was to happen to me. I was there, a spec-tacle to the spirits of men and to angels. My faith had failed me at the very last, and in the littleness of it I was to perish. There were wit-nesses of my wretchedness nigh me ; that I could feel ; and I could feel that there was sorrow amongst them. And within myself I thought,

" Thy unbelief was thy own misery on earth, and
now, at the very gate of heaven, it is a grief to
the angels, and it is what God has no pleasure in."
And now, at once, I was calm.   Hell might be
under my feet, but it could not open, except by
the will of God ; and that blessed will was what
I would pray to have done, though destruction
had hold of my feet the while.   I bowed my
head, and covered my face with my hands, and I
cried, " Though he slay me, yet will I trust in
him."   Then a voice of triumph said, " Now he
has overcome, and has got the victory ! "   And
other glad voices said, " The victory, the victory l "   But there was one which said, " Almost,
he has."

For a moment I could see, and then I was
blind again.   When I feared, then I was in a
horror of darkness ; but every hopeful thought
flashed through me, like lightning out of a midnight sky.   I wondered what was to happen.
But happen what might, I thought I could perish
gladly, if it were by the will of God, and for
God's good purpose.

And now, with this perfect love of God, my
fear was cast out.   And I was not in blindness
any longer.   The God whom I loved, I could see
by.   I could see ; and, O, by what a light !   For
there was no shadow in it, because it did not
shine from a sun or a moon, or from any one

quarter. But it was uncreated light, and was the visible presence of God, and was itself a joy to see by.

There were spirits standing round me. And some of them I knew, by their looks, were natives of the same world as myself. But towards others, I felt as though I did not know them, and yet as though I knew them well. O the blessedness which went through me from their looks! Compassed about with them, it was as though I could have remained for ever, and not have moved. But behind those who were nearest me, I saw standing a friend of mine, who had died many years before. His face was glorified; but whether it was changed or not, I cannot tell. His look made the same feeling in me that his best words used to do, and so it was I knew him, as I think. And I saw another person whom I knew. Then I said, "O my brethren, am I then amongst you, at last? And am I come out of the earth so safely?"

Then I learned that I had yet to die. And many high things were said to comfort and encourage me. I was in a tumult of glory, and joy, and wonder. Then I asked, " Shall I remember these great things when I come to die?" And then one answered, " No. Nor in the body will he remember them at all. For of the way of our spiritual life no knowledge can be kept by

5

a dweller of earth. But let them that have come out of the earth tell him what earthly words of theirs have proved the truest, and he will remember them."

And the first who spoke was one who had been a minister of Christ's in the town of my birth, but who had died a century and a half before I was born; for it was Richard Baxter who spoke, and it was as though he knew me. His name had been known and loved by me as a little child, with a love which I learned from my dear mother. And so, through earnest gazing on his face, I did not hear his words quite exactly. But as nearly as I remember, he said, " Never be persuaded that ever a soul will be cast out, which humbly, and earnestly, and with many prayers, has sought its God."

Then Robert Leighton looked at me and said, " You, in your thoughts, shut up death into a very narrow compass, namely, into the moment of your expiring. But the truth is, it goes through all your life; for you are still losing and spending life, as you enjoy it."

The next who spoke was one whom I knew to be John Wickliffe, and he said, " Men should not fear, except on account of sin, or the losing of virtues; since pain is just, and according to the will of God. And the joy which saints have, when they suffer thus, is a manner of bliss which belongs to them in the earth ; and it may be more of joy to them than all their worldly desires.''

And then some one said, ''You may not look, at your pleasure, to come to heaven in a feather-bed. It is not the way. For our Lord himself came hither with great pain and many tribulations ; that was the path wherein he walked hither. And the servant may not look to be in better case than his Master.'' He who spoke thus stood so that I could not see him, but by what he said I knew that he was Thomas More.

'' Reflect on death as in Jesus Christ, not as without Jesus Christ. Without Jesus Christ it is dreadful, it is alarming, it is the terror of nature. In Jesus Christ, it is fair and lovely, it is good and holy, it is the joy of the saints.'' These were Pascal's words to me.

Then one who stood next to Pascal looked at me. Him I did not know ; but when he spoke, I knew him by his words to be Thomas à Kempis. And he said, '' When the hour of your trial comes, do you pray, — O God, dearly loved ! this hour, it is right that thy creature should suffer something from thee, and for thee. O Father, the hour is come for him, which from all eternity thou hast foreknown would come, that thy servant should lie prostrate at thy door ; but, Lord, do thou let him in to be with thee, O, for ever ! For a little while must I be nothing, and

I must fail in the sight of men, and I must be worn with suffering and weakness. But it is all so that I may rise in the dawn of a new light, and grow glorious in heaven. Holy Father ! so thou hast ordered it ; and what is done and is doing on me is thy decree."

When this prayer for my learning was ended, Augustine exclaimed, " O this life which God has laid up in store for them that love him, — this life indeed ! This happy, safe, and most lovely, this holy life ! This life which fears no death, which feels no sorrow, which knows no sin ! This perfect love and harmony of souls ! This day that never declines, — this light that never goes out ! Think of its blisses and glories, and so find some refreshment from the miseries and toils of a perishing life. And at the last, recline your weary head and lay you down to sleep with joy ; for you know now that that sleep shall be shaken off again, and the blessedness of this life begin at once on your awaking."

Then a voice spoke ; and, O, it was so clear, and sweet, and grateful ! and it was the voice of Margaret Fox ; and she said, " Now these have finished their course and their testimony, and are entered into their eternal rest and felicity. I trust in the same powerful God, that his holy arm and power will carry thee through whatever he hath yet for thee to do ; and that he will be thy strength and support, and the bearer up of thy head unto the end, and in the end. For I know his faithfulness and goodness, and I have experience of his love. To whom be glory and powerful dominion for ever. Amen."

All that were standing by said Amen, like one voice. And with Amen upon my lips, I awoke.

I was sitting by the fire. And in my hand there was a book, into which I had copied many things from my reading. From this dream I inferred that we mortals have all the knowledge of the world to come which we can have, and all the assurance of it which is good for us, and that, for a believer in earnest, the right feeling towards the next life is hope, and not fear. And from my dream I learned that sympathy with saints gone hence brings us into that state of mind that is most firmly persuaded of the heavens, into which they have entered.

CHAPTER VIII.

Death is another life. We bow our heads
At going out, we think, and enter straight
Another golden chamber of the king's,
Larger than this we leave, and lovelier. —P. J. BAILEY.

And the pure soul emancipate by death,
The Enlarger, shall attain its end predoomed,
The eternal newness of eternal joy. —SOUTHEY.

MARHAM.

I HAVE been reading your dream, Oliver.
There is wisdom in it.   And I like it much, and
so I do the sonnet from the Italian.

AUBIN.

But of course you do not think it my translation ; for I am no poet.

MARHAM.

O, yes, you are, according to what you quoted
this morning, from some one : —

Poets are all who love, who feel great truths,
And tell them ; and the truth of truths is love.

AUBIN.

What book is that which you have been reading, uncle ?

MARHAM.

A treatise by Peter Huet, on whereabouts
Paradise was.   It was written in the seventeenth

' century, like many, and perhaps most, of the books on that subject. I think myself, that Paradise was in Asia, certainly.

AUBIN.

I dare say it was.

MARHAM.

You are not interested in the subject ?

AUBIN.

No, uncle ; or rather, I do not mind reading those books. Paradise is not so lost as is sometimes thought. The garden of Eden is now spread out into the width of the world. Our homes are bowers in it ; our roads are walks in it ; and always within reach hang forbidden fruits, though now they are such as are often their own punishment in the eating, — apples of Sodom, golden in the rind and dust inside. There is in the garden still the tree of the knowledge of good and evil, and this we may eat of now ; for it is full grown, and the fruit of it is ripe. And by eating of it, we, too, have our eyes opened, and so are able to recognize, as the very tree of life, what otherwise looks deadly, and itself dead wood ; I mean the tree of the crucifixion.

MARHAM.

That life is lost by seeking to save it, and is saved by willingness to lose it, is very hardly, and not very often, believed ; though most persons do think they believe it.

AUBIN.

The tree to be desired to make one wise may be eaten of now, and so men do not mind it; many of them do not, and so their eyes are never opened; and so, being blind, they fail of the fruit of the tree of life.

MARHAM.

You would say, then, that only by eating of the tree of the knowledge of good and evil can men know that the world is a garden of Eden, with the tree of life in it.

AUBIN.

But that now it is death who is in it, to dress it, and to keep it, none fail of knowing; though to some'he appears to be a spoiler of the garden; and he looks an enemy of God, instead of being a servant and one to be trusted in by us creatures, fully, if not fondly. And this is through men's not taking of the tree of the knowledge of good and evil; because if death came into the world with the forbidden eating of that fruit, it is the ordained eating of it that opens our eyes, so as to see in death an angel of light, toiling in earthly guise among us earthly creatures.

MARHAM.

Levelling us with the dust, out of which we were made.

AUBIN.

But into which we do not altogether, nor mainly, die.

MARHAM.

So we trust. But it is not what death does that makes us hope the more. It is with his soul in his face, that man can be believed immortal. But to me, a dead body ——

AUBIN.

Is no discouraging sight. For there is God about it. And his adorable will is as plain in the departure as it is in the presence of life. The body of a saint is a temple of God, from which the minister has withdrawn, and in which service is ended, and from which the Lord has accepted the prayer, "Now lettest thou thy servant depart in peace."

MARHAM.

You have so many pleasant images for death, Oliver, in talking of it! I suppose it is from your remembering death in your cheerfulness.

AUBIN.

Uncle, I would wish to remember it more familiarly. Eating and drinking, I would wish to remember death; not by drinking out of a human skull, as some have done in loving remembrance, and others out of hostile triumph; but I would eat my food, bethinking me often that any morsel may be my last. This would be a solemnity that from its very commonness could not continue mournful, but might be profitable always.

MARHAM.

Death never ought to be a painful thought with any one, because it ought to be so common, — such a dáily expectation.

AUBIN.

It ought not to be shrunk from for its novelty. It is not as though we were the first or the second of our race, or as though we belonged to the second or to the third generation of our kind. It is not as though none or only a few had ever died, and we were to be of the earliest. Only since the decease of Charlemagne, there have died twenty-five times a thousand millions of our fellow-creatures. Let us weep with the bereaved that weep, and feel along with those that are ill, and those that are dying ; and then down to the grave will be like a path we know well, and too well to be frightened on it.

MARHAM.

It is not by chance, but through God, that we come to an end. Many ways does God speak to us creatures of his, as in the events of life, from the Bible, and from within our hearts ; and I trust that we have listened to that Divine voice often enough, to know the tone of it at once and everywhere. Because, when we are spoken to, and have our souls required of us, we shall know then that we are spoken to by the loving voice of. our Father in heaven ; and we shall answer, as I hope, O, so willingly ! — " Lord, now lettest thou thy servant come to thee in peace."

AUBIN.

And that we shall say and feel, I hope, and no doubt we shall, if we have often said to God before, " Thy will be done." We live in one another ; father and mother in their children, husband and wife in one another, and some few friends in one another. So that we most of us die more than once, before we die of disease.

MARHAM.

In the same way as Erasmus said of his friend Sir Thomas, " It seems as though in More I myself had been killed."

AUBIN.

When death takes those we love, then we love death. Those who are alone in the world are as though they had been left for sleep ; and death comes over them like a sleep, for they are not unwilling.

MARHAM.

Not once, nor one thousand times, but more than fifty thousand times, I have been to sleep ; so that I ought not to be afraid to die now. And to my feelings, the evening of life ought to deepen on to the obscurity of the grave, as pleasantly as dusk gets dark.

AUBIN.

Yes, uncle, just so ; and exactly so. There

is no universal night in this earth, and for us in the universe, there is no death. What is to us here night coming on is, on the other side of the earth, night ending, and day begun. And so what we call death the angels may regard as immortal birth ; and so they do, as we may well believe.

MARHAM.

So they do, very often, we may be sure. In the early days of the Christian Church, what day a Christian died on was spoken of as that of his birth, — his birth into a higher existence.

AUBIN.

Through the body and its wants, I am held down to the earth's surface, and to its customs and employments ; and so I am kept out of heaven, and from off the bosom of God, and from the company of Christ, and out of the rapture of the angels.

MARHAM.

God help us ! God make us sure of that happiness at last ! God make us ready for it, — for that joy unspeakable !

AUBIN.

The day of our decease will be that of our coming of age ; and with our last breath we shall become free of the universe. And in some region of infinity, and from among its splendors, this earth will be looked back on like a lowly home, and this life of ours be remembered like a short apprenticeship to Duty.

CHAPTER IX.

This is the prerogative of the noblest natures, — that their departure to higher regions exercises a no less blessed influence than did their abode on earth; that they lighten us from above, like stars by which to steer our course, often interrupted by storms. — GOETHE.

MARHAM.

ANY thing a dead man leaves behind him, unfinished, makes one feel so strangely the nothingness of human purposes! I remember the pain in which I once saw what would have been a very beautiful picture, only it was not finished; for the painter had died very suddenly. And once I was in the studio of a sculptor who was lately deceased; and I was much affected by the appearance of a statue, the nobleness of which was just being brought out of the marble when the artist died. And whatever purpose death cuts a man off from has for his surviving friends a look ——

AUBIN.

As though it had been shone on by light not of this world.

MARHAM.

But it is sad, when genius dies with its work unfinished.

AUBIN.

I do not think so, uncle. Besides, when would genius finish its work, — all the work it could do ? For its growing grandeur would always have fresh excellence to show.

MARHAM.

Ay so, you are right. But Spenser's Fairy Queen, incomplete for ever ——

AUBIN.

Is a broken sentence ; and what ought to be the end of it is most eloquent silence. Spenser's writing is so vivid, that recollection of what he says is like a voice speaking in one's brain. I shut my eyes, and then the poet himself is with me ; and he tells me of Prince Arthur and his friends, in such a way as to make virtue itself feel more virtuous still ; then he stops, when he has only half told what he began ; then there is a word and half another word ; and then Spenser says no more. Then I am thoughtful, and an awe comes over me. For of the poet's having died I do not think. And it is as though Spenser had been changed while talking with me. And then I think how, to the angels, this whole earth looks like a Mount of Transfiguration. And feel afresh how this is a scene in which men become spirits, and blessed spirits, if they like.

MARHAM.

And such we will hope Spenser is.

AUBIN.

There have not been very many men of whom it could be better hoped than of Spenser, I think.

MARHAM.

I think he was certainly a good man, Oliver, because out of the heart are the issues of life ; and Spenser's heart was full of the beauty of a moral life.

AUBIN.

Now and then, he either has or makes occasion to say things, which, from most other men, would be lustful incentives ; but from him they do not sound so.

MARHAM.

Showing how, to the pure, all things are pure.

AUBIN.

So what you said of another we say of you, O Edmund Spenser ! your virtue is the brightness of your honor on earth, and elsewhere it is the reason

> For which enrollèd is your glorious name
> In heavenly registers above the sun,
> Where you, a saint, with saints your seat have won.

MARHAM.

He lies buried ——

AUBIN.

Not he, but his body does.

MARHAM.

In Westminster Abbey, I think.

AUBIN.

Yes, uncle ; and nigh the grave of the poet Chaucer.   Yes, and Geoffrey Chaucer was he

> That left, half told,
> The story of Cambuscan bold.

He is another of those who have gone away with the word in their mouths, and who have left us to feel as though that word were to be spoken yet, and we to hear it.

MARHAM.

I will read you ˊthe last lines that Chaucer wrote.   They are the end of what is called the Good Counsel of Chaucer, and are said to have been made by him upon his death-bed, while lying in his great anguish.

> That thee is sent, receive in buxomness.
> The wrestling with this world asketh a fall.
> Here is no home ; here is but wilderness ;
> Forth, pilgrim, forth !   O beast out of thy stall!
> Look up on high, and thank thy God of all.
> Waive thou thy lust, and let thy ghost thee lead,
> And truth thee shall deliver ; 't is no dread.

AUBIN.

Or, as I have seen the last line modernized,

> Truth to thine own heart
> Thy soul shall save.

A choice couplet, is not it, uncle ?

MARHAM.

Perhaps it is.   But I should feel the worth of it better, if you were to recite the poem itself that you quote from.   Now will you ?

AUBIN.

Yes, uncle ; what I remember of it, I will.

Britain's first poet,
Famous old Chaucer,
Swan-like, in dying
　　Sung his last song,
When at his heart-strings
　　Death's hand was strong.

" Earth is a desert,
Thou art a pilgrim :
Led by thy spirit,
　　Grace from God crave ;
Truth to thine own heart
　　Thy soul shall save."

Dead through long ages
Britain's first poet, —
Still the monition
　　Sounds from his grave,
" Truth to thine own heart
　　Thy soul shall save."

Chaucer of the fresh, green memory, — blessings be with him ! For him utterly dead, dead both in body and soul, we cannot think. And so he helps our faith in immortality.

MARHAM.

Thank you, Oliver. But what book are you looking for ?

AUBIN.

The Fairy Queen. I have found it. I want to see what were Spenser's last lines. Now, uncle, I am right, am I not, in having a liking even for the incompleteness of some of our greater authors ?   We hear a poet singing ; and while we listen, we are bettered, and silent, and we are enraptured.   Then, while we are listening so eagerly, the voice dies away into silence and into heaven. .And so for a while heaven feels the nigher us, and to our earthly apprehensions the more real.

MARHAM.

Oliver, you make me feel the same as yourself. Well, now what are the last lines of Spenser ? They are part of what was to have been a canto in a seventh book, I suppose.

AUBIN.

Now when you remember that Spenser was intending six more books for his poem, do not these very last lines look as though, while he wrote them, another hand had been laid upon his hand, and had guided it prophetically ?

MARHAM.

In the midst of life we are in death.

AUBIN.

And in the very middle of what Spenser thought was his great work, he died ; and the lines that happened to be the last from his pen are as though they had been meant against his death : —

> For all that moveth doth in change delight.
> But thenceforth all shall rest eternally
> With Him that is the God of Sabaoth hight;
> O ! that great Sabaoth God, grant me that Sabbath's sight.

Now, in the very midst of his work, is not it as though the poet's hand had been unconsciously guided into writing a prayer against the death that was just upon him ?

MARHAM.

In the midst of his diligence he longed for heaven ; and that instant, it opened to him. Some might call this chance ; but I would not, nor would any, I think, who have lived piously and watchfully ; for such persons know the power prayer has to bring us nigh to God, and they know how holiness can refine, almost into film, what separates our souls from the Soul they live in ; and so they know that, even in this earth, something of the light of heaven is possible, in some minds.

AUBIN.

Dear uncle, you have said what I quite agree with ; and it is a great truth.

MARHAM.

Oliver, do you remember any other authors who have died and left unfinished works behind them ? There must be many ; but I cannot re-member any of them.

AUBIN.

Jean Paul Richter died, leaving behind him a manuscript he had not been able to finish. It was on the immortality of the soul. And so while expressing his faith in an hereafter, Richter went away into the knowledge of it. Frederick Schlegel left incomplete what was to have been the second part of his greatest work. He was seized with death at his writing-desk, and the last word he wrote was But. And that is a word death scratches with his dart, at the end of the record of every life. A man's eyes are shut; his breath is stopped ; his last words are spoken, and have been written in the book of God's re-membrance ; but, — ay, " but after this, the judg-ment." Death means blessedness, and it means perdition ; and which meaning it shall have for us is left for ourselves to fix. There is given us the choice of two pages, for our lives to be writ-ten on ; but they are not quite blank, and if we will write on the wrong side, then we write our condemnation with our own hands ; for at the bottom of that page it is written beforehand, " But after this, perdition."

MARHAM.

Did not Keats leave some poem unfinished ?

AUBIN.

Some poem, uncle ! Hyperion he left, and it was as a fragment. Now I will read you what were his last lines.

> Thus the god :
> While his enkindled eyes, with level glance
> Beneath his white, soft temples, steadfast kept
> Trembling with light upon Mnemosyne.
> Soon wild commotions shook him, and made flush

All the immortal fairness of his limbs, —
Most like the struggle at the gate of death,
Or liker still to one who should take leave
Of pale, immortal death, and with a pang
As hot as death's is chill, with fierce convulse
Die into life. So young Apollo anguished;
His very hair, his golden tresses famed,
Kept undulation round his eager neck.
During the pain Mnemosyne upheld
Her arms as one who prophesied. — At length
Apollo shrieked: — and lo ! from all his limbs
Celestial ——

Celestial was the last word Keats wrote, and then he himself became it. Very singular, is not it ? And in telling what Apollo felt, is not it as though Keats had himself agonized into immortality ?

MARHAM.

He is a very vivid writer ; and he is a favorite of yours, Oliver, is not he ?

AUBIN.

Yes, uncle. For my experience in life has been not very unlike what his was. I have had worse things to bear than he, but I have had a stronger body to endure in than he was born with. What a thought this is ! —

Where soil is, men grow,
Whether to weeds or flowers ; but for me,
There is no depth to strike in.

This I used to say every day of my life, before I knew you, uncle. But now I do not, O, not now ! For I have your love, uncle, and I am at ease in my mind. I am so happy to what I was ! and sometimes it almost frightens me to feel how happy I am. But I must not talk of this.

MARHAM.

Oliver, my dear Oliver ——

AUBIN.

Uncle, you know what poor Keats's end was. He died of a broken heart ; or rather of consumption, brought on by wrongs done to him, and by anxiety, and by the want of any prospect in life, such as any one of ten thousand persons might have opened to him. His poems are testimonies of the world's strange character. They are loved, dearly loved, now ; but now the author cannot be honored nor helped in life. And all the greater truths that are in the world, — what are they ? They are what were coined by wise men out of their experience. And then did they pay them away ? No ; but they gave them, like charity, on the way-side of life. The noble spirits ! And then they were hooted, like the utterers of base coin ; and if any one of them had a fast friend, he was scowled at and' suspected. This wickedness, uncle, you and I have never been guilty of, I trust. But wherever genius is to be seen, we reverence it like light that is not without a something divine in it ; and we do not think the worse of a man, because, in the world's darkness, God has given him that light to hold.

MARHAM.

Genius often has ill success in the world.

AUBIN.

To the world's great shame; for genius is only a genial working of the mind, a conjoint action of the moral and the intellectual powers. A man of the highest genius is a highly moral and a highly religious man, and a man of infinite love. Is he disabled for success in the world, — for getting money and friends ? So he is in some respects; but it is in what respects are immoral and irreligious. Men of some genius have done wrong things; so they have, for they were men; but they would have done worse things but for their genius. A man of perfect genius is a man of trembling sensibility, of the greatest delicacy of feeling, of honesty most scrupulous, and of a temper to help the needy as much as he can. The conduct of such a man is like Christianity in action, and very often it is not very unlike Christ in its end, in this world.

MARHAM.

Oliver, you are, — but you do not quite mean —— Oliver, our Lord Jesus was crucified, and it was for his goodness. Perhaps it was impossible that there could ever be a greater contrast than there was between Jesus in the image of God, and the Jewish priesthood in their priestcraft. Nothing at all like such a moral contrast can possibly exist now.

AUBIN.

O, yes, uncle, there does ; and it is between
Christianity and the manners of the world. My
dear uncle, you know nothing of life, nothing at
all of the badness of it. I do not mean to say,
that there are not hundreds and thousands and tens
of thousands of positions, in which men may and
do act as Christians. But I do mean to say, that
there are very common circumstances, in which a
man fails, as a matter of course, if he does to
others as he would have them do to him.

MARHAM.

Do you think it would prove so, Oliver, if it
were tried ?

AUBIN.

Uncle, if you were to put a bit of gold into a
bushel of pease, and the measure were then to be
well shaken for a time, would not the gold go to
the bottom ?

MARHAM.

Yes, Oliver, it would, it would.

AUBIN.

Through having genius, does a man fail in the
world ? It is grandly, and like the dying of a
martyr ; and not because the man is not fit, and
the best fitted, for any work, the lowliest and the
highest.

MARHAM.

Oliver, I agree with you quite. I have been
provoking you to talk.

AUBIN.

O uncle, have you ? Then you will agree with me in what I am going to say.

MARHAM.

What is it ?

AUBIN.

That the way in which often genius gets treat‐ ed, in this life, argues there being a life to come. If there were no grounds given us for expecting another world, still it might be believed in, and it would be, by some few better persons, though it were only as a place in which for wisdom to be justified of her children.

MARHAM.

Yes, Oliver, I do quite agree with you.

AUBIN.

Of all the proofs of an hereafter offered by hu‐ man nature itself, to my mind there are none so conclusive as the sufferings of the righteous for righteousness' sake ; or as those miseries that are brought upon a man through his goodness. A man's nature has been too good for the sympathy of his fellow-creatures ; then how solemnly sug‐ gestive this is of what must surely be the great love of God for it.

CHAPTER X.

Still in the soul sounds the deep underchime
Of some immeasurable, boundless time.

For otherwise why thus should man deplore
To part with his short being? Why thus sigh
O'er things which fade around and are no more, —
While, heedless of their doom, they live and die,
And yield up their sweet breaths, nor reason why, —
But that within us, while so fast we flee,
The image dwells of God's eternity. — WILLIAMS.

AUBIN.

YES, uncle, I know what that feeling is.

MARHAM.

All the good I have done seems nothing, and all that I have attempted would go into a nutshell.

AUBIN.

A nutshell! The whole world would go into it, seas, mountains, and air. So Sir Humphrey Davy has said.

MARHAM.

And in one of the Psalms, David has said of God, that he takes up the isles as a very little thing. And we that live on the islands, what are we? Ants on molehills we are, and less still.

AUBIN.

What then? For the less we feel ourselves, the better; the meaner, the happier; because, like a medal, character has two sides, and humility is always the obverse of greatness. At times, not often, indeed, nor long, but still sometimes, none are so weary of life as they that can enjoy it most and that are worthiest, of it. For what is that weariness ? It is the pining of a great heart ; it is a soul craving for itself some work worthy of its pains. The feeling of life's nothingness argues a mind capable of heavenly grandeur, and if capable, then made for it.

MARHAM.

So we will hope.

AUBIN.

I am glad there is no everlastingness in the world, and that I know it. I am glad the world is only for a season, for me and my fellow-spirits to be in. It makes me feel myself. Do not we know, that chambers are furnished, and are beautified with gold and silk, for princes to lodge one night in, — the very shortness of the use being the greatness of the honor ? And so, because this beautiful earth is only for so short a time, I am sure of what must be my own royalty.

MARHAM.

Royalty !

AUBIN.

Kingly character, then. And so I only feel myself what Christ has made me ; for through him I am a king and a priest unto God and the Father.

MARHAM.

Now, Oliver, I never thought of that passage so. But so it is, that one man sees all heaven through a text which to another reader is blank of meaning.

AUBIN.

And one man feels himself nothing on the earth, while another feels the earth nothing under him. But both ways of feeling are right ; but they are quite right only when they are moods of the same mind.

MARHAM.

I think so ; for, in itself, life's emptiness is mournful and discouraging to feel.

AUBIN.

So it is. But, uncle, this life is more real to you now than it was in your youth. For now that you feel yourself a living soul, eternity feels your element, and it is what you live in ; for they are only appearances that change, reality in all things being eternal.

MARHAM.

I do not think I understand you, Oliver.

AUBIN.

You have looked through death, and beyond it, into life ; this you have done ; you have looked through what is darkest, and so now, in all temporal things, there is for you the feeling of what is beyond and eternal. But in this way, when life

becomes nothing to us, it is because we are ourselves sublimed.   You go into the city, and it is
to your better knowledge that luxury is a look only,
and not a joy : about the court men are fretting
for coronets and collars, but it is to your more
manly judgment that these things are bawbles :
in his study, the metaphysician is wearying himself with thought, and he does most of it in vain,
as you think now ; but this is because your spiritual experience is greater than it was once, and
because you are sure that all wise thinking about
the soul must end in the wish to have it become
as a little child's.   And this earth is beautiful,
very beautiful, but then you feel that it will perish.

MARHAM.

Vanity of vanities, all is vanity.

AUBIN.

Perhaps so.   But those words are themselves
no vanity.   For when I think this world away
into nothingness, then where is my soul ?   It is
somewhere.   Where is it ?   It is left face to face
with God.   This I have often felt for a moment ;
not more.   A trance-like feeling !   The very awe
of which made me remember myself, and so
brought the world back again between my soul
and God.   What are those lines, uncle, that you
quoted last night ?

MARHAM.

They are Samuel Daniel's : —

> That unless above himself he can
> Erect himself, how poor a thing is man!

And so he is.

AUBIN.

Something like that couplet is what Coleridge
has written in his biography, that we were indeed
πάντα κόνις, καὶ πάντα γέλως, καὶ πάντα τὸ μηδέν, if we
did not feel that we were so. Vanity of vanities
Coleridge would have been himself, only that he
knew he was; no! he felt he was. For because of
that very feeling, he knew that he must himself be
something better. That I am dust, and laughter,
and nothing, how can I tell? That I am not spirit,
I cannot know, but by some feeling of what spirit
is; and by my having that feeling, I must be myself somewhat spiritual. It is nobly said by Jean
Paul, that man would be altogether vanity, and
ashes, and smoke, upon earth, only that he feels
as though he were so.

MARHAM.

That is well said by him.

AUBIN.

So it is. And so we will conclude, with him,
at those times when the world is empty and nothing to us, that — O God! this feeling is our immortality.

MARHAM.

Amen, amen!

CHAPTER XI.

Awake, my soul! pour forth thy praise,
To that great Being anthems raise, —
That wondrous Architect who said,
"Be formed," and this great orb was made.

Since first I heard the blissful sound, —
"To man my spirit's breath is given";
I knew, with thankfulness profound,
His sons we are, — our home is heaven. — HAFIZ.

MARHAM.

O OLIVER! this is a lovely afternoon.

AUBIN.

It is, very. Uncle, this is May-day. We can not welcome the month along with the boys an girls, with their garlands of flowers, but we ca along with Wordsworth, in a verse of his.

Flattered with promise of escape
From every hurtful blast,
Spring takes, O sprightly May! thy shape,
Her loveliest and her last.

Uncle, I have been thinking of what we talke about yesterday.

MARHAM.

And what have you thought?

AUBIN.

That with a mind not diseased, a holy life is

life of hope, and at the end of it, death is a great
act of hope.

MARHAM.

This is what you mean, is not it, — that the
righteous has hope in his death?

AUBIN.

Hope, the growth of his life ; for this is quite·
another thing from the merely wishful state of
mind that illness may well cause.   I will tell you
what I mean, from my experience.   When I am
happiest, my spirit turns to God of itself.   At
the gain of a new truth, in the reading of some few
books, at the sight of mountains, in two or three
successful instances of worldly endeavour, two or
three times in hearing of good actions, and sometimes, uncle, in loving you, my delight has been
so great, that speaking it to God has been a relief to me.   Then, through thanksgiving, my happiness has grown greater still, but calmer, and
purified, and with something mysterious blending
in it, as though it were a foretaste of other higher
blessedness.   I wonder why this was.   Perhaps
it was in this way.   Through faith, the hand of
God is seen by us ; and so every gift that we
have from it reminds us of the infinite stores out
of which it was given us.   But rather, I think,
that hope in happiness is an instinctive accom-
paniment of trust in God.

MARHAM.

Commonly it accompanies it, and strongly, and perhaps always; and therefore, perhaps naturally.

AUBIN.

There is a hope in God that is merely despair of the world, but there is a hope that comes of having lived wisely; and that is the experience of a man who has seen on the tree of his life, as one after another its blossoms opened, how there was on them the dew of God's grace; and so when the tree begins to be bared in autumn, early or late, he does not fear but that it will live and be beautiful again, in that great spring-time that will be followed by no winter.

MARHAM.

We will be grateful to God, then, Oliver, more and more; and so, perhaps, at the last, be quite trustful in him.

AUBIN.

That is what I have been wanting to say; and it is what I think to myself, often. Morning and evening, in prayer, I will strive to feel God, and the whole day through I will be glad in him, and every pleasure, I will say to myself, is from him. So, through faith, I will see the hand of God above me, and I will see it often, and get used to the sight of it; so that when it shuts upon my

7

soul to withdraw it from the world, I shall not be afraid, but glad.

MARHAM.

Hope it for me, Oliver, and pray for it for me, as well as yourself. I wish I may not, — O, I wish I may not go hence in fear !

AUBIN.

Fear, uncle ! No, no ! we will not fear. For have not you been happy here, very happy, very often? And for a good man, what is death ? It is a door in our Father's house, out of one chamber into another ; and to fear to go through it would not only be doubt of what is beyond it, but would argue want of gratitude for what happiness we are now having, which is a thing we will not be guilty of. But, O ! our heavenly destiny is prophesied in this, that thankfulness for what we have makes us more trustful of what we may have. We count up our pleasures in the Divine presence ; and then, as we look up to heaven, it is as though God were smiling upon us, and encouraging us to think that our earthly joys are only the beginning of delight.

MARHAM.

Several times, in prayer, I have had such moments of holy confidence. I have often feared they might be presumptuousness ; but I hope your interpretation of what they mean is correct ; and I think it is.

AUBIN.

O uncle ! all our better moods are prophetic of eternity for us. Justice feels itself rooted more deeply than the mountains are ; it is of the very essence of love to be consciously everlasting ; and faith feels as though it could die death after death, and be only the nigher God with every change.

MARHAM.

And God would never let these holiest affections of our nature be false witnesses to us about our destiny.

AUBIN.

O, no ! For it is by the prompting of God they speak, and in the name of God ; and they are worthy of all belief.

MARHAM.

And we will believe them ; we will. And we will thank God for every way by which our faith can be strengthened.

AUBIN.

After achieving a hard duty, after a great act of resignation or of forgiveness, after a very earnest prayer, and after a kind action, I have sometimes had a strange, mysterious feeling, as though some great revelation were about to be made to me, — such a calm in the soul, as though God were about to speak in it. Draw nigh to God and he will draw nigh to you ; — this is corroborated highly and solemnly, out of the soul's own experience. There are, — yes, there are moments permitted us, that are an earnest of the certainty and the way in which our souls will be drawn into heaven, at last.

CHAPTER XII.

To some hath God his word addressed
  'Mid symbols of his ire,
And made his presence manifest
  In whirlwind, storm, and fire;
Tracing with burning lines of flame,
On trembling hearts, his holy name. — ANON.

Now for my life, it is a miracle of thirty years, which to relate were not a history, but a piece of poetry, and would sound to common ears like a fable. — THOMAS BROWNE.

AUBIN.

My birthday I make a thanksgiving of to God, that it was when it was ; and so I do of my birth-place, very devoutly, as it was not to be farther west than Europe.

MARHAM.

My dear Oliver, do not thank God with a reservation. But I know you do not mean it. Besides, you will feel as though you had been born very far towards the west, if you will think of yourself as a native of what St. Clement wrote of, from Rome, as the worlds beyond the ocean.

AUBIN.

Born in a Christian era, and among Christians, nineteen out of twenty of the human race have not been ; but I was. And as I was not to be one of the earliest disciples, nor a friend of St.

John's, nor a convert of St. Paul's, I am glad
that I was born when I was, and not sooner.
For, with my nature, it would have been ill for
me to have been born within the unmitigated influence of St. Augustine, of Gregory the Great,
or of John Calvin. There are scales that will
weigh to the five-hundredth part of a grain;
but for use they require the very temperature of
the room to be minded in which they are, and
in any wind they would never balance at all.
Now, I think that in the religious struggles of
the sixteenth century, and in the politics of the
seventeenth, my judgment might perhaps have
been false to me. I do think, that, if I had been
born twenty years earlier, I should, as a spirit,
have grown up like some sea-side trees, that
branch out and blossom only on one side.

MARHAM.

Prejudice blights most of us.

AUBIN.

So it does. And instead of our charities blossoming all round us, they do so only towards certain quarters; and they are the quarters whence
blow the breezes that flattered us in our opinions
or interests.

MARHAM.

Perhaps it is more so with ourselves than we
think; we will hope it is not, and we will endeavour it may not be so at all.

AUBIN.

I congratulate myself that my birth was when
it was ; for I might have been born in Greece,
and yet not—in Athens ; in Athens, and yet not
have been a Christian ; in the first century, I
might have been born a Christian, but have lived
all my life as a sand-digger, at Rome, in what
are now called the Catacombs.   But I was born
into a richer world than Milton was, or than Jeremy Taylor, or than Newton ; for I was born into
a world that was become the more glorious for
their having felt, and thought, and spoken in it.

MARHAM.

You knew the name of Jesus early, and so you
knew, as a boy, pure religion, and what truth
there is in philosophy, and what is best in the results of science.   But this you know.

AUBIN.

Yes, uncle, and I thank God for it.   And next
after early baptism in the name of Jesus Christ, I
thank God for my mother-tongue's having been
English ; for by this I was made heir to the mind
of Shakspeare ; owner of a key to the treasure-
house of Locke's thought ; one acquainted with
Sir Thomas Browne's worth and oddity ; free
of a church-sitting under Isaac Barrow ; a fishing
companion of Isaac Walton's ; and one to differ
from Bishop Ken, and yet to love him.

MARHAM.

No, Oliver, I did not speak.

AUBIN.

The house of my birth was in the outskirts of
a borough; and the front-door opened into the
town, and the back-door into the country. This
was a happy thing for my boyhood, because town
life made me think, and the country made me
feel. The town was like an atmosphere of
thought when I went into it, and the country,
when I was alone in it, was an ever-changing influence upon me, — like a presence of awe one
minute, and another minute, like a joy melting
into tears ; and then, again, it was as though my
soul felt itself whispered by the breezes, " Come,
let us away into the heavens, and worship together."

MARHAM.

Oliver, you make me feel that I have many
reasons for thanking God that I have never acknowledged yet.

AUBIN.

I think it much that I have lived in some of
the riper years of Wordsworth, and Thomas Carlyle, and Ralph Waldo Emerson. It is not a little to have learned what it is that Orville Dewey
preaches. It is something, too, that I have been
a reader of Alfred Tennyson, and that, from
over the Atlantic, I have heard Longfellow sing
his ballads. And it is as though I could die,
more confident of not being forgotten before God,

for having been of the same generation with John Foster, and Thomas Arnold, and Henry Ware.

MARHAM.

How do you mean ?

AUBIN.

In the presence of a good man, we feel the better ; and the better our mood is, the nigher God feels to us. So that, in thinking over the saints who have been of our generation, and half-known to us, as it were, we ourselves feel the holier, in our capacities at least, and so as though God were more surely with us.

MARHAM.

And with us he is always, from birth to death ; and in every moment of our lives, as much as in the first. Oliver, you look much better than you did. I wish you, and now I begin to expect for you, many happy returns of this day.

AUBIN.

Thank you, uncle. But there are many days I should be happier to see return than this, I think. I do not know though. But I will tell you what I mean. The birthday of the soul is greater than that of the body. And, besides, if a birthday is reckoned as what life was given us on, then I have had many birthdays.

MARHAM.

How have you, Oliver ?

AUBIN.

I will tell you, uncle. One October afternoon a person was drowning, and I went to his assistance.

MARHAM.

Was he saved ?

AUBIN.

Yes, uncle. But when I was exhausted, which I was very soon, I was caught by an eddy in the river, and I sunk.

MARHAM.

How were you saved ?

AUBIN.

The river was very rapid, and it rolled me on to a sand-bank, off which I was dragged on to the grass. When I was drawn in under the water, I struggled hard, but I could not rise. I was quite aware of my danger ; but I was as calm as I am now. I believed my life was ending, and I thought, " Well, it is strange that I should have lived all these years of education, and endurance, and hope, only to be drowned." Then I seemed to see, at a glance, all my life, from my earliest consciousness to the moment when I leaped into the deep water. It was as though there were a presence in me of all I had ever done, or said, or thought, or known. I remembered little things of my infancy, and I saw the meadows, and the trees, and the sky, just as they had last looked to me. Then I could not lift my hands any longer; and I felt as though sinking through an endless depth of feathers. I thought, " Now this is death. God receive my spirit!" And he did, for I became insensible; and I had no care of it myself, but God gave me my spirit back again. I was swept on to the sand-bank; my body was seen lying there, and it was drawn out of the water, and through the reeds, into the meadow. And now I feel, that, when I breathed again, it was with a life given me anew.

MARHAM.

My brave, good Oliver!

AUBIN.

When I was a school-boy, there was a build-ing on fire, and the doors of it could not be open-ed. I climbed up to one of the windows, and broke it, and got in through it. I let myself drop on to the floor, and groped my way along the wall to the doors, which I unbolted, and then I fainted; for I had not been able to breathe, for the smoke. And just then the flames burst out.

MARHAM.

Oh!

AUBIN.

Many other narrow escapes of my life I have had; once was while I was bathing, and another time was in a storm at sea.

MARHAM.

Your life having been renewed to you so often and so strangely, I do not wonder at your not feeling the beginning of it as so very special. And, indeed, when we think of what sleep is, it is as though every morning our souls have what is a resurrection out of more than oblivion.

AUBIN.

I will tell you another strange thing that happened to me. I had done, with some effort, and not without earnest prayers, what I consider to have been the most righteous action of my life. But by it I had alienated the only two or three friends I had, who could help me in any way. Besides this, I had intrusted a man in distress with all my little money, as a loan for a short time, and he had died suddenly, without leaving any thing for my repayment, though, if he had lived a few days longer, I should certainly have had my money. I had worked day and night for a week, in the hope of being a few shillings the better. But my labor had been all in vain. I was penniless; I was without a friend to speak to; and I was weak in mind, from grief, and anxiety, and hard work, and no sleep. My self-control was failing me; and I was going away from the town I was in, with I cannot tell what other notions, but certainly with the feeling that I was never to return to it again, when a man laid

his hand on my shoulder, and said, — "I want to
speak with you, and you must go back with me
to your lodgings, for I have come fifteen miles
to see you. But how ill you are! You seem as
though in a high fever. Would your surgeon
think it right you should be out of doors ? " I
answered, that I should be well soon ; for I could
not tell him that I was too poor to have medical
help. The man wanted to consult me on a case
of conscience ; for he said, that, somehow, he
thought he could trust me. While talking over
his affairs, I forgot my own ; and by using argu-
ments to strengthen his will, I got courage myself. When he left me, I fell asleep. And that
night I slept long and well, which I had not done
at all for five nights before. When I awoke in
the morning, I was quite another man from what
I was the day before ; and that day, there opened
to me the prospect of getting a little employment. My reason was failing me, and would
altogether have failed me, but for that man's having come to me. What was it brought him to
me, at the very last moment he could have found
me ; for in another minute I should have been
out of the town ? It was not chance ; it was
Providence. And if I am in possession of my
reason now, it is because my reason was, in that
time of need, renewed in me, and made mine, as
much afresh as when it was created in my soul at
first.

MARHAM.

My poor, dear Oliver !

AUBIN.

Once I did what was against the will of every person I was connected with, and nearly all of them disliked me for it. So that I did not do it easily, as you may suppose. The hardness of my struggle was great. It was not without tears, and an agony of distress. Very painful it was. O my God, what I felt ! And well I might feel ; for freedom of conscience was beginning in me. A nobler birthday for me that season was, than the day on which merely my lungs got free to play.

MARHAM.

It is a birth that not many of us ever have, Oliver.

AUBIN.

When a man, for conscience' sake, does what his acquaintance will hate him for, then his soul has its birth ; and till he does this, or is ready to do it when wanted, his mind is not a soul. What is meant by our having been born on such a day ? That that day we began to draw breath for ourselves, and to live in and through our bodily functions. So, for a long while, our minds live in the minds of others about us, only feeling what others feel, and wrongly per-haps, as well as what is called respectably. It is the birthday of a soul, when a man finds himself listening to conscience, as though to God calling him, when he follows the voice, when he goes out from his father's house, and from all that is dear to flesh and blood, and goes, like Abraham, not knowing whither.

MARHAM.

But to God, and nigher to God, he does go certainly. Ay, at such a time, such a man's soul is born anew within him. And the angels, as they look at him from heaven, see that he is become not of this world.

AUBIN.

There are, then, some days of our lives that are more to be thought of than our birthdays. Our birth is a beginning only ; and it is a commencement of what may perhaps prove perdition. But these other days are what man gets to be an heir of heaven in. The third heaven St. Paul was in once. One beyond another the heavens are, and differing from one another in glory, like stars. And in this world there are those, who, as children, were such as there is a kingdom of heaven for ; who, as youths, lived up to the holy height of the dwellers in the second heaven ; and who, as men, have days in which they are born into fitness for one heaven one year, and for a still higher heaven the next year.

MARHAM.

God give us such days, and many of them!
But every day might be such, if we wished it;
but we do not; we are not morally strong enough
to wish it.   The day on which one man is
crowned, another man has to stand begging in the
streets.   And the sun shines on the contrast, and
there is no help for it in the sunshine, nor in the
poor man himself.   But it is otherwise in the
world that is shone upon by the sun of righteousness.   For in that world, and in the light of that
sun, any man may make himself what he will, —
a brother of St. Paul's, a friend of Christ's, a
ruler elected to be over many things, an heir of
salvation, and a son of God.   But much of this
grace and blessedness we do not receive, because
we do not ask.   I believe this, but not enough.
Lord! help my unbelief.   O, it is sad to think
how seldom the voice of God is listened for,
though there are times and ways in which it makes
itself heard by the most careless!   When the
voices of pleasure are silenced about us, then we
are wretched, and we cannot help hearkening for
what comfort God may speak to us.   And through
the lips of a friend's dead body there comes to us,
out of the unseen world, a warning we cannot
help minding for a time.   And sometimes we are
touched so strangely, by words and by little things

which happen to us, that we cannot but confess God's power in them.

AUBIN.

When I was seven years old, I heard a hymn read from the pulpit ; and there was one verse of it that thrilled me so, that I could fancy myself hearing it being read now. I remember it to this day, though I have never heard the hymn, nor seen it, since.

> Youth, when devoted to the Lord,
>   Is pleasing in his eyes ;
> A flower, when offered in the bud,
>   Is no vain sacrifice.

With the invitation of that hymn, it was as though I was caught up into a heaven of resolution and hope.

MARHAM.

And that, I suppose, was one of the earlier of those days in-which you were born again. Well, it is a great day on which a man first draws breath ; but it is quite as great a day for him, perhaps, on which he first draws his breath in hope or in fear.

AUBIN.

Uncle, I shall never forget my finding a sermon of Channing's. I read it, unknowing of the author's fame, and I think from the beginning to the end without once looking off the pages. And when I had read the discourse, I said, " The

8

Father of spirits be thanked for this ! for now I can understand the Gospel, and now I shall be able to grow in grace." This was on one of the greater days of my life, one August afternoon, when I was a youth.

MARHAM.

Your spiritual experiences interest me very much.

AUBIN.

The other day, I was looking over some notes of my writing in a book, during a time of great distress with me. And I saw what I wrote one night after very earnest prayer, and perhaps the most effectual, fervent prayer I ever prayed. It is to me a record now of the beginning of a new era in my life, as a soul, a suffering soul, and a soul to be perfected. After the date of the day of the month and the year, these are the words : — " This night have I seen God for the first time." At that time of agony, in the earnestness of my prayer, I felt the presence of God with me, almost as though I saw it. I have now a feeling of what I felt then.

MARHAM.

Yes, it is strange how the feelings of some days of our lives do last on in us. Yet it is not so strange, either ; for we are in ourselves what those few days make us.

AUBIN.

Once I was not, and now I am. This is a thing to think of; it is a great, great thing. Up and down Syria the patriarchs wandered, and in their tents talked with their wives, in the valleys pastured their cattle, and here and there built altars, for sacrificing on to God; but in their way of life there was no part for me. At the building of the Pyramids, laborers crowded, and toiled, and shouted; and there was great earnestness; but there was no feeling of it for me. The hundred gates of Thebes were opened and shut; but there was no going in or out through them for me. Thousands of millions of men and women were born, and loved one another, and died; but in all that kindness, there was no share for me. Rome grew, and grew vast, and decayed; but there was never any place in it for me. In England, Britons dwelt together; and then Saxons sat round blazing hearths, and Norwegians and Normans had houses, in which they enjoyed themselves; and age after age men talked with one another, and worked together, and rested together, and were merry and sad together; and I was not anywhere. The sun shone on this very spot, and it was cloudy here, and it rained, and just as it does now time wore on; but I was not in it. And what thousands of years birds had been singing, and the flowers had been flow-

ering, and rivers had been flowing, and day and
night had been, while I was nowhere ! Nowhere ?
Alive I was not. But I was a thought in the
mind of God ; and now I have been made, and
now I am what Providence has care of. But
when I think of the time, the eternity, past in
which I was not, and then think of the day I was
born, I feel fresh from the hands of God ; I feel
as Adam may have done when he got up from
the earth, and knew himself that minute made
out of the dust of it.

MARHAM.

Fearfully and wonderfully we are made.

AUBIN.

Years, hundreds of years, thousands of years,
hundreds of thousands of years, for infinite ages,
I had no being, though God was meaning I should
have ; then, a few years ago, he let my life begin,
in his gift of a child to my father and mother.

MARHAM.

O, but it is a wonderful life, this of ours, when
we do think what it is ! Every child at its birth
is an Elnathan, a gift of God.

AUBIN.

And it is not for God to give and not to care.
Sometimes my soul is in darkness and mourns,
and it is as though God were far from me ; but he
never is, and I know he is not. For God is not
with us less one day than another, though there

are seasons in which our souls can feel him more. Yes, I know that what God has been to me at any time, he is always; and he is more to me than what I know, infinitely more. O, there are days that call to me out of the past, and one asks solemnly, "Dost thou not remember having been born again, and was not that change God with thee?" It was; and what I am now is because God is with me. And another asks, "Wert thou not as one dead once, and art thou not alive again?" Yes, and my soul's going out of the body will not be more terrific than many passages in my life have been. The day of my death will not be stranger for me than several days have been that I have lived through, through God; and so for which I have come to know God the better and the more happily. And I shall die, but only to know the more blessedly that God is the Father of us spirits.

CHAPTER XIII.

Mysterious Night! when our first parent knew
Thee from report divine, and heard thy name,
Did he not tremble for this lovely frame,
This glorious canopy of light and blue?
Yet, 'neath a curtain of translucent dew,
Bathed in the rays of the great setting flame,
Hesperus with the host of heaven came,
And lo! creation widened in man's view.
Who could have thought such darkness lay concealed
Within thy beams, O Sun! or who could find,
Whilst fly, and leaf, and insect, stood revealed,
That to such countless orbs thou mad'st us blind?
Why do we, then, shun death with anxious strife?
If light can thus deceive, wherefore not life?

J. BLANCO WHITE.

MARHAM.

PERSONS who have no faith themselves cannot understand in what way those who have it are the better for it.

AUBIN.

But whether we know it or not, we are all of us mysteries to ourselves and to one another. In our souls there is what is connected with God, and through that channel what may come, or how we may be quickened, it is not for us — no, nor for the angels — to say.

MARHAM.

It is very likely that hereafter some very slightest help or change may be enough to make us enjoy ourselves a thousand times more than we have ever done.

AUBIN.

There are landscapes by Paul Potter which are a delight to look at. But the Dutch scenery that he painted from, and painted exactly, is ugly and very dull; or rather I should say, it is so to most persons; but to Paul Potter it was not. Now I can believe, if some little want were supplied in my spirit, that the whole earth would be glorified to me, and God be seen throughout it.

MARHAM.

And so God be all in all, even to the eye.

AUBIN.

You remind me of another thing which I have remarked. A man has looked at a scene somewhere, and thought it to be very pretty; but when he sees it as a landscape in some great master's painting, he feels it to be spiritual, and his soul is the better for the sight.

MARHAM.

Is it so, Oliver? Well, how do you account for it?

AUBIN.

The artist is an interpreter of the earth's look, and such a helper we most of us need; just as the heathen cannot understand the Gospel without its being explained to their minds. However,

the more godly we are, the more we shall feel
the spirit of God in all God's works, and in all
his workings with us. The lily looked to Christ
more, and something diviner, than it does to us,
when he spoke of it as being so arrayed in glory
by God. God so clothing the grass of the field !
— there is a way of thinking of that which ought
to clothe our souls in faith.

MARHAM.

Faith, perfect faith ! That is the garment
which in the wearing would make life be like a
high festival, and this earth like the house of the
Lord, and our thoughts like Christ with us.

AUBIN.

That is what I am sure of ; and from my being
sure of it, my little faith serves me more than it
otherwise would. Troubles and pleasures and
death are about me. And they are about me like
a blessed home. Though this is what I do not
see ; but I do know it. So, in whatever my circumstances are, I can feel at home, and not like
a prisoner ; just as in this house I am sure that I
am at home, even in the dark, and when I can
only feel things about me and not see them.

MARHAM.

Whatever our darkness, God is in it ; and
through faith in him, if we have not light at once,
we have peace.

AUBIN.

Death comes to us in the dark, and so he is dreadful to many men ; but to the saint he is not. For though the Christian cannot see, yet he feels what the look of death must be ; and rightly, for in the light of heaven death looks divinely, and is one of the angels of God.

MARHAM.

I have been thinking that the fear of death is from thinking too much of one's self. At the last hour we will look up to God, and then death will come upon us as though straight from God.

AUBIN.

God is in the world and in all things more plainly than I can see ; but I can trust in what Christ saw. O, there is a song of triumph over our human nature, which day unto day is said about the earth, and which night unto night is chanted, and which the morning-stars sing together in for joy ! The song itself I cannot hear, but the joy of it I can believe in, and I do, and I will. So, at the last, I will feel as though underneath me the earth were glad, and as though the heavens were bending towards me from above, and as though there were joy among the angels at seeing in me what to them is birth immortal, though we mortals call it death.

CHAPTER XIV.

The tree
Sucks kindlier nature from a soil enriched
By its own fallen leaves ; and man is made
In heart and spirit from deciduous hopes
And things that seem to perish. — HENRY TAYLOR.

AUBIN.

You draw a deep breath, and fold your hands, and drop them a little, and sigh. What is it for, uncle ?

MARHAM.

It is an Eastern proverb, that the recollection of youth is a sigh.

AUBIN.

And so it may be in the tent of a misbeliever, and not without reason, with a man whose hands shake so that he cannot hold the lance, the tip of which was once protection for him, and bread for him, and glory, and gold, and the leadership of a tribe. But your Arabic proverb ought to be an untruth in England.

MARHAM.

Yes, the Gospel saves old age from being gloomy in itself ; but there are past pleasures that are a sadness to think of.

AUBIN.

Then they ought not to be, and in themselves they are not. With you, uncle, the recollection of youth ought to be quite another thing than a sigh.

MARHAM.

It is John Wilson who says, —

> How wild and dim this life appears !
> One long, deep, heavy sigh,
> When o'er our eyes, half closed in tears,
> The images of former years
> Are faintly glittering by.

AUBIN.

And falsely, if they make a Christian sad. Old men get from one another the habit of sighing over what is gone. What John Wilson wrote about a buried saint, we ought to say about youth when it is dead and gone, —

> The body in the grave is laid,
> Its beauty in our hearts.

And it is in the feeling of that beauty, that old men ought the more to hope for immortality. I say, uncle, that remembered joys are abiding joys ; for I am a Christian. But if I had no hope of heaven, then my memory would be like a charnel-house, and would be what I should not like to look into ; for then, in its chambers, all recollections of youth and happiness would be painful ; for they would be forms of perished pleasures ; and to think of them would be like opening a friend's coffin, only to see the body rot. But to Christian feeling, the remembrance of early delight is like some foretaste which has been had of the blessedness of heaven.

MARHAM.

With me, Oliver, the long, long past was so happy !

AUBIN.

And is become so poetical. To your mind now, the rod is what might have blossomed in the nursery any morning ; and a whipping at school is to you now as though it had been an emphasis of delight, which I do not think it ever was. What you are, you feel yourself to be ; but what you think you once were, that you never were. You should be thankful, uncle, that the past does become poetical ; but you should not therefore let the present feel melancholy. In the sunset of life, the path behind looks the more golden, the farther off it is ; but it only looks so, for it is not so really. Besides, uncle, there might be eyes in which your early would seem less happy than your present life. It is only to me that what befell me in my boyhood is so glorious.

MARHAM.

True !

AUBIN.

What troubles we have, we feel; but what are over, we do not even remember. For nearly every misfortune is like Janus, and has two faces; the one with which it comes is terrific to look at, but the face with which it passes away is that of an angel of God.

MARHAM.

Oliver, more than once, at a sudden appearance in my house, I have been frightened, and hid my face, and prayed God to hide the evil from me. And more and more dreadful it seemed to grow. But when I prayed for strength to bear the look of the calamity, then it became bearable, and slowly it grew bright; and at its vanishing there was a glory left behind. And so what I prayed against at first, proved at last to have been an angel with me, entertained unawares.

AUBIN.

Uncle, what terror you felt, you do not feel now; but the joy thrills on in you still. Of all life past, there was no one happy day the sunshine of which does not brighten us now, when we look back; but the clouds of the gloomy times are vanished as though they had never been.

MARHAM.

Well, it is so.

AUBIN.

Pleasures are pleasures for ever. You, uncle, are happy in the happiness of the past, in all that you remember of it, in the holidays, and sports, and adventures of your childhood, in the successes of your youth, in many a night's and midnight's conversation with learned men and dear friends, and in those watchful hours, when, from the firmament of thought, the greater lights first reached you with their glorious rays. Your times of delight are a delight to remember ; but your seasons of suffering are no pain to recollect. That they existed, you know ; but what they were, you cannot at all feel. Anxious nights, bitter disappointments, great sufferings, you have had ; but of very few of them is there any of the painfulness in you now.

MARHAM.

That is what argues the goodness of God very strongly, — that our pleasures are lived by us over and over again, but not our pains, or at most, not many of them.

AUBIN.

None of what I have been speaking of, for I have been meaning such troubles as are over.

MARHAM.

Our friends we grieve for many days and years after the day of their loss.

AUBIN.

That is because they are not a past, but a continual loss, for a long while. But of your friends who died many years ago, the very burials are not sorrowful memories now.

MARHAM.

Very dreadful life would be, if grief for the departed never wore out; but it does, and so as to leave no feeling of what it was. Or rather, I think, our departed friends become to us what we cannot weep for. And the longer we have been weeping, the more peacefully at last we give over; for those whom we mourn the most are they who become to us the most saintly to think of.

AUBIN.

Yes, they do. I had a dear friend waste away in my sight, week by week, and die. The agony of this, I know, was great; but I have no feeling of what it was, now. From me, at the time, he seemed to disappear in darkness. But my eyes were blinded with tears; and they were the darkness; for now, as I look back, it seems to me as though he had vanished like an angel of light, and as though he had left a track of glory along the years during which I knew him.

MARHAM.

So, then, you will have me think that it is my remembrances of youth which have been brightening, and not my latter years which have been darkening ?

AUBIN.

Yes ; and I think this, too. In your mind there have sprung up, from time to time, thoughts, of which you reaped the harvest in joy, but the seeds of which were sown in you in tears. These thoughts you remember, and the joy with which you had them first. But you have no re-membrance of how they first began to grow in you, in what was a time to weep.

MARHAM.

No, no ! We have not the same remembrance of pain as of pleasure.

AUBIN.

The recollection of pleasure is itself pleasure ; but the recollection of pain is not pain. And if the suffering be quite over, the memory of it is more than agreeable ; it is blessed. For, to a Christian, the after-taste of the cup of sorrow is like a draught from the river of water of life. But indeed, excepting of sin, all recollections are more or less pleasant ; some like a thrill of the nerves, and some like the reading of poetry ; while others make mournful music in us, and others, again, are like the holy fervor of a thanksgiving.

MARHAM.

The past, then, may sadden us, and what one now is may sigh for what one once was ; for you say that there are recollections that may make a mourning in us.

AUBIN.

Mournful music in us, uncle. And there are masses for the dead, which, to listen to, are full of the spirit of immortality ; and so ought all an old man's memories to be. My life I would not live over again ; would you yours ? Why, then, should you sorrow for what you would not wish to have ?

MARHAM.

Few and evil are the days of the years of our lives, say the Scriptures.

AUBIN.

The Scriptures say it ? No, they do not. They only say that Jacob said it. And when he did say it, he did not mean that life was evil with him, when seven years of service seemed only like a week, for the love he had to Rachel.

MARHAM.

When he said that his days had been evil, I suppose he meant that life, as a whole, felt so to his aged feelings.

AUBIN.

About life, my dear uncle, whatever Jacob may have said and felt, you ought not to feel and say the same ; for though of the same flesh as the patriarch, you are not of the same spirit ; for every man, in Christ, is a new creature.

You are right, Oliver. And I was wrong in using as my own Jacob's last words about life. And so you say, I think, there is a fashion of speaking mournfully about old age ; and of speaking comes feeling.

AUBIN.

Good and evil are the lot of old age, and so they are of youth. Does it seem now as though youth had been all good? Is not it, then, in some things because early life has resulted in abiding good? And, perhaps, behind you many of the points that catch the light of heaven most blessedly are what were once shuddered at as mountains of hardship to cross.

MARHAM.

No, no! When óne thinks of it, it cannot have been. And early life never was what it now looks.

AUBIN.

Pardon me, uncle, but I think it was.

MARHAM.

You do! Then I have not understood you.

AUBIN.

Yes, uncle, you have, I think. What I said, or more certainly, what I meant, was this. Youth was what it looks to have been ; but in the spending, it never felt what you fancy it did. Ay, youth would be something, and a something not

of this earth, if it were what it feels to you. But
that would be for a boy to have at ten years of
age the mind that grows in a man only at seventy.
To all men, youth would be a little more nearly
what it looks, if there were more faith in them
while it is passing. ⸱ And there is a greatness of
faith, in which it would be possible for a man to
wear his old age like a vesture, which unem-
bodied spirits might, some of them, envy.

MARHAM.

⸱ Lord ! increase our faith. St. Augustine said,
that he would not change places with any angel,
if only he could attain the station assigned to
man.

AUBIN.

O that station ! And yet when we have
reached it, and when we are ensphered within it,
everlastingly, this very day will be a fond memory with us. For it will be a pleasure, in the
city of God, to think how we used to die daily
in the earth. These are our latter days, and the
ends of the world are upon us now ; but in heaven
any recollection of our present feelings will be a
zest to our immortality, and what will make us
look up to God and thank him.

MARHAM.

And for me, this may be before the year ends
its round.

AUBIN.

It is more likely to be for me, uncle ; that is, if
I am worthy of heaven on my dying. And for us
both it will be before Saturn finishes one' circuit
more. And then we shall be untouched by what is
planetary, — by heat and cold, and the changes of
day and night. And the light of the sun and moon
will be nothing to us when we are citizens of the
New Jerusalem ; and on our becoming immortal,
days and years, the shadow that moves on the
face of the dial, the hammer that strikes the hour,
and the marvellous clock-work of the stars themselves, all will be nothing to us.

MARHAM.

And then the last enemy will be nothing to us ;
for death we shall have undergone, and found to
be birth. O God ! may our certainty of what
death will prove to be strengthen us against what
it seems to be.

AUBIN.

And it ought to do so. For in itself life was
better than what it felt in our passing through. In
your youth, uncle, no doubt you were troubled
about many things, and you took more thought
about the morrow than was right, and you were as
anxious as though of your life you had the whole
guidance, and God had none ; and so, through
littleness of faith, the eyes of your understanding
were withholden, so that you could not see things

about you as they might have been seen, and
as they look now that you have passed through
them.

MARHAM.

Now I see them beautiful with the light of God
about them ; but that light I had little feeling for
once. Ay, and I must remember that in these
old days of mine the light of God is on all things
round me, as much as it ever was. Faith, more
faith, is my great want. The Lord is my salvation ; why or what should I fear ?

AUBIN.

I will think of the past, and so be brave for
time to come. Adversities laid hold of me, but
I said, Whom the Lord loveth he chasteneth ;
and so they became angels with me unawares.
And moving in remembered scenes, what are
those forms I see so beautiful and smiling, and
with the light of heaven shining from them ?
They are friends, who, the last time I saw them,
were bodies wasted and convulsed ; rather, so
they seemed to me to be ; but now they are to
me what in their agonies they were just becoming, — they are saints of heaven. Sufferers they
were, and now they are saints ; and so I think of
them, though at first after losing them my thoughts
of them were as painful as their last days were.
It is not the past has changed, but myself ; for I
judge of it more wisely now than I did.

MARHAM.

Even while passing, life was more beautiful than we know of ; and so, in coming, death, without doubt, is diviner than we feel.

AUBIN.

Week by week I am nearer the end of my life, and time pushes me on towards death, out of one day into another.   But after prayer in an evening, I have a thought that comes into my mind with a feeling as though it were sent ; and it calms me with a peace not of this world, and it says to me, " It is through night that the day begins anew, and it is through death that life will be thine afresh." Misfortunes seem to call to me from places where I met them, " Evils we were at the first look, but in thine eye of faith we changed into ministers of God ; and so will death."   And there are solemn seasons, in which, from heaven, holy and departed friends make their witness felt within me, " Our last agonies did but make us immortal ; for death is Christ's, and Christ is God's."

CHAPTER XV.

Now this is why, in my old age,
  No sorrow clouds my brow,
No grief comes near me, and no cares
  Disturb me here below.
Serenity broods o'er my mind,
  'For I daily pray to Heaven,
That when the hour of death arrives
  My sins may be forgiven.
No anxious fears disturb my breast,
  My days serenely roll;
I tarry till it pleaseth God
  To heaven to take my soul. — JEAN MICHEL.

AUBIN.

THERE are some who grow to be men, and almost old, without the knowledge of suffering. And their thanks to God are for their many pleasures ; and for their sorrows, when they come to thank him, they are not the men they were. For, in the mean while, they have eaten of the tree of the knowledge of good and evil, and found Eden vanish from about them, and the world feel like thorns, and thistles, and dust, and a curse. And there are some who do not get the better of this sense of desolation ; for they are angered by it, and not humbled. But those who, having lost the feeling of Eden, get that of earth's being Gethsemane, soon find life rise heavenwards under

them, like a Mount of Olives; and when they
look up on high in the thought of Christ's ascen-
sion, heavenly longings rise within them; and
their souls clouds cannot darken any longer, and
what is commonly the darkest of all is to them a
cloud of glory, for it is what will receive their
souls out of earthly sight.

MARHAM.

Yes, sometimes a man may be thirty or forty
years old before his first grief; and when it does
come, what a change it makes in the tone of his
mind!

AUBIN.

A great change, if the sufferer proves to be a
saint; and a great one, too, if the sufferer becomes
a reprobate concerning the faith. For affliction
separates men to the right and to the left, like
Christ from the throne of his glory. For I have
known some who seemed to worship God zeal-
ously; but it was not the true God, but the God of
their good fortunes. What they worshipped in
was founded upon the sands of pleasure; and so,
when the floods of misfortune came, their temple
fell; and then they said there is no God.

MARHAM.

Instead of saying, as they ought to have said,
" Mine was an idol, and God Almighty pardon
me the wrong worship." Ever more and more
do I myself thank God, — God! I do thank

thee for what troubles I have had ; they were
touchstones of my faith, and now they help to assure me of heaven. And yet, — O God ! in
merciful affliction let thy will be done upon me, if
unknowingly I am serving thee for wages and not
for love. Oliver, I have been thinking of what
we talked about two or three days ago. And it
seems to me that old age is meant to be a further
and a last chance for those who have not been
made wise before.

AUBIN.

There are those whose minds are so small, that
this world is enough for them, as it would seem.
To a man of this character who is a tradesman,
the earth was made for his shop to stand on, and
to be a street for his customers to come up ; and
to him life is a long market-day, and the safety of
a bank is in the place of Providence ; and his
sorrow for a bad bargain is an anxiety greater
than ought to be felt for any thing else but sin.
And sinful his state of mind is become, for it is
without God. And now memory, calculation,
activity, fail him ; and so his love of trading fails.
And now he says, " I thought existence had
been a mart for trading on, but it is not, though
it is only so I have used it. Lord, have mercy
on me ! "

MARHAM.

Better late than never, infinitely better. But

it is sad to see a man begin to serve God only because he cannot serve Mammon any longer. That is more melancholy than seeing a man's faculties fail. Though the decay of the mind is very distressing to witness. To know that very probably your own or some friend's mind will be enfeebled by old age ———

AUBIN.

Mind, mind enfeebled ! Body you mean, dear uncle. Mend the decaying body, and the mind would show itself again. It is not the soul, but only the manifestation of it, that fails with the brain. My hands are palsied, and I cannot use them ; but my mind is as lively as ever. My brain is torpid, and is useless for thinking ; but my soul may be the same as ever. An aged relative of mine had been childish for many years, and knew none of her family. But for an hour or two before she died, she was herself again. And she knew all her friends, and asked after her absent children. And through her watery eyes and blank expression, her soul looked out on the world again as loving, and knowing, and peaceful as ever. That I myself saw.

MARHAM.

In her body, some change against death had excited her brain a little, I suppose.

AUBIN.

And made what was not brain be brain, and what her soul could make itself felt in.

MARHAM.

For years she had been imbecile, do you say?

AUBIN.

Yes, uncle. Of the day of her life the latter part was as dark as night; but it was with fog and clouds, not with an extinguished sun. For in the evening, the sun of her reason was seen again, and seen to have been always shining in itself, though not into the world.

MARHAM.

Why, why, — what can be the reason, — this, of the soul's being allowed to be so eclipsed?

AUBIN.

There are many good reasons for it, I have no doubt ——

MARHAM.

Dear Oliver, I do not ——

AUBIN.

It is a great thing for us to be made sure sometimes, that, though the soul is darkened, it is not put out. And if we see for ourselves that the soul can be eclipsed, and yet shine on again, then we can so easily trust how the shadow of death will pass over it, if righteous, only to leave it shining forth as the sun in the kingdom of our Father.

MARHAM.

Thank you, Oliver. But I was going to say, that I had asked just now what I should not; perhaps it was more my feeling which was wrong, than what I said. For it is better to trust in the goodness of what God does with us, than for us to be anxious about what his purpose is. Yet, Oliver, do you know it sometimes feels as though it would be a relief to me to know what certainly are the uses of old age which God intends?

AUBIN.

In regard to old age, I think what you have been saying. I think that there is a purpose in it, and a privilege higher than our thoughts, and above what we could have understood from the Son of God, if he had spoken about it.

MARHAM.

Age makes leisure for reflection, whether we wish it or not.

AUBIN.

The years of old age are stalls in the cathedral of life in which for aged men to sit, and listen, and meditate, and be patient till the service is over, and in which they may get themselves ready to say Amen at the last, with all their hearts, and souls, and strength.

MARHAM.

And so to depart in peace. Old age has been called a disease of the body, and perhaps it is; but very certainly it ought to be consecration of the soul. Oliver, you are looking for something. What is it you want?

AUBIN.

O, I can do without the book. I will tell you a saying of Martin Luther's. He said, that God assembles to himself a Christian church out of little children ; for that when a little child dies, of one year old, that always one — yes, two — thousand die with it, of that age or younger ; but that when he himself, who was sixty-three, should die, there would not be a hundred of his age die with him ; and that he believed that old people live so long in order that they may see the tail of the Devil, and be witnesses that he is such a wicked spirit.

MARHAM.

I would sooner believe that men live to be old so as to know for themselves the truth of the text, that even to our old age God is the same, and that even to hoar hairs he will carry us.

AUBIN.

Age does for the whole character what can be done for it in youth only by one adversity on one side, and by another on another. Even with the best man, rule is apt to run to self-will, and high health to self-reliance, and knowledge to pride, and unblemished morals to self-satisfaction. But when the man grows old, he finds age to be a corrective of all this. His sight and hearing fail, and so he has to rely on the eyes and ears of persons about him. His memory fails, and so he has to depend on other men's recollections. His body leans, — ay, and so would his soul, and be bowed quite down, only that, as he grows weaker, he feels more and more a divine arm about him upholding him. And upon that arm he leans, and the more lovingly the longer he lives.

MARHAM.

There is good, Oliver, there is great good, in old age ; more and more I hope to know of it for myself.

AUBIN.

The ancients might call old age sad, but that is what we Christians ought not to do. And if about any old man there are things that might sadden nim a little, let him be a Christian, and his melancholy will be changed into what will be like a gentle prayer, always rising from within his soul. In a sermon which I once wrote ——

MARHAM.

A sermon, you said ?

AUBIN.

Yes, uncle ; I thought once of writing and publishing some ten or twelve sermons on the religiousness of daily life, but I only wrote one.

MARHAM.

I should like to see it, Oliver.

AUBIN.

You shall have it, uncle, this evening.

CHAPTER XVI.

Where there is no vision, the people perish. — PROV. xxix. 18.

THIS text was a proverb once, and its meaning
was accurately known a hundred generations ago ;
but now it is not, and it never will be known quite
exactly ; for this proverb is a something of the
spirit, and the world of spirit is not to be scruti-
nized like that of matter.

From a few marks studied upon limestone,
from a few rocky appearances, from a few fossils
and bones, and other like proofs, will a man, after
the manner of Baron Cuvier, rightly infer what
this earth was before it became what it now is ;
what its climate was and its plants, and what the
aspect of its forests ; how the mammoth looked
and moved amid tall trees, and in and out of their
shadow how there went creeping things innumer-
able and monstrous ; at what swiftness the bird of
prey flew upon its victims, and what its victims
were ; how it rained then as it rains now, and
how the tide rippled on the sea-shore then as it
ripples now, and how the shells were mostly then
what are not to be found now. And the look of

what all this was, science will make out from a few vestiges.

And vestiges of ancient thought the book of Proverbs is. Our text is one of these spiritual remains, and for us it has a meaning plain enough, though perhaps not exactly what the author meant; because what his state of mind was in thinking it we do not know, for at that time the human mind was under another economy than the Christian.

" Where there is no vision, the people perish." There may be hidden meaning in these words, perhaps, but there is plain truth. Most of the Proverbs are easy to be understood, though some of them are of no use in our English circumstances, and some others are too shrewd for Christian simplicity. But all of them are interesting as spiritual remains. Vestiges they are of an era in the human mind, long, long back; words of caution, spiritual armour, fashioned for the use of the young in the anxious minds of experienced sages; proved advice for behaviour in the house, the city, and the field; and immortal truths which wise men coined out of their mortal sufferings.

" Where there is no vision, the people perish." Whence came this proverb among the Jews, for had not they their prophets always, and visions always? No, for the school of the prophets in Ramah was sometimes attended in vain; and as

in the latter days of Eli, the priest, often there was
no open vision. And why was it, at any time,
that the prophets could "find no vision from the
Lord"? It was because the people had disabled
themselves for such grace, and not because God
was changeable, as some of them thought, and so
withheld his free spirit from them. God never
withdrew from them who had Abraham to their
father; but withdraw from Him they did, not over
Jordan, but farther still, down the steeps of vice,
into that thick air of sensualized thought, which
hardly a ray of spiritual light can shine into.

Among the Jews, when there was no vision,
they perished, and with ourselves spiritual ruin is
very common, for want of spiritual insight. Spiritual insight into life is the subject of this sermon.

I. Let us think about life as activity. In God
you live and move and have your being. That
not a breath do you draw, nor a pulse do you
feel, nor a step do you take, but in dependence
on another will besides your own, — this you do
not doubt. Nor can you doubt that in God your
spirits live, as far as they live at all; for like the
church of Sardis, they may have a name that
they live, and be dead.

Our human is no empty existence. The circumstances of our lives are not unmeaning, but
infinitely otherwise; but this we very often do not
see for want of vision. High as heaven and wide

10

as the earth is the atmosphere of holy opportunity, in which our souls have their being. Is not it felt? Then it is only because it is not wished.

Not every hour, nor every day, perhaps, can generous wishes ripen into kind actions; but there is not a moment that cannot be freighted with prayer. But do you say that you cannot pray except when night solemnizes your spirits, or before the day's business begins? Begins the disorder of your souls; say that, and so you finish your excuse. But do you establish it? No. For that would be unchristian business, and to be shunned like hell itself, that could not be done in a quiet, loving, and devout spirit.

What! you have perverse wills to deal with, have you? And these evils you do not, some of you, overcome with goodness, but oppose with heat. Firmness, principle, do you call it? But it is not. For be sure of this, that, in any circumstances, a right temper towards your fellow-creatures is what would any moment pass freely into prayer. Do you object, then, that business is not and cannot be made religious? Theological it cannot be made, but religious it ought to be. Do you say that labor can be executed rightly, only by minding it and thinking of nothing else? But is not it done sometimes sulkily, and sometimes cheerfully? And cannot it also be done trustfully? And would it be done any the

less thoroughly, if the laborer felt himself something better than a machine, if the ploughman felt
himself more than a continuation of the plough-
handle as he holds it, and if he were glad at being
a worker together with God, — God in the elements, and himself in the flesh ? Does any one
still contend that in trade a man cannot be spiritu-
ally-minded, and that in the throng of domestic
cares the spirit is quenched, and does not and cannot live ? Then the old anchorites were right in
retiring from town and home into solitude. For
is not this the worst thing possible, and the most
horrible, to be without God in the world ?

To be born in heathen ignorance of God is the
worst misfortune. But, whether in a counting-
house, or handling tools, or busied with domestic employments, to remain in circumstances that
close the avenues of. the soul against God's Holy
Spirit, — and this through nearly the whole of six
days out of seven, and therefore through nearly
the whole of life, — this is not misfortune, if it is
what we know ; for it is crime. Crime those
early anchorites felt it, and so they left their
homes and their old places of business and pleasure. And criminality there is in us, if we are
living large portions of time in a way that is without God. But in all probability it is not what
we have to do, but it is our spirits, that want
changing. And they may be so changed, and be

made so familiar with loftier views of life, and so eager after righteousness, that, in the field, and the shop, and the house, what is now a monotony of work for them may itself become an exercise unto godliness.

God forces man to toil, and it is well; because, without life were laborious, much of what is best in it would never be. But in exertion there is what is not often thought of. This less-heeded virtue of it I will now speak of.

There are kinds of action that are specially favorable to the formation of a good character; such as relieving those who are in want, risking life in good causes, and devoting one's days to such works as are, like virtue, their own reward, all unrewarded else. But the merest toil, the merest muscular exertion, draws character out and helps to fix it. Every stroke of the hammer on the anvil hardens a little what is at the time the temper of the smith's mind; if blasphemous, he is morally the worse for working; but if hopeful, trustful, then, though the blow rings only on the iron, it is a blow for goodness, and it is struck against sin and on the side of God; and because struck in the faith and cheerfulness of the man's soul, his faith and cheerfulness are in that way exerted, though indirectly; and so those divine feelings are strengthened in him a little. The toil of the ploughman furrows the ground, and so it does his brow with wrinkles, visibly ; and invisibly, but quite as certainly, it furrows the current of feeling common with him at his work into an almost unchangeable channel.

What exertion a man makes from day to day makes intenser his ordinary mood. It makes the sensual man more brutish still ; and him in whom there is little vision it makes still blinder to God and goodness, and what life is ; while at hard work, along with deep breath the saint draws in holiness.

The monks of old knew that, for willing persons, there is a religious use even in manual labor. It was a saying with one of the fathers of the Church, and with some monasteries was a motto, that to work well is to pray well.

Bodily exertion makes mental earnestness ; — earnestness in what you will, — what you choose to let your working mood be. Be discontented with your lot in life, — in other words, be dissatisfied with God, — commonly work in that state of feeling, and then every day your mind will darken, and every effort of your arm will help to rivet on your soul the chains of perdition. Chains of perdition ! The metaphor does but hide the truth. For your soul's godless, joyless temper is itself perdition ; and the stripping your soul of the flesh would itself leave you in hell.

What ! hell for what is hardly called a crime,

— for what is less than fraud, lust, and falsehood !
But with no joy and peace in believing, is a mind
guiltless ? and shut against the Holy Spirit, is not
a soul sinful ?   In the vision of judgment in the
Revelation, St. John counts as the victims of the
second death, the abominable, and murderers, and
whoremongers, and idolaters, and all liars.   But
these are not all whom he names ; there are two
other classes, and in his mention of them they
precede the abominable and the murderer, and
these are the fearful and the unbelieving.   They
are the first in St. John's list of the wicked, and
theirs is the state of mind in which all wickedness
begins.   Murder, lust, lying, are manifestations
of an evil spirit ; of which evil spirit the very essence is unbelief.   Passion throws a shade against
the sun of righteousness, and in that eclipse the
benighted man sins ; for no man ever did wrong,
feeling full faith in God the while.

Quite away from all feeling of God no man
ever quite escapes ; and into the most darkened
spirit a few rays of the Divine Majesty will flash.
And most persons are accessible to religious influences for an hour or two on Sunday, and for a
few minutes on other days.   But this does not
show religious character, but only religious capacity.   The cheater and the debauchee have times
of mournful longing for their lost innocence.   But
this does not show that they are virtuous, but

only that they are capable of becoming so. And
so with many a one, his regular prayers betoken,
not that he is religious, but that he might be so if
he were to will it. The holy spirit is a spirit,
and not one mood of the mind ; it is not sabbat-
ical, but daily ; it is not a morning and an evening temper, but a perpetual presence in us.

O, there is a spirit that Christians have, that
makes domestic and mechanical work be more
devout than what service often a priest per-
forms ; making it be done heartily, as unto the
Lord, and not unto men. There is a spirit that
is quickened, and not quenched, by vexations ; a
spirit of forgiveness, enforced, and free, and rejoicing : for he that is forgiving in this world is
blessedly conscious of being himself forgiven in
another world, and for ever. And no one ever
hushes what he might think his just anger into
silence, without feeling that there is another life
dwelling in his little life, — God in his soul. And
so in his soul he has the peace of God rise and
spread over what would otherwise have been the
disorder of his passions. Most lives are thronged
with anxieties ; but there is a spirit that is not
overcome of these things, but that bears with them
in the high thought of being in fellowship with
God ; for if we have to endure evils, God bears
with their existence too.

Whether or not this Christian spirit is his, ev-

ery one knows and cannot but know. Now this
spirit is being. strengthened within you, or it is
being shut out from you, in every thing you do,
— by the pleasures you take, and the labors you
undertake. You are capable of being, and some
time you may will to be, what as yet only your
enthusiasm thrills to in a hymn, or some better
hour now and then ; but you are yourself what
your common mood is, and that only ; and that
mood is made more abiding in you by every yes
and no of your speaking, and by whatever use
you make of your hands.

II. Let us now consider what is the spiritual
effect upon us of the outer world. The sights
and sounds of nature stream into our minds, a
force for good to the good soul, and for evil to
the soul that is evil. Nor is this so strange, if we
think on some experiences of our own. Perhaps
with us all there have been mysterious seasons,
— summer evenings, oftenest, — in which all nature about us has felt instinct with meaning ; when
our spirits have thrilled into the same tone with
the wind in the tree-tops, and rock, and river, and
the distant stars have felt as though struggling with
their dumbness for speech with us.

There is some incitement of nature upon us
nearly always, perhaps, though we may not know
of it. Like our bodies, our souls are affected
by gloom and sunshine, day and night, summer

and winter. For instance, a bright day makes us decided in our minds, and it shines precision into our purposes. While in the evening we may notice that it is with some states of our spirits as it is with some plants, which flower only in the night-time. With the twilight our hearts begin to soften, but in what way, darkness has nothing to do with. For while one man is softened into pure affection by the evening, another has his feelings relax into debauchery.

Also, when the limiting world is shaded from our eyes, the feeling of the infinite is freer within us, and it blends with our other feelings and makes them stronger, and passionately full; and so our spirits feel sublimed by the awfulness of night, and the world around us is transfigured; and so much so, that to our altered mood vice itself is altered, and is not the odious thing of mid-day, but a fruit, forbidden indeed, but hanging still on the tree of knowledge, and not fallen into the common mire of sensualism. And so damnation is often plucked and eaten under the spell of night, by those who would never have so sinned in the day. Never have so acted the sin, is the truth; for the sinfulness itself must have been in them before, because outward circumstances do not make any feeling in us, they only quicken it. And often a good man will thrill with holy zeal from the same cause that makes another man's heart throb only with selfish anxiety. Thus, too, night does not appear one thing to one man, and another to another; for it has the same look to every human eye; but it has not the same feeling to every spirit, but much otherwise. For in many things our souls feel only what they are ready to feel. And so darkness is to one person like the shadow of God's hand upon the earth, and under it he rejoices with trembling; while another man feels it like a disguise to walk in, and he loves it better than light, only because his deeds are evil.

To the evil-disposed, the whole world is a temptation; and all the changes in it are so many vicious allurements; and the very voice of nature is turned into fleshly suggestions. While, to a Christian, nature is as pure as her Maker, and is full of his expression. David's feelings may be ours. May be? They must be. They will be ours, if in this world of God's we are God's children; and we shall feel how the heavens do declare the glory of our God, and how the earth is full of his goodness. Yes, there is a state of mind in which God's presence everywhere is what is felt, as well as known, and in which the Maker of heaven and earth is more than a devout phrase, — is a living reality, a felt Godhead, the indwelling spirit of the green earth and the fiery stars.

Only let us love God, and then nature will compass us about like a cloud of divine witnesses; and all influences from the earth, and things on the earth, will be ministers of God to do us good. The breezes will whisper our souls into peace and purity; and in a valley, or from a hilltop, or looking along a plain, delight in beautiful scenery will pass into sympathy with that indwelling though unseen spirit, of whose presence beauty is everywhere the manifestation, faint, indeed, because earthly. Then not only will the stars shed us light, but they will pour from heaven sublimity into our minds, and from on high will rain down thoughts to make us noble. God dwells in all things; and felt in a man's heart, he is then to be felt in every thing else. Only let there be God within us, and then every thing outside us will become a godlike help.

In the morning, we shall wake up to work "while it is called to-day," and more deeply every night will darkness solemnize our spirits; and the four seasons, as they change, spring into summer, and autumn into winter, will ripen our little faith into "joy and peace in believing"; and every year, more and more clearly, the world will be for us " a glass, in which we all with open face, beholding the glory of the Lord, shall be changed into the same image from glory to glory, even as by the spirit of the Lord."

III. Of action in life and of the scenery of life we have thought; now let us think of participation in life, — of life as shared with others.

" He that loveth not his brother abideth in death "; so wrote the Apostle John; and thus Jesus Christ said : — " I say unto you, Love your enemies." But out of the circle of our acquaintance, and beyond those to whom we can reach a gift with our hands, what is Christian loving ? It is not merely not hating, as the common notion is, but it is spiritual sympathy.

" What is my neighbour's misfortune to me ? for he was no friend of mine." So says Respectability. And what said William Hazlitt, who dared to speak out many things that most men feel, but only few confess ? Now Hazlitt was a kind-hearted man, and yet he has written that men never hear of the ill-fortune of their friends without being secretly pleased. And with Christian exceptions, this is a thing to be believed. For perfect friendship is impossible in any but a Christian spirit. It is not to be felt out of social instinct only, joined though it may be to intellectual refinement and a quick sense of honor. This is the friendship of the world, and it is what may be enmity with God.

Man, the child of God, may be a true friend, but not the man of Hazlitt's observation, not the man of the world, not a man merely, though thoroughly, well educated.

' scenery of 1
ik of partici- -i
1 others.
r abideth in n
a; and thus a
you, Love a
e of our act- ·
om we can t
...an lov- ·
he common t
me to me? !
} says Re- ·
n Hazlitt,
that most l
w Hazlitt :
las written l
le of their '
And with l
be believ- ·
...e in any
...: out of
may be to
· of honor.
! it is what

ve friend,!
r. not the
...gh thor-

There is pleasure in the sight of the same faces day by day ; and so there is in the intimacy of those who can be helpful to one another, as they contrive and labor in the same corner of the earth ; but for true friendship, the world must be felt as something more than a workshop ; it must be the busy porch of infinity.

This is the feeling that perfects friendship ; and it is what perfects that love which is the fulfilling of the law. Sympathy, fellow-feeling with one another as spirits, immortal spirits, — this makes the temper, which, when it has opportunity, does, and is glad to do, good unto all men ; which rejoices with them that do rejoice, and weeps with them that weep. Is this our mind ? For if it is not, we are perilously wrong. Our state is not only not right, but it is what gets worse every day.

It is not enough for a man to love his family tenderly ; it is not enough for him to love a friend or two, so as to be willing to halve his property with them ; and to the poor, it is not enough for him to give alms, for this the Pharisees did, and freely ; and domestic love and friendly attachment a man may feel who bitterly hates his enemies.

Christian love not only relieves a poor man's nakedness and hunger, but it strengthens his soul with sympathy ; and domestic and friendly affection it sublimes out of capricious instinct into a feeling, which, for an unfailing fountain, has the depth of infinity itself, and for brightness, God's smile upon it, and for warmth, hopes that glow with immortality.

God! of what grandeur this life of ours is made capable! In the eye of faith, what a glory it often wears! Spiritually we are what we will be, and the meanest of us may have a day such as kings and prophets longed for once, but never saw. For now God is known in Christ, and now in Christ our spiritual nature is regenerate, larger in capacity, and richer in opportunity, and what may become in all of us that which Jesus felt, as he prayed, "I in them, and thou in me, that they may be made perfect in one."

Look at the life of a saint. It is honorable and beautiful outwardly, but inwardly it is nobler still; just as behind the very brightness of the stars is hidden the exceeding and indwelling majesty of God. In the heart of a saint, how sweetly all his anxieties are soothed into peace, mysterious and "not as the world giveth"! No, not as the world giveth! For when heaven and earth shall have passed away, that peace will have outlived the disorder it controlled among the passions, and will have hushed for the soul her fears for a perishing universe.

In the mind of a saint, there is not a thought but has the most wonderful relations. It is holy,

because God Most High is holy ; it is solemn
with the unknown, but fast coming, day of judgment ; it is self-denying in and through the spirit
of Christ upon Calvary ; it is trustful with the
faith of many days' past prayers ; and it is cheerful with that joy of God with which the whole
universe is instinct, but which on earth wells up
nowhere so freely and purely as into a believing
mind. While over the head of a saint, the meanest cottage has heaven open ; and nigh him always
is a door to be opened by prayer, and at which
to ask is to have given him a wealth of goodness,
and comfort, and assurance of heaven. " For
every one that asketh receiveth, and he that seek-
eth findeth."

Faith is the inspiration of nobleness ; it is the
strength of integrity ; it is the life of love, and is
everlasting growth for it ; it is courage of soul,
and bridges over for our crossing the gulf between
worldliness and heavenly-mindedness ; and it is
the sense of the unseen, without which we could
not feel God nor hope for heaven.

Faith is the very life of the spirit ; how shall
we maintain it, how increase it ? By living it.
Faith grows with well-doing. What little faith
you have, only live it for one day, and it will be
stronger to-morrow. Live with your fellow-creatures as their brother to-day, and to-morrow God
will be felt by you as your Father in heaven the

more tenderly.   We become children of the Highest, through loving like our brethren the dwellers
of the whole wide earth.   And it is a law of our
spirits, that, in many ways, what we regard others
as being we ourselves become.

If you treat another as having no feeling, you
harden your own heart.   If you are suspicious
commonly, what does your temper betoken ?   It
means that you want faith in goodness.   And you
may allow yourself to doubt your friends so much
as to have but little faith in God at last, and so
as yourself to become worse than your own sus-
picions about your acquaintance.   Disinterested
you cannot continue, nor become, if you are to
be thinking often as to whether other persons are
selfish or not.   A man that is in want, you shall
treat as a suffering brother, and not relieve as a
beggar, else your own soul shall be beggared of
delicacy.   Here is a fellow-creature in reach of
your hand, and in want of help, which you could
give if you would ; now if you do not, it is because to you the man is not even as the least of
Christ's brethren ; and so every time you see
him, you are spiritually the worse ; for to shut
the eyes against virtuous opportunity weakens
virtuous perception.   Here is another man whose
most earnest thoughts are of Mammon, whose
pleasures are of eating, and drinking, and vanity,
and whom the world loveth as its own.   Now if

you have a love for that man that is not pity,
then

"His spirit shall have power to weigh thy spirit down."

Here is a good man who is poor; now if you
withhold your regard from his virtue on account
of his being poor, poor will you yourself grow in
worth. Here is another fellow-creature; he is a
servant of yours, perhaps, and perhaps you feel
towards him not unkindly, and yet only as though
he were some contrivance of flesh and blood.
So much the worse for you, then. For the man
has a living soul within him, — a soul despairing
and hopeful, suffering and enjoying, loving and
praying, and not without a looking for of judgment. And some little it is through sympathy
with his soul that yours is meant to grow. Here
is some bad or ignorant person within the reach
of your influence; now if you are heedless of
his crown of immortality, then the fine gold of
your own will grow dim.

> "And he that shuts Love out, in turn shall be
> Shut out from Love, and on her threshold lie,
> Howling in outer darkness. Not for this
> Was common clay ta'en from the common earth,
> Moulded by God, and tempered with the tears
> Of angels to the perfect shape of man."

Think of what St. Paul has written, — "We,
being many, are one body in Christ, and every
one members one of another."

11

This is the manner of our being ; it is of God,
the way of our spiritual growth now, and perhaps
for ever ; that morally we make ourselves what
we treat others as being.

Yes ! for the spirit, all things have spiritual effect. All actions, — such as occur only once in a
lifetime, and such as make up our daily business,
and even what are only momentary, — all actions
are expression, unavoidably. But it is for ourselves to will what they shall be expressive of,
and so strengthen in us, — whether apathy, self-
will, discontent, sensuality, or a spirit hopeful, and
cheerful, and loving, and joyful in God.

Yes ! for the spirit, all things have spiritual
effect. Nature is an excitement for us, more or
less, almost always ; but whether for good or evil
is according to what our spirits are. One man is
made moody by hearing the winter's wind, while
another is sublimed by the almightiness that flies
upon its wings. Silence is a spiritual power to
feel ; and in it one person feels the more inclined
to sin, while another man, as it were, hears from
on high the music of the spheres, known only to
those who are being taught by virtue

"How to climb
Higher than the sphery chime."

Yes !- for the spirit, all things have spiritual
effect. Sharing in life, along with others, has.
Very largely we ourselves become what others

are to us. If to our regards they are not spiritual, then we are not spiritual. If others are to us living bodies only, then very nearly of the flesh, fleshly, we must be. But if in others we honor the image of God, then upon our own souls it will come out and brighten. Love truly, and then other men's souls will be sources of your soul's growth. Sympathize with the good in their endeavours, and you will yourself be morally the stronger. Revere the wise, and yours will be the state of mind into which wisdom comes most freely. Love little children, and something of their innocence will come over your mind, and whiten its darker spots. Love them that are old, and your soul will be as though the longer experienced in life.

This life that we are living in is not empty of power, but full of it, — power that is on us and about us always, and into the nature of which we have vision given us, that we should not perish.

Wish to be a child of God ; and then sunshine and frost, and friends and enemies, and youth and age, and business and pleasure, and all things, will help to make you.

CHAPTER XVII.

Our many deeds, the thoughts that we have thought, —
They go out from us thronging every hour;
And in them all is folded up a power
That on the earth doth move them to and fro;
And mighty are the marvels they have wrought
In hearts we know not, and may never know. — F. W. FABER.

MARHAM.

I LIKE your sermon, Oliver. Why did not you go on with your purpose, and write the volume which you meant, on the religiousness of daily life?

AUBIN.

Because I became too poor to pay for the printing of it. Instead of my making sermons to others, I had myself to listen to one every day, preached to me out of a stone pulpit, by poverty. One day the text was, "It is good for a man that he bear the yoke in his youth"; and another day it was, "Man that is born of a woman is of few days, and full of trouble"; but on the festival days of the soul, it was, "As dying, and behold we live; as sorrowful, yet always rejoicing; as having nothing, and yet possessing all things." It was a course of sermons that lasted with me a long, long time. But I am the better for it. At first, the voice of the preacher was distressing to me, but my ear got so attuned to it as to hear it like a voice, the tones of which God was using to talk to me with. And now I am another man for what I learned then. I am not the same as I was, either in mind or heart, nor in my way of expressing myself. So at least I thought, on lately looking over the sermon which you have been reading.

MARHAM.

What I am sorry for is, that you have deserv-ed to have a name ——

AUBIN.

To be printed in catalogues of old books ; and I have not got it. But what does that matter ? Why should one covet being forgotten as an au-thor as well as a man ? Since nearly all of this generation will be forgotten, both the men and the books of it.

MARHAM.

A few years, a very few years, and of us two all that will be left in this earth will be a little dust, and in a few men's minds a few distant rec-ollections of us.

AUBIN.

Ay, in one man there will be a recollection of your having shown him a curious book; on anoth-er's tongue there will be some faint after-taste of a very good dinner of your giving ; in another, there will survive the way you looked in your morning-gown ; while in the memory of another, there will be living the tones in which you said he was a good boy. In men's minds a faint remembrance of us, and, six feet deep in the ground, a little blackness in the mould, will be all our remains in the world.

MARHAM.

Then a little while longer, and they will have vanished ; and then, ah ! then there will be no trace left of our lives ever having been.

AUBIN.

Been what, uncle ? Not spent in vain.

MARHAM.

I thought, Oliver, you were saying that we should be forgotten soon.

AUBIN.

So I did. But I did not mean that our lives would ever be unfelt; for in this world they never will be. Babbage says, that, with every word spoken, the air vibrates, and the particles of it are altered as to their places ; that the winds, north, south, east, and west, are affected every time I speak ; that, with my voice, the atmospheric particles in this room have their places changed, not so as to be any thing to us, but so as, ages hence, to witness to higher minds than ours what we have been saying this afternoon.

MARHAM.

In that way, there is more truth than was intended in what came to be used as a Christian epitaph, — *Non omnis moriar*, I shall not, all of me, die. For so our idlest words are as lasting as the earth.

AUBIN.

And so are our actions, and so are our thoughts.

MARHAM.

And more lasting than the earth they are ; for by them our everlasting souls are the worse or the better.

AUBIN.

True. But what I mean besides is, that our influence will last as long as the earth.

MARHAM.

Ours will !

AUBIN.

Yes, and so will any peasant's. Because, of course, I do not speak of the endurance of names. For they are only one or two persons in a generation, and not ten out of a whole people, who stand in the sun of life in such a way as to have their shadows lengthen down all time.

MARHAM.

You mean, then ——

AUBIN.

That my cousins, go where they will, are living impulses in society, and of your beginning.

And just as there is something of your grandfather in you, there is something of you in your
grandchildren ; and there will be something of
them, some time, in their children.

MARHAM.

No doubt, men's lives do live on in their de-
scendants.

AUBIN.

In their flesh and blood, their beating hearts
and pliant limbs ; but so they do in other ways,
and in other men.   For every good deed of ours,
the world will be the better always.   And perhaps
no day does a man walk down a street cheerfully,
and like a child of God, without some passenger's
being brightened by his face, and, unknowingly to
himself, catching from its look a something of religion, and sometimes, not impossibly, what just
saves him from some wrong action.

MARHAM.

The stream of society is such, that often a
pebble falling into it has altered its course.
Many times, words lightly spoken have been carried against thrones, and been their upsetting.
And many a little event has had in it what in its
unfolding filled towns and countries, and men's
minds, and ages.   I say, that, under Providence,
it has done this.

AUBIN.

An ark of bulrushes fetched from among the

flags of the Nile was the saving of Moses, and the deliverance of the Israelites, and an event through which the Saviour of the world was born where he was. The way of thinking which St. Paul got as a youth influenced his way of viewing and arguing the Gospel as an Apostle of the Gentiles, so that when Saul of Tarsus was listening at the feet of Gamaliel, it was as though the whole Christian Church had sat there. And very certainly Augustine would never have been heard of in the world so much and so long, and even now so reverently, but for his mother, in whose warm temperament he shared, and after whose earnest prayers on his behalf, year after year, he became Christian.

MARHAM.

Yes, there have been men of such a character and standing as that, through happening to them, even slight things have, in their effects, become stupendous, and as wide as the world. But we were speaking just now of common life and ordinary men.

AUBIN.

And without common men, there could be no uncommon ones ; and every extraordinary event has its roots in quite ordinary places. Days and years are linked together, and so are men's lives, by chains of cause and effect, and sometimes curiously and most wonderfully. So that it is possible, that to-day in a shop what an artisan is working at with a song may be the cause — no ! one means — of filling a palace with grief fifty years hence, and of changing a dynasty. Or one word of your speaking to a boy this morning may prove to root and thrive in his spirit, like good seed, and to become what will bear fruit for a whole neighbourhood, and perhaps for a nation, and for ages.

MARHAM.

That is not a thing that could ever be known.

AUBIN.

Not in this world, perhaps. Nor would it be good for us to know such things ; for we are weak creatures, and we might get to do what is right for the sake of its grand effects, and not for its own dear loveliness. But though much of the greatness of the life we are living is wisely veiled from us, yet we cannot believe too much of it. And now, uncle, rays from the stars come millions of millions of miles together, and there are millions of them in the breadth of an inch, yet they are not lost in one another ; and it can be told of any one of these rays whether it shines from a sun or a planet, or whether from a solid or a liquid mass. Man can know this with his eye of flesh ; so that it is not impossible that an angel may be able to trace a thought out of one mind into another, from people to people, and down generations.

MARHAM.

It is not so unlikely ; and, Oliver, it is perhaps even probable.

AUBIN.

Perhaps when death shall make us spirits, the spiritual world will be open to us, and all the movements in it ; and great thoughts will look like angels going from soul to soul ; and noble feeling will seem electric, as it spreads ; and some words will be echoing for ever, out of the recesses of one soul into the chambers of another.

MARHAM.

The watchwords of liberty and right.

AUBIN.

Hated, and wronged, and blind, and nearly friendless, was John Milton, during the latter part of his life. His sufferings were great, and so was his faithfulness ; and he has sat down in the reward of them. And perhaps, now and then, he hears from his throne in heaven the refining music in men's minds which his poetry makes round the earth, unceasingly. I knew a mother, who died with her arms round her child, praying God, the while, to guard it. And now, along her son's path, shining more and more as though unto perfect day, is to be seen what perhaps gladdens her with the certainty that the fervent prayer of her righteousness did avail him much. And many years hence, there will be to be seen

among men some little trace of my having lived ;
and perhaps I shall myself see it. O, that would
be a tender delight ! It is not impossible, I think.

MARHAM.

In heaven every sinner that repents is known
of ; and, very likely, so are the means of his conversion ; and if so, then nearly all the holy influences there are in Christendom must be known of.

AUBIN.

I shall not live long ; nor shall I be in the
memories of men very long. But out of the
characters of men I shall never die, quite : no,
not in many ages. I like the thought of lasting
on in the earth, any way. It is pleasant to me
to think even of leaving my body behind me in
the world.

MARHAM.

O, is it ?

AUBIN.

Out of this world into another my soul shall go,
through death. Soon this earth will be to me
what my body was buried in. My body will rot
and become dust ; but it will be my dust. And
always it will be in the earth ; and I like to think
so. Dear world of my birth, that I am to remember for ever and ever ! I have had pain in
it often, and pleasure often. And, O, what I have
learned in it ! God, and Christ, and my immortality ! And I have got the knowledge of the
Good, the Beautiful, and the True.

MARHAM.

And of Human Brotherhood.

AUBIN.

The blood of which God has made all nations of the earth is not much felt yet, as being one blood. But our having shared in it will be a near relationship when we human creatures have scattered ourselves thinly among the hosts of heaven. Then to have been of the same generation will be like having been of the same family; and, down long streets of stars, we shall look back upon this earth as the little home we all lived in once. When I think how I shall remember this world after death, sometimes there are moments in which I do love the very dust of this dear earth.

MARHAM.

I feel so sometimes, Oliver.

AUBIN.

Years ago, a beggar and I exchanged looks on a road-side, and we have never seen one another since; and we never shall again, in this world; but after many ages, perhaps, we shall find ourselves standing side by side, looking up at the throne of God.

MARHAM.

There lies no despised Lazarus at my door; but perhaps I have not searched far enough into my neighbourhood. I could help the poor more than I do, I think. There are some things, —

luxuries they may be called, — which I might deny myself, and perhaps ought to. I will think of this, and to-night I will ——

AUBIN.

Uncle, are you speaking to me, or only to yourself ? for I do not hear you.

MARHAM.

I was thinking something to myself, and aloud, too, I suppose. But, Oliver, go on with what you were saying : now, do.

AUBIN.

I shall die soon. The hand of God is on me. My feelings are not much changed, perhaps ; but they are stronger than what they were, I think. Now, every man I part from is a soul to be met again, and every face I see is what will be bright with the light of heaven some time, and in my sight. Duty reaches down ages in its effects, and into eternity ; and when a man goes about it resolutely, it seems to me now as though his footsteps were echoing beyond the stars, though only heard faintly in the atmosphere of this world, because it is so heavy. Yes, dear uncle, and in this way I shall still hear you, though soon you will hear me no more. But often when you are doing a good action, you will think the light of it is to be seen in heaven, and that perhaps I am seeing it. And sometimes after your prayers you will think that, some way, I may know of them, and perhaps join in some of them ; for now and then I may be near the elders spoken of in the Apocalypse, as having every one of them golden vials full of odors, which are the prayers of saints. What, then, is death ? It will be a concealment of me from the world, but not a hiding of the world from me. Always there will be something of me lasting on in the world ; and to the end of it the world will be known to me in some things, I think. Yes, it certainly will be. What is it, then, to die ? It is not to be estranged from this life utterly. O, no ! For it is to be taken into the bosom of the Father, and to feel his feelings for this world, and to look back upon it from under the light of his eyes. Death is this, and it is beauty and it is peace.

CHAPTER XVIII.

Silent rushes the swift Lord
Through ruined systems still restored,
Broad-sowing, bleak and void to bless,
Plants with worlds the wilderness,
Waters with tears of ancient sorrow
Apples of Eden ripe to-morrow. — EMERSON.

I, the heir of all the ages, in the foremost files of time. — TENNYSON.

AUBIN.

O FOR a day of ancient Greece ! O to have been quickened for a week at Rome, in Cæsar's lifetime ! O that I had had a day with the priests of Egypt ! and then I should have known what intelligence the Sphinx is meant to look. O to have had an hour with the Druids of Stonehenge, and so to have learned what soul was in their doings there ! O for one of the days of the school of the prophets at Ramah !

MARHAM.

They are wishes which you would be none the better for having, Oliver ; for if they were good, they would not be impossible.

AUBIN.

I should like to have had a week at the court of Lorenzo de' Medici, and a month at Alexandria in the second century, and a day or two with the sand-diggers at Rome when they were become Christians, and were making their excavations in the earth, into churches, and tombs, and hiding-places against persecution.

MARHAM.

They must have been a very interesting class of men.

AUBIN.

I should like to have had a day's talk with Abelard. And, O ! I should like much to have been a Moor of Granada for a while. Human nature I should like to know in all its varieties. I should like to be an Italian for a week, and a Norwegian, and a Hindoo, and I do not know what else.

MARHAM.

Nor I either, to any purpose. For such experiences would not be of any use, or else God would have made them possible. So I think, Oliver.

AUBIN.

My dear uncle, you are quite right. And besides, when we look beyond the clothes, and deeper than the skin, civilized nations are not so very different from one another. Betwixt five nations there are not greater diversities than there often are in the tempers of any five members of an Anglo-Saxon family ; only in the household these differences do not seem so great, because

12

all the members of it dress alike and are drilled into like habits. If a man loves the twenty persons nearest him, and so sympathizes truly with their peculiarities, then with the reading of a few books of travels he knows almost as much of human nature as though he had been amongst all nations.

MARHAM.

It is only with our eyes and through telescopes that the stars are to be known, and it is by much travelling and searching and comparison that the various kinds of flowers and plants are to be known that grow on the Andes and along the Oregon, in the West Indies and in Australia. But it is chiefly out of a loving heart that mankind is to be known. There are good men who have never been out of their native valleys, who are wiser in human nature than thousands are who have traversed the world.

AUBIN.

Nearly wise, I would say, they are. They have just what is almost wisdom, and what would be wisdom at once, with a very little experience of men. I have known one or two such persons, and in talking with them I was always expecting something wiser than what they said. It was as though they were always just about to become great. I think the state of mind of such persons is what will enlarge in heaven, and brighten very fast.

MARHAM.

I quite think that. And in that way many that are last now will be first hereafter.

AUBIN.

They are seraphs elect, as is sometimes even to be felt in talking with them. A man of this character I knew once, who was a pauper ; and I never saw him without my soul being humbled in me. For, in presence of his goodness, I myself felt so unworthy ! I assisted him a little, and only a little, for I was myself suffering some want at the time. But that he should be accepting relief from me made me feel that there must be a world to come, in which for him and me to be in juster places. And when he thanked me, with humble words, I trembled in myself, — because it was as though, all round me, the universe were calling out against me for my enduring to be less of a sufferer than he was who was a better man than myself.

MARHAM.

He must have been a very extraordinary man, Oliver, I should think.

AUBIN.

So he was, uncle ; and so he is now. He became known to a gentleman, by whom he was befriended and brought forward in the world, and so well, as that he is now a man of station and some public repute. In his profession he is very eminent; and he exemplifies, to some extent, the truth of what we have been saying.

MARHAM.

I am so persuaded, Oliver, that, though a man can be cunning without a heart, he cannot be wise. It is against the Gospel to suppose he can be. And humble, humble, we must be, if we would know any thing to any spiritual purpose.

AUBIN.

And especially if we would know human nature; for one way of learning it is out of our own hearts, and they are books that can only be read in humility.

MARHAM.

Yes, humble we must be, before we can know ourselves, and be willing to see that in our own hearts are the beginnings of what might be like the vices of every nation in the world.

AUBIN.

There is one soul in all us human creatures. In my mind are the elements of all other men's characters; and my many moods are so many national tempers. In the middle of summer and in the heat of the day, now and then, I am a Brahmin; and sometimes in the middle of winter, with the wind roaring in the wood, I feel like a Scandinavian. A word or two from some one, some little event or other happening to me, a little bile more or less in my system, the sort of day,

— sunshiny or foggy, — these things change me ; and one day my temperament. is of one country, and another day it is of another. It is manifold. I have in me a Frenchman, a Dutchman, and a Spaniard, a German, an Italian, and, alas ! an Otaheitan, a savage.

MARHAM.

No, Oliver, no.

AUBIN.

I am an Egyptian, a Greek, and a Roman. I do not look like any one of them ; but that is because I am more than any one of them was. For what knowledge the priests of Egypt made a secret of would be nothing sublime to me. Nay, I have no doubt that I have it, — though, out of all my treasures, exactly which it is I cannot say. For in the schools at Alexandria all the wisdom of the Egyptians must have been known ; and out of those schools came some of the fathers of the Church, and many of those ways of thinking and feeling that began to obtain among Christians in the second and third centuries. For at one time Alexandria was the great school, the famous university, of the whole world. The way the Egyptians were ready to view the Gospel has had its effect on the Christianity of every nation ; and still it has, and not without having caused me some darkness, and so made me sorrow, once.

Errors are so lasting in the world ! It makes one almost despair.

Despair ! No, uncle, but most firmly hope. For then surely truth must be immortal, if, by only being a little like her, falsehoods can live a thousand years. And truth is immortal ; and there is living in me all of it that was known to those who were solemn among the sphinxes, and thoughtful in the vast temples of Egypt. On one of their symbols of the godhead were the words, " I am all that was, that is, and that is to come ; and no mortal has ever unveiled me yet." This was at Sais ; and these were not words to be seen and thought of for hundreds of years without many a person becoming the readier to say, " Show us the Father, and it sufficeth us." And the way in which educated Egyptians were readiest to view the Gospel affected their understanding of it, and so also the interpretation of it by the Fathers, who were of the Alexandrian school, and so even my own religion a little.

The Christian religion was sadly corrupted by that Alexandrian philosophy ; though I think Christianity would have had a very much worse history, if, in the second and third centuries, the preachers of it had been Persian, or merely Ro-

man, in those respects in which they were Alexandrian. But, Oliver, we were talking about the
knowledge of human nature.

AUBIN.

So we were, uncle ; but it was with a view to
seeing that in no age or nation has there ever been
a day to be envied by us for its brightness. However, uncle, what is the wisdom that comes of
much experience among men ? Is not it the certainty that all men are born with hearts very like
one another ? So that a man who is fit to rule
knows all kingly feelings without his going up
the steps of a throne, and sitting down with a
crown on.

MARHAM.

Would you say, then, that any one man understands all other men ? Hardly, Oliver, that.

AUBIN.

For that is what can be said only of " the first-
born of every creature " ; and of others it is true
according as they are more or less Christian.
What I mean is, that if two men are equally
acute in their faculties, and have had the same experience the one as the other, they may still differ in their knowledge of human nature ; and if
they do, it will be because the one is more Christian than the other. By no bad man, by no man
conceited or in any way affected, is the soul of
man to be known, but only by a good man, a man

of love and honesty and holiness, and who has made it religion to himself to keep simple in heart and manners. This man understands the good; and he knows the bad better than they know one another.

MARHAM.

Then would you affirm that Shakspeare was a good man?

AUBIN.

No saint, but a good man he was, certainly. But if a saint he had been, he would have been a poet of still larger spiritual insight. Sometimes I fancy that I can feel this while reading his plays. A man of falsehood, or selfishness, or injustice, or habitual sensuality, Shakspeare never can have been. Measured by the common height of principle among men, he must have been nobly minded. And this I believe more surely than if I saw it; for he might have deceived my eyes, but through his writings he has put his soul in contact with my moral sense.

MARHAM.

And is there nothing in him offensive?

AUBIN.

Yes, uncle, there is. And there is to be read what is offensive in regard to one writer, at least, who is called a saint, and not undeservedly. In estimating what Shakspeare was in himself, what time he lived in must be remembered. There are stains on his pages, but they are of his age's making, and not his own. And we should not ourselves have noticed them if we had been of his century and his birthplace, or even of the court of Elizabeth.

MARHAM.

It is just as though we were at her father's court, and at other times as though we were along with her grandfather, while reading some of Shakspeare's plays.

AUBIN.

Yes; we Englishmen have transmigration of souls through Shakspeare. In reading him I am of Athens, and I am Timon, and I know and scorn what hollowness is in many men; then I lay down the book, and I am myself again; but my soul is the wiser for having been in Timon's body and lived his latter life. Another time I am Hamlet, and sometimes I am Romeo, and King John, and King Lear, and Wolsey. I go out of one man's mind into another's, into a wider, and still widening, experience.

MARHAM.

Yes, in Shakspeare you are the man you read of for the time.

AUBIN.

And so you are the hero, and the saint, and the thinker, while reading their lives. The well-written lives of great men are things to thank God for ; for in reading first one and then another, we learn how great we are ourselves, — how much there is in us that is unacted and unsaid, for want of opportunity, — and how we are, all of us, not so much living in this world as getting ready to live.

MARHAM.

In another world.

AUBIN.

Yes, and where there will be no such limits on our movements as are about us now, and where there will be no fear to chill us, either of enemies or friends, or to-morrow, or death.

MARHAM.

Thank you, Oliver ; for I like what you have been saying.

AUBIN.

Sometimes thinking of myself as only one in a thousand, it is as though I could not, in the eye of God, be any thing ; but then I am what he will care for, when I think that in my soul there are a thousand unacted lives. Because, in some few moments of little faith, one may have misgivings for one's self ; but never for a village with a thousand inhabitants in it.

MARHAM.

And you may say this, too, that one soul is with the Lord as a thousand souls, and a thousand souls as one soul.

AUBIN.

That thought is like a lens, uncle. There shine through it a thousand rays of light from heaven. And it brightens with looking at. Yes, it does. Sometimes, when I have thought of myself as one of a million persons all unlike one another, I have felt, in the sight of Heaven, as though I were lost, and nothing. And then, again, I have had faith as strong as that of a multitude when I have been in a crowded city, and have looked up to heaven, feeling along with Wordsworth

That we have all of us one human heart.

MARHAM.

Yes, one heart, always and everywhere ; now in our European civilization, and in the extinct spirit of ages past.

AUBIN.

Extinct spirit of past ages ! What you say chills me, uncle. It is as though the light of my own spirit might be put out.

MARHAM.

No, no ! Your soul, Oliver, is not to be worn away by time.

AUBIN.

Nor is the spirit of Rome, nor that of Greece, nor that of Egypt, nor that of the Hebrews ; for what are those on your shelves ? They are not bones from a Greek tomb ; they are the very spirit of ancient Greece; they are what was grandest in the mind and to the judgment of Plato, and Sophocles, and ——

MARHAM.

Well, in a library here and there, that spirit lives.

AUBIN.

And in more libraries now than it ever did in men in Greece.

MARHAM.

So it does. But in the world it does not live.

AUBIN.

The whole world is this day better than it would have been if Greece had not been. I need not tell you how the civilization of Greece widened into that of Rome, and so over the whole world; and how impossible it is that Grecian books should have been read and studied for ages by the best minds, without the minds of the whole world being the better. In the spirit of ancient Greece, the great characteristic was the feeling of the beautiful. Now for you to be sure that the Greek spirit is living in the world still, I need only ask you to think what the history of art has been. Some one has said that there is not now a sign-board but witnesses, I think, that Rubens was a painter. And it is still truer that Greece is living, not in colleges only, but in every town, and is to be felt in the common talk of men.

And in our laws, and in half the words we speak,
Rome is living in us English people.

MARHAM.

It is so, Oliver ; it is so.

AUBIN.

And so is Judaism ; for in some things we are
Jews, and rightly, or else we could not be Christians. For Christ came not to destroy, but to
fulfil the law of the prophets. Undestroyed, they
survive still ; at least the use, the purpose, of
them does. Of Jewish opinions, and Grecian
feeling, and Roman manners, it is none of the
truth, but only the falsehood, that has perished.
All the truth of them is in the human mind now,
and is everlasting. And myself, I am of Egypt,
of the time of even the earlier Pharaohs ; and I
am more than an Egyptian, for I am a Greek ;
and I am more than a Greek, for I am a Hebrew ;
and I am more than a Hebrew of the Hebrews,
for I am a Christian.

MARHAM.

I like your idea, Oliver, very much.

AUBIN.

It is what makes me consciously immortal. I
am of many ages past, so that it is not for me to
fear perishing in a day. And on my very death-
day I only can seem to perish. Before the world
was, God had me in his mind ; and with being
shut out of his mind what shall frighten me ?

Not death. For not a sparrow shall fall to the ground without my Father.

MARHAM.

What a saying that was of Christ's ! It filled the woods and the air with witnesses of Providence.

AUBIN.

My body will be dust; but desolation and ruin are the buildings of Athens, yet the spirit of Greece lives on, as I myself feel, and that most blessedly; for so, out of my own experience, I can trust in being myself immortal when disembodied.

MARHAM.

Yes, what Greece was must be living on in the human mind as inspiration and unsuspected wisdom. But in ancient statues, and in the engravings of Greek ruins, Greece is everywhere present, so as to be looked at. Lycian and Xanthian marbles have been brought to London from amongst bushes and trees; and not by chance, I think, — no, not by chance. The bringing of Grecian remains to England seems, under Providence, like the gathering up of the fragments of ancient civilization for nothing to be lost.

AUBIN.

In the Campagna, near Rome, the shepherds live in old tombs ——

MARHAM.

Horrible lodgings they would have been for an old Roman ; but not so for those who have faith in Christ.

AUBIN.

Ay, and with our larger souls, if we had been Romans, the world itself would have felt like a tomb, to live in ; and the earth would have been to us a mere floor, for nations to be laid under. Life, to look at, is mortality from moment to moment ; but it is not so to us, because there is plan, there is purpose, there is hope, to be felt in it. And there is not a thought of ancient wisdom ——

MARHAM.

Yes, this life is lit up with the manifest presence of God in it, for those the eyes of whose understandings are not blinded. And to feel the presence of God is to feel his spirit and ours for ever related.

AUBIN.

It is so, dear uncle. And, indeed, for a Christian, every thing human is suggestive of immortality. The kingly form of David has been vanished from this world thousands of years ; but his psalms are here still. Many a noble head is dust ; but what thoughts were wrought out in it are alive now, and will be for ever. As long as a thought has such immortality, the life of my soul is not a matter to be feared for.

MARHAM.

For our souls live in God far more safely than thoughts in the mind ; because in him there is no forgetfulness.　And from what you have been saying, I think this : that if the Past lives on in us, we may well hope ourselves to live on in God.

AUBIN.

On account of our souls, we might perhaps have feared a little, if what was good in Athens had perished ; but it did not.　The old ages are gone by, but the spirit even of them did not go into nothingness ; nor will my soul, then, ever, by any likelihood.　In the rise and fall of empires there is Divine purpose.　There has been growth in the successive forms of civilization, in the Greek over the Egyptian, in the Roman over the Greek, and in Christian Rome over Pagan Rome, and in every age of the Christian world over what has been before.

MARHAM.

O Oliver ! ours has been the midsummer of the world's history, to live in.

AUBIN.

There is in us and about us what is the science, the wisdom, the religion, and the worth of all the centuries since Adam.　Yes, in my character there are the effects of Paul's journey to Damascus, and of the meeting of King John and the barons at Runnymede.　There is in my soul the seriousness of the many conflicts, and famines, and pestilences of early English times. And of my enthusiasm, some of the warmth is from fiery words that my forefathers thrilled to, in the times of the Commonwealth and the Reformation. There is in me what has come of the tenderness with which mothers nursed their children ages ago, and something that may be traced to the resolute talk of Cromwell and his cousin Hampden ; and there is that in me which is holy, and which began from a forty days' fast in a wilderness in Judea, now eighteen hundred years since.

MARHAM.

In a sense, all the ages that have ever been are now ; they are with us now.

AUBIN.

The Past, the infinite Past ! My soul was born of it, and I am spirit of its spirit. O, as I look back at the Past, and think what it is to me, I feel as Apollo did as he gazed upon Mnemosyne, and said, —

Mute thou remainest — Mute ! Yet I can read
A wondrous lesson in thy silent face ;
Knowledge enormous makes a God of me.
Names, deeds, gray legends, dire events, rebellions,
Majesties, sovran voices, agonies,
Creations and destroyings, all at once
Pour into the wide hollows of my brain,
And deify me, as if some blithe wine
Or bright elixir peerless I had drunk,
And so become immortal.

13

O, the way of my soul's growth argues eternity
for her life ! The Past ! — as I think of it, and
how wonderfully I was born of it, I do feel in me
a something infinite, that persuades me of my immortality. Thou glorious Past, thou suffering
Past, thou dear, dear Past !

I can read
A wondrous lesson in thy silent face.

MARHAM.

It seemed to die every day, but it did not. And
we men, — we seem to die, but we do not. It is
only to one another that we die ; for we do not to
God, nor to the angels.

AUBIN.

God ! this life of ours is much too wonderful
to be despaired of, even at its end.

MARHAM.

And through Christ, that end has itself become
so hopeful, — so divinely hopeful !

CHAPTER XIX.

A trance of high and solemn bliss
From purest ether came ;
'Mid such a heavenly scene as this,
Death is an empty name. — JOHN WILSON.

MARHAM.

A DELIGHTFUL day, is not it, Oliver ?

AUBIN.

Yes, uncle. But how calm it is. It is so profoundly quiet. A blessed day it is ; and the great peace of it reaches into the soul.

MARHAM.

It does ; and it feels like the peace of God ; and so it must be, in some way ; for a troubled spirit never feels this calmness of nature.

AUBIN.

That is true ; and, uncle, I would widen what you have said, and say, that when the soul is most nearly what it ought to be, it is then fullest of faith in what it will be. When we are most heavenly in temper, we are in belief surest of being immortal. Our highest moods are higher than any fling of death's dart.

MARHAM.

It is the goodness of God that exempts our

best experiences from the taint of the charnel-house. But you seem as though you had another explanation, Oliver.

AUBIN.

No, uncle, I have not. The mind is like a harp, in which many strings thrill, on one being struck ; and the feeling of the beautiful and that of the infinite are nigh one another. What I mean is, that beauty is to the feeling as though it were everlasting.

MARHAM.

Evanescent, surely, Oliver. For of all beauty there is one emblem, — the grass, which is in the field to-day, and to-morrow in the oven.

AUBIN.

Trees please me much to look at, and walk amongst, and sit under. But that they will rot and fall never troubles me.

MARHAM.

That is because most trees are as long-lived as we men, and some are a hundred times longer. But over and over again we see the flowers fade. And the more we like them, the more decaying this world must feel.

AUBIN.

No ; but the fresher and the newer. For do not the flowers, when they have gone out of blossom, come into it again ? What decays in flowers is the pulp, which is not what you care for ;

but the beauty in them, that you love, never perishes, and every year it is fresh to look at. O,
to me flowers are words about a life more spiritual than is plainly to be signified in this earth by
things springing out of it !

MARHAM.

And they so frail !

AUBIN.

When Jesus spoke, his words thrilled on the
air a very short time ; and yet there was an everlastingness in them, which an angel would have
known at once.

MARHAM.

Yes, what the Pharisees thought was only gentle breath did outlive their boasted temple, as
some of them lived to know ; and will survivé the
very earth, as we live late enough to be sure of.
In Galilee and in Jewry, many centuries ago,
there were low sounds on the air for little spaces
of time ; but there were ears through which they
proved to be doctrines, and revolutions, and the
coming of the kingdom of God on the earth.
Things are not always what they seem, even to
all men.

AUBIN.

So much depends on the way of regarding
them. And so what are emblems of decay to
some men are to me suggestive of eternity and
youth. Sometimes, in looking at a flower, my

mind is drawn into a mood that is like a firm persuasion of immortality, it is. so largely thoughtful
and full of peace.   That word which was made
flesh is the greatest word that God has spoken to
the children of men ; and there are many ways in
which he never leaves himself without witness in
the world ; and I like to think that flowers were
meant to be what I feel them, — the undertones
of encouragement, in which the Creator speaks to
us creatures, in a world in which sometimes the
thunder is his voice, and fire and hail and stormy
winds the fulfilment of his word.

MARHAM.

Once I had been gazing up at a very high rock,
for some time, in awe ; and at the foot of it, I remember the pleasure, almost the relief, it was to
me to notice and examine a little pimpernel ; for
that I think it was.   It rested my strained eyesight and overwrought feelings.

AUBIN.

And did not it rest your spirit, to see that
Providence, in its works, is infinitely minute, as
well as awfully vast ?   For that is no small comfort to know.   I think the discoveries of the telescope would have been dreadful, but for the mi-
croscope.   God's throne has risen above this
earth inconceivably high ; but, another way, the
Divine condescension is to be seen reaching un-
expectedly and infinitely low.   In a field, or on

the side of a brook, when I see a forget-me-not, I think to myself, He has not forgotten even thee.

MARHAM.

In a writer of the fifteenth century, I remember that there is a passage in which he says that the universe is the handwriting of God, and all objects are words in it.

AUBIN.

And very significant words some of them are. At the end of winter, the snowdrop comes out of the ground quietly, and like a word that is expected, and renews the promise, that seed-time shall not fail. And in autumn, the ears of corn, yellow, and bending heavily on the stalk, are themselves the certainty that harvest shall not cease.

MARHAM.

Our Lord says, "Consider the lilies of the field." And no doubt there is more in a lily than has been considered yet, and very much more than colors and leaves. To most men, there is in the stalk only sap ; but there is really in it the presence of God every moment, arraying the plant in glory.

AUBIN.

And that is blessedness to know ; for with every feeling of that truth, God is felt in ourselves, and the feeling of God is that of our immortality.

MARHAM.

Yes, in our minds any thought of God may be almighty in its effects.

AUBIN.

I have God to believe in, and so I am immortal. Sometimes I feel this, O, so strongly ! and then at other times there is no meaning in it. And sometimes I am made conscious of my immortal nature by such beauty as comes and goes in a moment, — summer lightning, a shadow's passing over a sunlit valley, the smile of a woman ———

MARHAM.

Oliver !

AUBIN.

It is so, uncle. In the feeling of beauty there is no taint of decay or death.

MARHAM.

A painting is colored canvas, and an engraving is paper printed on ; and both are very perishable.

AUBIN.

So they are, and so are the leaves of the Bible ; but the Gospel is not.

MARHAM.

But the Gospel is not in the ink and paper, but in the meaning made in the mind of the reader.

AUBIN.

And in art beautiful objects are things by which

souls understand one ᐧ another. There is York Minster. I look at its western front, — I go through the door, and up the nave, and into the choir, and up to the east window. And round my head I am conscious, as it were, of the sublimity of the stars, and under my feet the floor feels as though it were low, very low, down in the earth. I experience what the builder meant, — how humility is the basis of that character which has glory for its crown. I return down the aisle in the spirit of the place, and I feel that, while walking humbly with God, there is heaven above a man very soon about to open. I understand by York Minster what the man who built it wished.

MARHAM.

That Minster is a noble thought made into stone, and he who feels it does feel what was the mind of a Christian artist five hundred years since.

AUBIN.

And so this earth is a thought of God's, and to know and feel what it is is to understand something of the mind of God. Now to me, uncle, the loveliness of this scene from the window is like the smile of Almightiness. It feels so, and it is so. See under that tree how the shadows play! O, how very, very beautiful it is!

MARHAM.

Yes, it is pretty, very.

AUBIN.

Pretty ! It is beautiful. Yes ! and there is that to be felt in it that is like learning the mind of God, and finding it to be love, infinite love.

MARHAM.

Trees and flowers, turf, ground a little undulated, and yonder a brook ; that is what you see, Oliver.

AUBIN.

A little earth shaped into a pair of cheeks, and pinched into a nose, and made into lips, chin, and forehead, and with some humors mixed together for eyes, — these are a face. But though only clay, yet they are expressive of faith, hope, and love, despair and hatred, and every passion.

MARHAM.

And every degree of every passion ; the face is so wonderfully expressive of the mind within.

AUBIN.

And so is nature of what is Divine within it. This morning I sat alone in the garden ; and all about me things looked so lovely, so imbued with spirit, that I felt myself circled with love and beauty ; and my soul within me yearned like a child in its mother's arms.

MARHAM.

I saw you, and I was coming to you, but I fancied your thoughts were making you good company.

AUBIN.

What Godhead is in nature I feel about me, though not familiarly, but with something of awe and distance in it.

MARHAM.

But is not it the mind itself which colors the earth with meaning ? for it is not always, nor to many men, that nature is what you speak of.

AUBIN.

Because we are not always, nor often, in our best moods ; and they are our best that are our truest. If you had Leonardo da Vinci's Last Supper in this library, how often would you experience the spirit of it ? Not every moment you were here, nor every day, nor rightly even every week, perhaps, but only in some more exalted seasons.

MARHAM.

True ; and what we felt at our best would be most nearly what the painter meant.

AUBIN.

And it is the same with the meaning that comes out in a landscape, or in any view of nature, in our best moments. Now this morning, as I sat under the tree, — indeed always, when my soul is in sympathy with nature, my feeling is that of a joyful recognition of God. It is as though out of some infinite distance the face of the Father Almighty were becoming visible, smiling upon me in encouragement and love.

MARHAM.

And do not you feel that the truth of all truth is God, and that the goodness of all good things is God, and that God is the inspiration of all excellence, and that every good and perfect gift is from above ?

AUBIN.

Yes, uncle. And so in reading a good book, the truth and beauty of it are witnesses to me of my relationship to God, as his child. What is true to my mind is true to God ; and what is goodness to my feeling is good in the eye of God. But how do I know this ? By inward feeling. I am strongly persuaded of it from within myself. But it is from what is outside me, as well as by inward feeling, that I know that what is beautiful with me is beautiful with God ; I know it by what God has made.

MARHAM.

And God made the human soul, and he proportioned its feelings like the strings of a harp ; and in its better and believing seasons the music it makes is what the Father of spirits listens to and loves.

AUBIN.

That is blessedly certain.

MARHAM.

In the hearts of little children there is many a feeling, the strain of which their angels do often hymn before the face of their Father which is in heaven. And in silent chambers there are those whose thoughts at night are like organ-music in the ear of God, they are so beautiful, and great, and solemn ; though, as being pure worship of the spirit, they must be more acceptable to him, infinitely, than any music made with hands.

AUBIN.

The knowledge of every such man is very dear. Because over every one out of whose heart the Spirit cries, " Father ! Father ! " Christian faith hears the voice of God making answer, " My son ! my son ! "

MARHAM.

I like what you say, Oliver.

AUBIN.

I was thinking of you, uncle.

MARHAM.

I only wish, — but ——

AUBIN.

And that I was thinking rightly, I know by the calm effect your company has on my mind.

MARHAM.

You were going to speak about the spiritual witness there is in the beauty of nature.

AUBIN.

When tree, or river, or rock shows beauty, and my soul answers to it, it is as though the spirit of nature said, " We understand one another ; and so thou art mine and I am thine." And then every thing in nature feels dear ; and death, if not very dear, feels beautiful, and worthy of infinite trust.

MARHAM.

Always may we feel it so !

AUBIN.

Summer and winter, sunshine and darkness, rolling seas and high mountains, — unlike one another though they are, there is that in me that is like them all. They are witnesses to me of myself. For the beauty of each one of them I feel, and the spirit that is in them all I am akin to. If only flowers, or only trees, or only some one class of objects in nature, were beautiful to us, then their perishing might infect us with mortal fears. But now all things are made beautiful to us in their time ; all things of God's making are. And the feeling of this is fellow-feeling with God. And in any thing, but very strongly in all great things, fellow-feeling with God is persuaded of co-eternity with him. Now at the view from this window I can look and look till I feel inwardly immortal.

MARHAM.

I cannot say that I have ever felt it much myself, but from the temples and the religious history of all ages I should suppose that there is a state of mind in which beauty is to be felt like a Divine presence.

AUBIN.

Beauty in nature, and as felt by a Christian spirit, — this 'is what I think is a manifestation of God. Uncle, look at the garden ; see the flowers, and the apple-trees, and the lilacs in blossom. And in the field beyond how white the hawthorn is ! And then there are the poplars, so leafy and straight, and as though standing against the sky behind. Now does not the sight of a scene like this make in the mind the peace of God ? And this peaceful feeling must be God's meaning, and not mere chance in us.

MARHAM.

But may it not be mere contentment of the soul, and not what is any way a promise of an hereafter ?

AUBIN.

No, uncle ; I think not. And that is nearly all I can answer you. O, yes, there is something that occurs to me ! If in our souls there were no feeling of infinity, mountains would not be sublime to us ; they would only be craggy steeps, and no more to us than to the goat and the chamois.

MARHAM.

And that something of the infinite which there is in the soul betokens a higher relationship than what the grave can close on.

AUBIN.

The mountains make in us a feeling sublimer than of what they are themselves. But they are what they are to us, because there is that in our nature through which height beyond height might rise before us in the universe, and so our souls grow grander and more solemn ; but only to feel more grandly and more solemnly at further higher sights, for ever.

MARHAM.

What there is of infinity in our souls does lay hold of the gates of heaven for us.

AUBIN.

While we have been in valleys, and on mountains, and the banks of rivers, what feelings have grown in us in this England of ours will be the beginnings of our delight in the fields of heaven. Sometimes, at the sight of a sublime scene, or a beautiful landscape, or a glorious sunset, first my feeling is delight, next it is worship, and then it is a presentiment of heaven ; for I think to myself that this earth, at its loveliest, is hardly even the forecourt of the temple. And certainly, than this it is no nigher to himself that God has admitted us earthly worshippers. But though not called so, death is that Beautiful gate through which we shall pass on into the temple, and towards the Holy of holies, where the pure in heart are blest with the sight of God.

CHAPTER XX.

A Healer, a Redeemer came,
A Son of Man, with love and power;
And an all-animated flame
He kindled in our inmost soul.
Then first we saw the heavens unfold;
They seemed an ancient father-land:
And now we could believe and hope,
And feel we were akin to God. — NOVALIS.

MARHAM.

You have been looking at your watch these five minutes. What do you see, Oliver ?

AUBIN.

More than I can speak of; and I hear more

gone, gone ! As fast as this watch goes, men die, — a man a moment.

MARHAM.

Is it so ?

AUBIN.

Yes, very nearly.

MARHAM.

Oliver, it is a thing to think of. And the more one thinks, the faster time seems to go ; and faster and faster it seems as though men were dying. As one listens, it is as though the watch were

14

saying all manner of warnings, — now then, now
then ! — thy turn, thy turn ! — 't will be, 't will
be ! And so it will be ; and God knows how
soon.

AUBIN.

And only he knows the witness this watch
might witness about me, for I have forgotten myself ; or rather, my brain has, for my spirit has
not, because it will be all surviving in me hereafter. Round the face of this watch, every min-
ute-mark has been the date of some impulse I
have felt and followed, right or wrong, and that I
shall remember hereafter, and, as I trust, when I
am in glory ; and every such recollection will
make me feel myself then, more and more devoutly, a miracle of grace. And that will soon be,
perhaps. On, on, on ! says the watch ; on, on,
on ! And on it goes, and on time goes, and on
the world goes. Tick, tick, tick ! And only
with this, Venus is a hundred miles farther away ;
and it is another part of the sun that shines on
Mercury ; and girdled about with rings, and circled about with moons, Saturn is not where he
was ; and perhaps out of a million stars, there is
not one but has changed its place. And all with
less noise than the going of this watch, and with
less effort, perhaps ; and, indeed, certainly ; for
with Almightiness there cannot be any effort at all.
I do not discern it, for I am in the flesh ; but on

the face of my watch, here, among these twelve, one will be the hour of my death , and there is a minute here that will be my last breath. This finger moves on slowly and surely, and over the whole face it will turn, and many a time, perhaps ; but for all that, like a finger along the lines of a death-warrant, it is moving on to point the time of my departure hence. And the next minute afterwards some one will take up this very watch, perhaps, and remark to himself the hour and the minute of my death. But the very moment that I breathe out my last breath, somebody will draw his last. And before it will be well known that I am dead, quite a company of spirits will have come forth with me out of this earthly life. And then where shall we find ourselves, — ay, where ? Day and night, summer and winter, life and death, — these our planetary changes will be over. But if we shall have done with this earth, shall we have done with our planetary system ? But why not ? for shall we not have already learned the great starry lesson ? and are there not some human minds in which the material system exists almost as clearly as it does in the eye of God, — both the stars in their movements, and the earth in what it is ? Such knowledge has God allowed us, and it is very wonderful.

MARHAM.

In the heathen it would be ; but it is not in us Christians, to whom he has given the knowledge of his Son.

AUBIN.

Right, uncle. For that knowledge is deeper, and higher, and wider, and more enduring, and of quite another nature, than what is got through the telescope, and perfected by mathematics ; for, indeed, it is infinite.

MARHAM.

That is a sound thought, Oliver.

AUBIN.

The stars differ from one another in size, and some of them in color ; and what any one of them might be to visit, there is no knowing. But I think they are an unlikely home, any one of them, for us Christians, on whom the ends of the world have come, as some Apostle expresses it.

MARHAM.

It is a thing I never thought of ; but why unlikely ?

AUBIN.

Unlikely is perhaps too strong a word. And it is possible, before being free of the universe, that we may be surrounded awhile with " the bands of Orion," or be bound within " the sweet influences of the Pleiades." But why should we ? For it is likely that their starry elements

are not very different from these of our earth.
And this of our earth is a way of life we are experienced in now ; though many die out of the
earth, knowing little or nothing of it. Then how
many thousand nights we have seen the stars, and
seen them with bright eyes, and with tearful eyes,
and in every mood, so that, perhaps, there is
nothing new to be felt in their sight ! But of that
one cannot be sure ; for they may wear quite
another look in the sight of creatures redeemed,
immortal, and crowned, to what they do in eyes
that have weariness, and passion, and tears in them.

MARHAM.

And dimness and watchings, an older man would
add. But, says the Scripture, there remaineth a
rest.

AUBIN.

Now blessed be Paul for that one word, — rest.
It makes one feel like a child in the evening of a
summer's day, and it makes one's death-bed as
soft to think of as going to sleep. Rest, rest !
Is not the sound of the word so soothing ? It
will be a world of rest ; and so it will hardly be
a world like this earth, with clouds driving over
it, and with seas in it ebbing and flowing, and
never still, and with winds rising and falling, and
blowing now one way and now another.

MARHAM.

Green pastures are what David ——

AUBIN.

Many objects in this earth are what things in heaven will be like. Meadows we shall lie down in ; and there will be in our ears the murmur of the river of water of life ; and over us there will be a tree of life, and through the leaves of it, some rays of the light of God will shine upon us in that blessed shade ; and we shall eat ·of the fruit of the tree, because it is for the healing of the nations : and just at first we shall not venture to look into the full glory beyond, for we shall be only fresh out of the darkness of this earth.

MARHAM.

And God will be all and in all, and ——

AUBIN.

All and in all ! He will be in the river of life, flowing alongside us ; and he will be in the tree that shades us, and in the light that shines through it ; and he will be in us, ourselves. He will be everlasting growth of spirit in us, and he will be peace and joy. Ay, there will be then one soul of joy in us and in God. We in him, he will be in us. We shall be nerves in his infinite blessedness, and for ever be thrilled with delight. And, perhaps, what is done divinely on one side of heaven will gladden us on the other ; for we shall be in God, and God will be then, as he is now, glad in all things. Ay, this, — this is the thing to think of. God in us, and we in God, —

this one certainty of what heaven will be is enough for us. For of the manner of the future life we do know nothing. There is nothing told us. Perhaps there could not be. And, indeed, why should it be told us how we are to live the first instant after death, any more than what fresh experiences we shall have age after age in eternity? Sufficient for our day is the light we have; and to-morrow, if we have things to do not of this earth, then we shall be lighted for our work in another way than we are now.

MARHAM.

Ay, if we would only walk by what light we have, instead of standing still to wonder how it shines, and whether we might not have had much more of it than what we have! In all things it seems to be a rule, that we should have no greater light than what we can use, and ought to use. I suppose it is for knowledge always to feel the same as duty.

AUBIN.

Yonder shines the sun, looking as though he were only the light of our sky, and not as though he were to be seen in ten or twelve other firmaments. It is all as though he rose in our east, and went round our sky, and down in our west. And the look of it quite agrees with what our state is. For we are only dwellers of this earth, and not creatures of the solar system. What duties am I made to owe in Jupiter, or Mars, or any of the other planets, that my eyes should have been fashioned in such a way as for me to see at a glance what look the sun has as he shines in their skies? No doubt, astronomy has proved profitable knowledge; but it is not holiness. Why the sun shines for us is to light us to our duties, which are all to be done on this earth. Hereafter, there may be purposes for which we shall see the sun shining in another way than he does to us now. Ay, and does not this suggest how God will grow for ever on our gaze? O, many are the thoughts about him, and many are the ways of feeling towards him, that are withheld from us as yet; because, though he is in himself from everlasting to everlasting, still, to our experience, he is no more than the Father of our as yet earthly spirits. Let our thoughts be as familiar only with a few ages as they are now with years; let us see another world or two beside this earth, and sympathize with some forms of spiritual life, and know a few of the truths that shape into existence in seraphs' minds; — and all this let us learn, loving God the while, like his children; and we cannot even think the grandeur, and the strength, and the rapture, with which the thought of God will quicken in us.

MARHAM.

True, very true. And very glad I am at what

you have been saying, Oliver. For, Oliver, why
I cannot tell, but always the greatness of the universe has been to me an oppressive thought.
Astronomy is no delight to me, but appalling.
Our earth is not the only planet that belongs to
our sun, nor the largest; it is only one out of
many, and it is a thousand times smaller than
some of the others. In thinking of the solar system, this earth feels to be nothing; and it is painfully nothing, in comparison with the thousands of
suns we know of, and the myriads of other suns
that are shining beyond the reach of our eyes.
The rays of the sun are swift, and the light of the
stars is quite as quick. So that sometimes my
heart has almost withered in me, as I have thought
at night of the rays of some stars having been
travelling towards this earth longer than my life.
It is light from such a distance, as makes the
word *infinite* sound dreadfully. Sometimes when
I have been thinking astronomically of this earth
and the sun, and the millions of other suns there
are, and of what I am in it all, I have been as
though lost, — I have been quite overwhelmed
with my nothingness.

AUBIN.

Now, uncle, that has not been my feeling ever.
For the sun could not shine long without me,
nor this earth continue. For in the universe elements and forces are so exactly proportioned,

that the least change in one would disorder the rest, and so destroy the creation. It is said that not an atom of matter could be struck from existence, without being the ruin of the universe.

MARHAM.

It may be true ; and it would be indisputably true, if the universe were no more than the curious machinery which it is often thought. But its working is more than that of mechanism ; it is that of an infinite spirit.

AUBIN.

I quite agree with you, uncle. And so we ought to be hopeful and cheerful ; for in all things about us, is not there the presence of a spirit, wise, loving, and almighty ? Providence is infinitely careful, as well as infinitely vast. It is not more likely that I should be forgotten by God, than that a star, a world, a sun, should be. In the universe I am not a mere accident. Nay, the very hairs of my head are all numbered, and not one of them can fall without my Father ; and if it could, it would be into annihilation ; and through that, there would be a time when this earth would begin to shake, and the planets to err upon their orbits ; and from star to star, and from one constellation to another, the heavens would begin to wear toward their destruction.

MARHAM.

And pass away they will, some time.

AUBIN.

Your mind can think the blotting out of the stars ; and so the light that is in you is greater than what is in them all, — greater in its kind. A destructive blast might go forth and extinguish our sun, and other suns, one after another, down infinite space, but your soul be swept over, and be left behind, a light undimmed.

MARHAM.

What you have said this afternoon will do me good. The vastness of creation has been to me an oppressive thought : and yet it ought not to have been ; for I might have been sure there was some cheerful way of thinking of it. For even of clouds, the darkest have all an edging of light, showing that there is the sun behind them.

AUBIN.

And there is this consideration, uncle, in which I am sure you will agree. As I have said before, to us earthly creatures the sun looks, and was meant to look, as the sun only of our sky, and not as the luminary of ten or twelve or more firmaments. For my seeing him shine on other worlds would be of no use to me for what I have to do in this earth, nor would it make me more loving, or dutiful, or devout. And so I know of God what is good for me ; but there is knowledge of him withheld from me, — such knowledge as in my present circumstances I should not be the better for having, perhaps ; but yet such as for not having I may be the wiser, that is, the humbler.

MARHAM.

Many things we are ignorant of in this world. And how should it be otherwise with us ? And many things will never be known of in this earth at all. There are directions into which inquiries might be made, were it not for the darkness. But it is holy darkness ; and what makes man the holier, when it is rightly felt.

AUBIN.

I know that darkness is good for me, as well as light, and that it is good for me not to know some things, as well as to know others ; and for myself, I can pray to God out of my whole heart and with the strength of my understanding, " Thy will be done on earth, as it is in heaven " ; else there is not a flower, nor an insect, nor a bird, nor an animal, nor a day, nor a man, but might make me question myself to madness.

MARHAM.

Yes, Oliver, you have felt the same as I have.

AUBIN.

Why was not yonder butterfly created an angel ? for it would not then have taken up more room in the universe than it does now. One reason of its life may be for me to wonder about it. For if we grew up in the knowledge of every thing, we should never grow devout. In every way of thinking of it, and in every question which can be asked regarding it, this world is mystery; so as to shut us up on the only truth which can be answered about it, — the will of God. But O the wondrousness of that answer! for in the earnest making of it we ourselves are made god-like, — are made to feel ourselves children of the Highest.

MARHAM.

You have said the very thing, Oliver, which often and often I have wanted to know; though I do not know that I ought to have been in want of it; and indeed I have tried not to think of some things which have come into my mind.

AUBIN.

I can so easily bewilder myself about the De-ity, if I think of him as the God of the hosts of heaven, — every host a myriad times, ten myriad times, more numerous than the inhabitants of this world; also if I think of him as the Creator of angels and archangels, and so the God of many a million worlds besides this of ours, and as a Being from everlasting to everlasting, and as almighty, yet allowing of death in this world of his. All this is true, and I know it to be true: but such thoughts are too high for me; for I can gaze at them, and strain my eyes after where they lead, till I feel blind, and could grow so. In every way God is infinite, and so I never could have learned him of myself.　But he has shown himself as the sun of our firmament.

MARHAM.

As the Father of our Lord Jesus.　Stars, and ages, and infinities, — these are not the way to think of God.

AUBIN.

They can awe a spirit, but enlighten it they cannot.　At least they cannot be the beginning of light in the soul ; but Christian belief, when it has begun, draws into itself light from almost every thing.　To understand at all what life means, one must begin with Christian belief.　And I think knowledge may be sorrow with a man, unless he loves.　It is my right, and there is some duty in it, too, to learn all that is to be known of what the ages and the great men of this world have been, and of the worlds beyond worlds which are round us every way.　But the look of the firmament itself hints wisdom to us ; for bounded by the horizon, all the world round me is only a few miles.　From which I may feel, that for me the world is specially meant to be what is just about me, — what I can see and talk with men in, and be kind in, and do duty in.　Let me be right with the world about me, and the whole world beyond will then look right towards me.

MARHAM.

Thank you, Oliver ; for you have instructed

and you have delighted me very much this after-noon. And your imagination is not lawless, as I have sometimes feared it might perhaps be, a little, a very, very little : but it is not. It is religiously chastened ; it is hither and thither, but it is to do Christian work : it is lowly service at the door of the church ; and it is a noble hymn in the choir; and it is a voice from the pulpit like a clarion ; and in quieter moments it is a vision of heaven and hell, and unearthly things.

AUBIN.

You are yourself imaginative, uncle.

MARHAM.

I ! not I ! No, Oliver, no !

AUBIN.

Yes, you are, my dear uncle ; and now and then very beautifully so ; but more so in talking with me than with any one else, I think.

MARHAM.

What time is it, Oliver ?

AUBIN.

Ten minutes to five. Which time of the twenty-ninth of May, of the year eighteen hundred and forty-seven, will never be again, — never, — not ever. Every day the world is ripening against that harvest which is to be at the end of it ; slowly, perhaps ; and yet not so very slowly considering what the fruits of it are to be, for they will be eternal ; they will be souls, — everlasting souls.

MARHAM.

A very beautiful afternoon ! And so sweet the air is ; is not it, Oliver ?

AUBIN.

O that lark ! He is up, singing his thanks after yonder cloud, for having dropped a few big rain-drops on the field ; for his nest is in it ; and so the grass smells more sweetly to his mate.

MARHAM.

It must have been on an afternoon like this that holy George Herbert first sung his four verses on virtue ; playing the while on the theorbo.

AUBIN.

I should like to hear them, uncle. Will you repeat them ?

MARHAM.

Now you must like them, Oliver ; for I do very much.

> Sweet day, so cool, so calm, so bright,
> The bridal of the earth and sky ;
> The dew shall weep thy fall to-night ;
> For thou must die.

> Sweet rose, whose hue, angry and brave,
> Bids the rash gazer wipe his eye ;
> Thy root is ever in its grave,
> And thou must die.

> Sweet spring, full of sweet days and roses,
> A box where sweets compacted lie ;
> My music shows ye have your closes,
> And all must die.

Only a sweet and virtuous soul,
Like seasoned timber, never gives ;
But though the whole world turn to coal,
Then chiefly lives.

George Herbert! Holy George Herbert! It is more than two hundred years since he was living. Since he was living, did I say? As though he had been any thing else but living! Between him and me there have dawned and darkened nearly eighty thousand days; and yet he is to me as though he lived yesterday. And if he is this to me, then, very certainly, he is more than this to God. It is long, — long, — a space of two revolutions and many wars, since George Herbert lived at Bemerton. And yet through eighty millions of English people who have lived between him and me' do I feel him, feel his feelings, feel his having been in the earth. I am only one of so many brothers of his, but his spirit has not died to me ; and if to me his spirit has not died, then how it must be living on to God! O Lord, thou lover of souls! You look at me, Oliver, as though you thought those words were my own ; but no, — they are not. They are from the Wisdom of Solomon, and very beautiful they are. I like repeating them, — O Lord, thou lover of souls!

15

CHAPTER XXI.

Praise God, creature of earth, for the mercies linked with secrecy,
That spices of uncertainty enrich thy cup of life.
Praise God, his hosts on high, for the mysteries that make all joy;
What were intelligence, with nothing more to learn, or heaven, in eternity
    of sameness? — M. F. TUPPER.   •

MARHAM.

THERE is no knowing what a day may bring
forth.

AUBIN.

There is many a one for whom that is almost
all the happiness of his life, uncle.

MARHAM.

In the midst of life we are in death.   Life is so
uncertain !

AUBIN.

O, this uncertainty is great wealth, and it is
the freshness of existence.   And there are those
who could not keep living from year to year without it.

MARHAM.

Do you think so ?

AUBIN.

To-day I am poor, ill, and friendless.   But
to-morrow I may be, — ay, what may I not be ?

All over the world there will be changes; and why not so in my lot? Next week there may chance to me some mechanical discovery that may enrich me; or I may be reëstablished in my health; or I may meet, and from the other side of the world, perhaps, a woman who may become my wife; or I may have thoughts come into my mind that will be for the good and the love of multitudes of men. These are possible things, though not likely. But this is no improbability, — my dying to-morrow. I may never be rich, married, famous, healthy; but I shall be still more changed; for a spirit I shall, I must, become some time. Die, — I may die to-morrow, and so to-morrow prove heir to a crown immortal, and feel in my soul the look of eyes purer and more loving than any that have glanced at me yet; and have throng into my mind thoughts, O, so beautiful, and blessed, and great! And any day this may happen to me; for death keeps no Jewish Sabbath any more than the sun does. And sometimes I could be glad of it; for to some moods of my mind that would be a gloomy day indeed, on which the earthly could not become the heavenly. But now there is no day forbidden to immortalize man. To-day, to-morrow, the day after, any day, gates may be thrown open, and I enter in, and gems and sapphires be poverty with me, and kings and princes an unheeded company. Any day I may die, and so there is no day but feels like a porch that may, perhaps, open into the next world. Yes, death, — the hourly possibility of it, — death is the sublimity of life.

CHAPTER XXII.

In some hour of solemn jubilee
The massy gates of Paradise are thrown
Wide open, and forth come, in fragments wild,
Sweet echoes of unearthly melodies,
And odors snatched from beds of amaranth,
And they that from the crystal river of life
Spring up on freshened wing, ambrosial gales!
The favored good man in his lonely walk
Perceives them, and his silent spirit drinks
Strange bliss, which he shall recognize in heaven.

COLERIDGE.

AUBIN.

O THIS earth, this dear, green earth, this happy, happy earth! It will be happy and beautiful without us soon. We shall be out of the earth soon, — out of this world, but not out of its beauty. The grace that rises from the earth in many a tree; the fascination that eddies and murmurs in flowing water, keeping the gazer standing on the river-side; the beauty that lives along the plain, and sometimes that draws man's outstretched hands towards itself, as though in recognition; the loveliness that in a valley is round and over man, and embosomed in which he feels unearthly and sublimed; the dear and fearful beauty of the lightning; the wild grandeur of a September sunset, various, and living, and glowing; all these we shall see again ; no, — not see ; for these things themselves we shall not see ; but what is in them all we shall feel again, and drink into everlastingly. And it will be a dearer delight than it is now, and intenser and fuller. For then, O God, we shall be in thee and of thee ; and thou wilt be to us like an ocean of delight, our little spirits being bathed in thine infinite spirit.

MARHAM.

Amen, O Lord, Amen !

AUBIN.

And it will be ; just as we are sure of loving again, because God is love. O, I have sometimes felt, in the country, what I fondly think may be not unlike the way of our feeling in the next world !

MARHAM.

Why, Oliver, what can you mean ?

AUBIN.

When I was a boy I used to ramble into the country, and oftenest into a quiet valley, for blackberries and nuts. But I never got many when I went alone. For in the woods I seldom was long, before becoming possessed by a spirit, like what the Greeks imagined was Pan. A fearful pleasure ! At first it seemed as though the low wind whispered me ; and then, as though it waited about me and curled round my face. If a branch waved, it was toward me; and if a leaf fluttered, so did my heart. It was as though my spirit had melted into the spirit of the woods. Then I would sit down and wonder at myself in awe, and joy, and tears. And the awe in my spirit would deepen, and the joy too, and my tears would fall faster, till I felt as the child Samuel may have done in the temple, while waiting for the Lord to speak. And there was speech from God to me at those times; because, from my feelings then, I am now sure, even of myself, of the blessedness with which God is to be felt by the pure in heart.

MARHAM.

There are many of the feelings of childhood little understood, and some of which, I do not doubt, are vague yearnings after God.

AUBIN.

On the Rhine, and overhanging it, is the Lurleiberg, a rock. One evening in August I sat upon it. Up and down the river, on one side, were vineyards, and on the other, thick trees, and across it was the little town of Bingen; but from where I was, it seemed to contract into nothing, as I looked at it, and so did my worldly thoughts. And into my soul slid the calmness of the scene, and then the sublimity of it. The air was like a living presence about me, and the rock underneath me was like that of my salvation; and from above, it was as though there were descending into my soul an exceeding weight of glory.

MARHAM.

Some seeds of glory fell into your soul then, no doubt. For the invisible things of God are to be understood from the things that are made.

AUBIN.

And there is an enjoyment of heaven, for which our joy in nature is a preparation. And there is a love of the beautiful arts, which a man will be the better for, hereafter. Beauty is of God, as much as love is, or truth.

MARHAM.

It must be ; and the earth and the skies are the school in which for us to learn it.

AUBIN.

I shall die without having looked on the Mediterranean in the Bay of Naples, and without having known the magic effect of a Milanese atmosphere. I have not seen the valley of Chamouni, in the Alps, nor had a look from the Pyrenees. The gloom, and the grandeur, and the worship of American forests have not been felt by me ; nor have I ever rejoiced in the flowers, and the luxuriance, and the deep green of the West Indies. I have never heard Niagara roar, nor, at sight of the Mississippi, thought of God, and been devoutly glad, as I should have been if I had ever seen it ; for the sight of any great power in nature is to me like God's felt presence; and during thunder and lightning, I cannot so well pray as sing hymns.

MARHAM.

The powers of nature are the almightiness of God; and so they are what can be triumphed in.

AUBIN.

I have never seen the Southern Cross, nor felt the beauty and the mystery of the Northern Lights. These things I shall die without having known. There are picture-galleries, in the neighbourhood of which I should like to have lived a little while. There are books of engravings that I wish I could have owned years ago. And Athens and Rome I wish I had had opportunities of visiting. But I shall die, my soul not enriched by the greater marvels of the world, and poor in beauty.

MARHAM.

Not poor, though not as rich as it might have been. And sometimes, Oliver, I think, under other circumstances, the world might have been the better for you. Such things as you have been speaking of are to be seen for money. Now, as I know myself, one pecuniary prospect you declined, on account of your scruples of conscience. And you were right in doing so, feeling as you do. There are grand and lovely sights in the world, and some of them you might have, had the

means to visit, if you had not been quite so scrupulous. You might have seen more than you
have seen ; but, Oliver, I cannot think that your
sense of beauty will prove to be the weaker· for
such actions as have strengthened your conscience.

AUBIN.

There is in the world fearful wonder, that we
have never thrilled to ; but before us, there is the
great mystery of death, which we shall not miss
of.   Then what is beauty in nature ?   It is God ;
so that it is what we shall feel more sublimely
hereafter, than we could anywhere at present.
The greatest loveliness of this earth we may never
see ; for we are here so short a time, and we are
so restrained by circumstances ; but the beauty
of the everlasting and ever brightening heavens,
we are sure not to fail of.

MARHAM.

We trust to see it.

AUBIN.

And we shall not only see it, but feel it, and
enjoy it.   That we certainly shall do, though in
this world we may not have been much refined
by the study of art, or by travel ; for he who is
sensible to the beauty of a moral life wants little
towards loving well and wisely all beauty else.
In the neighbouring town there are many saints,
in whom taste has never been cultivated, because
necessity has kept them laboring at one spot, as

though in chains, and poverty has shut them out from the doors of many opportunities. While among them there is one, perhaps, with an eye like Raphael's, and another with feeling like what Turner has ; and there is another, perhaps, whose mind would be like Bryant's, only there are no woods in which for the man to strengthen his soul. But now, in these laboring saints, will God let the feeling of beauty become extinct ? No, never. Nor is there any chance of its dying out in them, because they feel the beauty of holiness. Beauty is manifold in form, but in spirit it is one ; it is one and the same in poetry, music, art, nature, and character. Out of primitive rudeness, he who has fashioned a soul after the Christian model is an artist, not for one age of flattery, nor many years of wonder, nor for time at all, but for eternity.

MARHAM.

And so in that way, and often, many that are first will be last, and the last be first.

AUBIN.

There are rich owners of statues and pictures, and who besides can talk about them critically ; yet they have less of the eternal essence and soul of beauty in them than there is in some herdsman on their grounds. Pictures will perish, and the science of them ; so alas for him who does not feel most the beauty of the human soul !

MARHAM.

It is all over now, Oliver; and I have you
here; and we are so happy together!　And now
you are getting well; and you will be well, I hope,
in a few months, though perhaps not very strong;
and so now we can think of the past, and talk
about it.,　It does seem to me such a pity, such
a misfortune for society, I might say, that you
should ever have been in want of any means for
study, or for self-improvement in any way!　O
Oliver! for a man like you, it must have been
very, very sad.　Now it is all past, and there is
no help for it; but we can believe that it was not
all evil; cannot we, Oliver?

AUBIN.

Yes, uncle.　Three years ago I was mournful
with the thought of mine being a wasted life, — of
no use either to myself or others.　Not covet-
ously, but I did long for a little of that money
which so many waste on luxuries, to their own
hurt; for with that I could have got books to
read; and matter to think about.　I tried to bor-
row books from two or three persons; but I could
not get any lent me, which made me wretched.
And many mournful things I said to myself.　I
said, I am in this world along with the works of
great, old writers, and I cannot have them to
read; — I am going away beyond the stars soon,
and I shall know nothing of what truth is new in

this earth ; — books for refinement and instruction
are lying useless in libraries and on booksellers'
shelves, while my soul is wanting them for her
good ; — the world about me is full of knowledge,
and I, in my innermost self, am perishing for lack
of it ; — I am made for wisdom, I am anxious for
it, I am called upon to get it, both by God and
Christ, and yet I am unable to be learning ; —
O, the end of my life, and the great purpose of
the world, is spiritual good ! and I cannot get
any ; and I am as though I were made in vain.
So I thought at times ; and sometimes my grief
was great, — very bitter, — too great to be wept.
I said to myself, that the world was not right,
some persons being far too rich for their good,
and others too poor for it. And then I thought,
if it was ill with me, it was worse with some
others, for that they did not even wish for knowledge. Well, now, I said, there is opportunity
for my being useful, and for my learning something myself. So I persuaded some rude and ignorant persons to let me teach them ; and my
books were what they read to me ; and their
minds were books, out of which I read to myself.
And in this way I learned what is not to be learned any other way. And in my teaching, what
knowledge I made use of was improved for me,
as iron is when it is made into steel. And from
experience I know, that, if a man is loving and

earnest, what feeling he has of beauty is to be
kept alive in him, and even strengthened, by
every soul he knows of, and in the most unlikely
places; just as the beautiful rose blossoms and
lives out of black earth.

MARHAM.

Tell me, dear Oliver, was not that sermon of
yours written about the time which you have been
speaking of ?

AUBIN.

Yes, uncle.

MARHAM.

I thought it was very likely to have been.
Oliver, you have been a very noble ——

AUBIN.

Sometimes, and sometimes very unworthy, pos-
sessor of what light God has given me to live by.
For sometimes I have bitterly wanted to have
things as other men have them; and I have not
always been contented with that Christian ownership through which all things are mine, whether
things present or things to come. And uncle ——

MARHAM.

Nay, but Oliver, speak about the feeling of
beauty; say what you were going to say when I
asked you about the sermon.

AUBIN.

No, uncle, I have nothing more to say. Only
I believe, that, for the enjoyment of heavenly

beauty, a Christian spirit is better readiness than a well-educated eye. There are acts of forgiveness that will hereafter prove to have refined a man's soul more than the ownership of a gallery of paintings by Correggio and Raphael.

CHAPTER XXIII.

So works the man of just renown
On men, when centuries have flown:
For what a good man would attain,
The narrow bounds of life restrain;
And this the balm that Genius gives, —
Man dies, but after death he lives. — GOETHE.

MARHAM.

WELL, Oliver, what books have you been
reading while I have been away ?

AUBIN.

The Song of the Soul, and a portion of the
Ennead of Plotinus.

MARHAM.

Henry More was a Platonist, as well as Plotinus ; but More was a Christian, which Plotinus
was not.

AUBIN.

This edition of the Ennead was printed in
1580 ; and on the title-page Plotinus is de-
scribed as being easily the Coryphæus of all
Platonists. His style is wonderful ; it is almost
magical in its effects ; for it is so very clear.
The book is as though it had been written
with a diamond ; it is like cut-glass, like a
very rich vessel of it, — so very rich, and beauti-

ful, and labored, that you doubt your senses, and you agree with yourself that it cannot be only a drop of water that is held in so costly a vessel, but some elixir.

MARHAM.

What is the character of his argument, Oliver ?

AUBIN.

This edition of the Ennead was edited by Marsilius Ficinus, and is dedicated to Lorenzo de' Medici. At the end of the chapter on the immortality of the soul, the editor asks Lorenzo whether he would not like to have a summary of the long argument ; and then he gives it, and says the soul is immortal ; first, because she is mistress of her perishing circumstances, and is able to resist bodily impulses ; secondly, because she often thinks of many things which are distinct from bodies of all kinds, either because they are separate naturally, or because she herself distinguishes them in that way ; thirdly, because by nature she desires eternal things, and indeed often foregoes things temporal in her confidence of those which are eternal ; and fourthly, because she worships the Everlasting God in the persuasion of an unending life.

MARHAM.

And how do you like the Song of the Soul ?

16

AUBIN.

O uncle! very much, very much indeed. Yours is the only copy of it I have ever seen; and I have been delighted with it.

MARHAM.

It is very ruggedly written.

AUBIN.

So it is; but now and then there are lines which are more than smooth, and quite musical, — though they are not many; but I will read you two or three.

MARHAM.

I would rather you would give me some account of the book, and here and there read me such passages as you think I may understand. Once or twice, many years ago, I tried to read the book, but I could not. On the title-page it is said to be Christiano-Platonical, is not it? What year was it printed in? For sometimes from the date of a book one can understand the spirit of it a little better.

AUBIN.

It was in 1647.

MARHAM.

And this is 1847. It is singular, is not it? I think that must have been one of Dr. More's earlier works.

AUBIN.

I think it was; for it was printed at Cambridge,

which would seem to show that the writer had not at that time left the University. Then there is this ; — the author dedicates the book to his dear father, Alexander More, Esquire, and says that he pleases himself with embalming his name to immortality, who next under God is the author of his life and being.

MARHAM.

I like that ; for it is affectionately, and reverently, and simply said.

AUBIN.

There is what is affecting in loving words like these, outlasting so long the hand that wrote them and the eyes they were meant for. The right hand of the philosopher and affectionate son is dust, but his ideas are living still : and one is willing to think of this as being in accordance with the immortality of the spirit, and as some effect of it.

MARHAM.

Yes, it is exactly two centuries since Dr. Henry More published this book, perhaps this very month, or even day. But what a season it was in which for a poet to sing his Song of the Soul ! For it was a time of civil war ; counties, and towns, and many houses, divided against themselves ; doubts in men's minds, and troopers on the high-roads ; King Charles at Hampton Court, the Parliament in London, and the army

at St. Albans, all three powers being opposed
to one another. Ay, and 1647 was the year
in which George Fox got spiritually enlightened. But for one minute, let me look into
his Journal. Yes! At the beginning of the
year he says that his troubles continued, and
there were many temptations over him; that
he fasted much, walked abroad in solitary places
many days, and often took his Bible and sat
in hollow trees and lonesome places till night
came on, and frequently in the night walked about
mournfully by himself. But before the end of
the year he records that he had great openings,
and that he saw the mountains and the rubbish
burning up, and the rough, crooked ways and
places made smooth and plain, for the Lord to
come into his tabernacle; that he saw the infinite
love of God; and that he saw, also, that there is
an ocean of darkness and death, but an infinite
ocean of light and love which flows over the
ocean of darkness. And, O, then, he says, he
saw his troubles, trials, and temptations more
clearly than ever he had done; for as the light
appeared, all appeared that is out of the light;
that darkness, death, temptations, the ungodly,
the unrighteous, all were manifest and seen in the
light. He says soon afterwards, that he was come
up in the spirit, through the flaming sword, into
the Paradise of God; that he knew nothing but

pureness, innocency, and righteousness, being re-
newed up into the innocency of God by Christ
Jesus ; so that he was come up to the state which
Adam was in before he fell.

AUBIN.

There was great likeness between Fox and
More, both in their minds and views. But that
is a thing which would not have been readily believed by George Fox, the despiser of colleges
and the enemy of steeple-houses. Of this Song
of the Soul, the first part is a Christiano-Platonical display of life, which I have read, but which
I cannot easily give an account of. But, O ! in
the description of the character of God there is
one line, quaint but endearing, and which is very
good : —

Father of lights and everlasting glee.

Is not it a happy line, uncle ?

MARHAM.

Yes, Oliver. But is not it in a passage which
I can understand ? What is the subject of it ?

AUBIN.

The Triad of Plato. In the notes to the
poem, Dr. More says that the third person of this
Triad is Love ; and that Peter Lombard held
that the Holy Ghost is the same. To be influenced by this Divine Love is for our souls to be
baptized with the Holy Spirit ; and this is the
baptism which is salvation. Baptism in the name

of the Father, the Son, and the Holy Spirit is
of more consequence than the reading of all the
learned and acute tracts about the Trinity; for
that is what might be permitted to the Devil, but
the other is the privilege only of the good and
pious man. Baptism of the Christian spirit,
coming from the Father and through the Son, is
the certainty of salvation.

MARHAM.

And so I believe. Now you have turned to
what seems another part of the poem.

AUBIN.

And it is what pleases me most; perhaps because I understand it best. The immortality of
the soul is a truth which is not bright except to
the pure in heart. The soul has power rising
from within itself; but is it therefore eternal?
Man cannot be sure of it, and the more he thinks
of it, the more he doubts. It is night, and a miserable man walks in it, for he cannot sleep. An
angel comes to him and tells him the manner of
spiritual life.

> And more for to confirm this mystery,
> She vanished in my presence into air;
> She spread herself with the thin, liquid sky.
> But I thereat fell not into despair
> Of her return, nor wailed her visage fair,
> That so was gone. For I was waxen strong
> In this belief, that nothing can impair
> The inward life, or its hid essence wrong.
> O the prevailing might of a sweet, learned tongue!

The soul is not a body, nor a spread form, nor any quality of a body ; so it is not subject to the laws of matter, and therefore not to death.   Also that the soul is not corporeal, and is not mortal, is to be proved from the nature of our rational powers, and especially from our being capable of religion.   Now are not these two stanzas admirable ?   O, they are, very !

> But true religion, sprung from God above,
> Is like her fountain, full of charity,
> Embracing all things with a tender love,
> Full of good-will and meek expectancy,
> Full of true justice and sure verity,
> In heart and voice; free, large, even infinite ;
> Not wedged in strait particularity,
> But grasping all in her vast, active spright.
> Bright lamp of God! that men would joy in thy pure light!

> Can souls that be thus universalized,
> Begot into the life of God, e'er die ?

MARHAM.

That is well asked ; and that description of what religion is is truly Christian.

᛫AUBIN.

Can souls ever die that have been living in God, and in some manner like God ?

> Can they fly
> Into a nothing ?   And hath God an eye
> To see himself thus wasted and decay
> In his true members ?   Can mortality
> Seize upon that which doth itself display
> Above the laws of matter or the body's sway ?

Now, uncle, excepting in the Bible, a finer thing has never been said than this asking if God could bear to see souls perish. O, it is boldly, and tenderly, and grandly asked !

MARHAM.

A good man Henry More was, we may be sure, for it was out of the treasure of a good heart that those thoughts came.

AUBIN.

Ask the soul whether God is one thing, and she answers that he is not ; or whether he is another thing, and she says that he is not ; or whether he is sometimes in one place and sometimes in another, or always present everywhere, and she makes answer at once, that God is omnipresent.

> So that it is plain, that some kind of insight
> Of God's own being in the soul doth dwell ;
> Though what God is we cannot yet so plainly tell.

But we can tell from this what we ourselves are. We are souls. For it is not with our hands, nor with any of our bodily senses, that we feel God ; nor

> Can aught born of this carcass be so free,
> As to grasp all things in large sympathy.

Reckon up all the properties of the human body, and they will not account for all the feelings that we have. There is, then, a soul in man ; and she

> Foresees her own condition. She relates
> The all-comprehension of eternity;
> Complains she is thirsty, in all estates;
> That all she sees or has don't satisfy
> Her hungry self, nor fill her vast capacity.

This alone might persuade us of our being destined to a higher life. Only what we most long for we are so slow to believe ! We can never be sure enough about it; if we are well convinced of it, then we want to be more strongly convinced ; and if ourselves we are certain, then we want to have the mouths of all doubts stopped, both in men and books. We may believe ourselves immortal, from the nature of the connection between the soul and the body. The soul was not made for the body, but the body for the soul ; and

> when this work shall fade,
> The soul dismisseth it as an old thought.

Then reflect on the difference there is between the influences which act upon the soul ; for some of them are from this outward world, and others are from the spiritual world.

> When we are clothed with this outward world,
> Feel the soft air, behold the glorious sun,
> All this we have from meat, —

and from bodily feelings that are kept alive by food. But our mouths open themselves through appetites created in us, which appetites are the natural man. That is first which is natural ; but afterward there is that which is spiritual ; for

there are created in us spiritual capabilities. And
what earth and sky are to our bodies, the world of
spirit is to our souls. And so we may know ourselves to be closely related to the everlasting ; for

> In the higher world there is such communion.
> Christ is the sun, that, by his cheering might,
> Awakes our higher rays to join with his pure light.

> And when he hath that life elicited,
> He gives his own dear body, and his blood,
> To drink and eat. Thus daily we are fed
> Unto eternal life.

And now comes a long proof of the earth's revolving round the sun.

MARHAM.

But what can be the purpose of that, in an argument on the immortality of the soul ?

AUBIN.

If the strength of outward impressions is to be
corrected and conquered by our right reason, then

> ·we see
> That we have proper, independent might,
> In our own mind, behold our own idea,
> Which needs must prove the soul's sure immortality.

And now against the fear of death, the consciousness of justice is of great help ; for

> Strange strength resideth in the soul that 's just.

Then man may expect a happy immortality from
the character of his Maker. For it is blasphem-
ing the name of God to say that he does, or can
do, any thing else than love us human creatures of

his. For an instance, suppose it possible that our Creator does not care for us, and lets our souls be at the mercy of enemies, and then feel the consequences. Now are not these lines very touching? They are not to be believed for a minute, and yet they might almost make one weep. God! God, my Maker!—

> I feel that he is loved
> Of my dear soul, and know that I have borne
> Much for his sake; yet is it not hence proved
> That I shall live. Though I do sigh and mourn
> To find his face, his creature's wish he'll slight and scorn.

> When I breathe out my utmost vital breath,
> And my dear spirit to my God commend,

I shall find that God does not care for me at all; I shall be wretched, and without help, and be the victim of enemies;—

> Though I in heart's simplicity expected
> A better doom, since I my steps did bend
> Toward the will of God, and had detected
> Strong hope of lasting life; but now I am rejected.

That a good man should die a death like this is what cannot be. And then we must believe that God is good, or there can be no faith in any thing. So that predestination and its kindred doctrines are not even to be mentioned, nor

> such odd thoughts, that thus pervert
> The laws of God, and rashly do assert
> That will rules God, but good rules not God's will.

And then, in reference to the doctrine that some men are elected to perdition, he says,—

O horrid blasphemy!
That heaven's unblemished beauty thus dost stain!

There is nothing God possibly can wish, but the good of his creatures. There is nothing in us he can intend, but happiness; for there is nothing God can want for himself, because his own nature is sufficient for him, being infinitely full and glad and excellent. In order to be saved, a man has only to be willing, has only to be sincere and without hypocrisy, has only not to be excusing his sins to his conscience, and extenuating them to his friends. For God, with his spirit, is everywhere, and always and anxiously he is trying to win

<blockquote>
Unto himself such as be simply true,
And with malignant pride resist not him;
But strive to do what he for right doth shew;
So still a greater light he brings into their view.
</blockquote>

God is the life of all lives, and the strength of all things; and so he is to be firmly trusted in. But holy trust is not a thing to be argued step by step; for what it is, words

<blockquote>
Cannot declare, nor its strange virtue show.
That's it holds up the soul in all her woe,
That death, nor hell, nor any change, doth fray.
Who walks in light knows whither he doth go.
Our God is light; we, children of the day.
God is our strength and hope: what can us, then, dismay?
</blockquote>

MARHAM.

That is true and to be trusted. Yes, —

<blockquote>
God is our strength and hope: what can us, then, dismay?
</blockquote>

AUBIN.

Here are ingenious answers to such questions
as why Adam was made with such a loose will as
to have forfeited Paradise so foolishly ; if souls
can exist of themselves, why they should be in-
closed in wretched bodies ; why the world was
not made larger than it is, and much sooner than
it was.

MARHAM.

These are the greater secrets of the Divine
counsel. Christ never spoke of them. And
with these infinite questions, we finite creatures
are worse than water-flies thinking to struggle up
the falls of Niagara. But you are turning over
the pages very fast, Oliver.

AUBIN.

From old age, it might be thought that the
spirit might very likely live without the body.
For often, while the body weakens, the soul
strengthens.

> Mild, gentle, quick, large, subtile, serene,—
> These be her properties ; which do increase,

though the body may be losing strength. In old
age, a man may not have passion set through his
soul like a whirlwind, nor like a breeze ; —

> But the will doth flower
> And fairly spread ; near to our last decease,
> Embraceth good with much more life and power,
> Than ever she could do in her fresh, vernal hour.

This is said not without some beauty, as well as truth ; is not it, uncle ?   We are sure of a future life.   But of what kind will that life be ?   It will be like what we are ourselves.   At death, the souls of men are drawn, through their feelings, into their right places, quite naturally and exactly ; for

> God, heaven, this middle world, deep glimmering hell,
> With all the lives and shapes that there remain, —
> The forms of all in human souls do dwell.
> She likewise all proportions doth contain;
> Which fits her for all spirits.

And so, like a bad man drawn into bad company in an evening, the soul that is bad will in the future world be drawn into the outer darkness. But heaven will draw into itself what souls are good ; and also these souls will be drawn into places fittest for them ; and those that have been holiest will be drawn nighest to God.

> What now remains, but, since we are so sure
> Of endless life, that to true piety
> We bend our minds, and make our conscience pure,
> Lest living night in bitter darkness us immure ?

MARHAM.

It is day with us yet ; it is what we can call to-day ; and while we can call it so, we will work.

AUBIN.

While in the body, if the soul were to keep her attention

> fast fixed on high,
> In midst of death 't were no more fear or pain,

Than 't was unto Elias to let fly
His useless mantle to that Hebrew swain,
While he rode up to heaven in a bright, fiery wain.

That is a noble image, is not it ? It makes me
feel as though this garment of flesh might be slip-
ped at the last easily, and like a cloak.

MARHAM.

Thank you, Oliver. Your account of the
book has pleased me, and I hope it may do me
some good;

AUBIN.

At the end of it, the book states its purpose to
be to make the readers of it think two things ;
one of which is, that every holy soul hereafter
shall enjoy a never-fading felicity in the invisible
and eternal heaven, the intellectual world.

MARHAM.

But what else is the book to prove ?

AUBIN.

That this world is a commixture of light and
darkness ; but that God will through his power
rescue those souls that are faithful in their trial,
and that prefer the light before the dark, deliver-
ing them from living death and hell by that strong
arm of their salvation, Jesus Christ.

MARHAM.

It is a good book. I have long wished to
know what was in it ; I might have read it for
myself, and I ought to have done so, perhaps ;

but I was frightened at the Platonic words in it, and at its being in not very good verse. But by your help, Oliver, I like the book.

AUBIN.

And by that liking, you may know yourself to be a living soul, and so a soul to live for ever. Throughout the book there is the spirit of immortality, which you feel, and that is because you are yourself immortal ; for

Only the spirit can the spirit own ;

just as the light can only be seen by light.

MARHAM.

That one line is a thing worth thinking of.

AUBIN.

So it is ; and by itself it would make us fellow-debtors with Abraham Cowley. For you and I, uncle, — we feel what the poet would seem to have felt at a time of life when he knew how much he had been bettered by the philosopher ; and so we will say that we have learned things of infinite advantage from the admirable Dr. Henry More, of Christ's College, who is to be looked upon as one of those bright stars which God permitted to shine on a darkened age, — stars whose lustre he has never suffered to be entirely wanting.

MARHAM.

I do not know why, but always I have had some affection for the name of Henry More.

AUBIN.

Uncle, it is because you are the better for him. And you are not one of the multitude who are unwilling to return, or even acknowledge, any good which is done them without their asking. Some time since, when we were reading the Divine Dialogues, you said you should like to know where Henry More was buried, so as to have his tomb cared for. But if he had been living, and been in want of bread, you would not have been the friend to have only intended him a stone after his death. In the latter part of his life, high preferment in the Church was offered him, but I suppose his conscience hindered his acceptance of it. However, he always lived easily, though, as it would appear from his own words, not quite as prosperously as he might have done, if he had not been the earnest, pure thinker that he was. But who asked him to philosophize in religion, instead of making money for himself, or taking his pleasure? Who asked him to write on the grounds of faith in religion, and on the mystery of godliness? The Song of the Soul, — who asked it from him? It might be answered, that the prophets became such without any man's asking them; though, after having been stoned, they were commonly reverenced for having been inspired. Here are these books about us for which the world is the wiser, and through the writing of

17

which men are not the Calmucks, and the Hot-
tentots, and the Cossacks, they would otherwise
have been ; and yet in many a one there is the
question, as to why he should be grateful. Who
asks authors to write ? To this worldly question
one of them says, that he has no share in the
choice of his lot as a thinker, except his readiness
to be an organ for God to work with among men ;
and another makes such a helpless, yet such a
touching answer, —

> This is the thing that I was born to do;
> This is my scene ; this part must I fulfil.

MARHAM.

If it is not for fame, nor money, nor for self-
interest in any other way, that a man of genius
writes, then it must be because he is constrained
to the work from within himself, and in a manner
that I can well believe to be quite strange and in-
credible to a selfish man.

AUBIN.

These great thinkers, then, we will love like
brethren of ours ; for so they are ; — not after the
flesh, indeed, but they are our kindred after the
spirit, and through God. And by our loving
them, they are to be understood the better, and
they make us very much the better. Because
it is only from the height of our nature that we
can love those of a high nature. And we ourselves grow gentle, by loving a writer of gentle

thoughts. And there are devout men, the affectionate remembrance of whose names makes the soul ready for prayer. So God be blessed for the great men we know of !

MARHAM.

And make us be like them in all good respects !

AUBIN.

A truth cannot be rightly felt without love, — without the author of it being to us a brother to be proud of. The foolish homage to great men that the multitude sometimes show comes of rightful impulses in them, — of a way of feeling which God has made in them for their good ; and that will be shown more becomingly, and lovingly, and wisely, in wiser ages. A man makes himself closely akin to excellence, does himself grow excellent, by making a noble thinker, or a hero, or a saint, be his brother if he can. This is a great truth ; and it is what reaches farther and higher than would often be believed. For even if there is a mere sufferer from pain, or for righteousness' sake, and there is sympathy felt for him, then there are other men who are the better for him, and with his stripes who are healed. What I mean is this, uncle, — and it is what my soul feels, like a truth of God, — that through fellow-feeling with them that are great in soul there is to be caught a temper, a frame of mind, a spirit, just ready to be great, and that will open into greatness at once in the world to come.

MARHAM.

Oliver, what you have said — I mean — I
have a strange feeling of its being right ; but how,
I do not know.   But it is a strange power which
we men have over one another.   Oliver, my
mind is growing more like yours.   I am sure it
is.   It is as though — however, what you have
been saying is true — yes ! it is reasonable, quite.
Men may like reading the New Testament as
well as any other book ; and may be fond of the
excitement of religion ; but they are saved through
our Lord Jesus Christ only by their loving him.
And from the Scriptures it would appear that in
Apostolic times by some men the truth was received with pleasure, yet not in love, and so not
unto salvation.

AUBIN.

Hereafter the multitudes of souls will show like
cities that have been ruled over by the good and
faithful men of ten talents and of five.   And it
will be seen how our minds are profiting now
under the rulers of the world of thought ——

MARHAM.

And not ungratefully, I hope, Oliver.

AUBIN.

No soul can profit much while it is ungrateful ;
for while it is so, it can be the better neither for
a friend to talk with, nor for a poet to feel with,
nor for a philosopher to think with, nor even for

that first-born of every creature whom men are saved by. Praise to the men, then, for whose writings I am the better! I have in me thoughts of their thinking, and they have from me dear love of mine ; and so we are members one of another, — yes, we are, though we have never seen one another. And so we are members of the kingdom of heaven, and none the less surely for our never having seen it. But it is to be felt by us, of ourselves, and, O, so plainly and so happily by the help of some few greater souls from amongst us ! Blessings on them, whether in this world or the next ! Blessings on them from the Highest !

CHAPTER XXIV.

We are what suns, and winds, and waters make us.
The mountains are our sponsors, and the rills
Fashion and win their nursling with their smiles.
                              W. S. LANDOR.

The soul of man is larger than the sky,
Deeper than ocean, or the abysmal dark
Of the unfathomed centre.   Like that ark,
Which in its sacred hold uplifted high,
O'er the drowned hills, the human family,
And stock reserved of every living kind,
So in the compass of the single mind
The seeds and pregnant forms in essence lie,
That make all worlds. — HARTLEY COLERIDGE.

AUBIN.

O THIS summer day! It is a great calm in
nature.   There is not a bird in the air that I can
see.   Listen! How still it is!   There is nothing to be heard but the two or three flies in the
room here.   So quiet, yet so earnest, life feels to
me just now.   There is such sublimity in a day
like this.   To me the stillness of it is like the
peace of God.   I feel as though brooded over
by almightiness.   And the bright light is God's
presence about me, looking my spirit through and
through.

MARHAM.

To me sometimes a calm like this feels awful
almost, — and like a lull in a storm.   The world
is so vast, that ——

AUBIN.

The universe is great, but it is greatness of my own that I see in it; it is glorious, but it is glory of my own that it is bright with; it is wisdom in motion, but it is knowledge of mine which it moves to; for the mind that is in it all I am made with, and the Maker of it is my Father.

MARHAM.

It is better to speak of the grandeur of the soul in Scriptural language; for so it sounds less presumptuous, and perhaps is so. We men are made in the image of God.

AUBIN.

And so more nobly than the universe. For there must be a something of infinity in what is a likeness of the infinite. Yes, man's is a destiny more lasting than that of suns and planets. Nay, I do not doubt but that, in the eye of an angel rejoicing over these lower treasures of God, there are some souls that already are counted before the earth and the sun. My nature, — it is not only what I am, but what I may be. Ay, what I may be! To the greatness of that, this world is little; Alps and Andes though it be, Mediterranean and Atlantic, American woods and Arctic snows.

MARHAM.

Perhaps so, Oliver. But something else is true. You may see thousands of other worlds at night, but you cannot visit one. Earth owns you, and holds you to her ; and she scorches you by turning you to the sun, and freezes you by letting her north wind against you. With her west wind you are gladdened, and with her east wind you are withered, and with her speed you are carried captive over the fields of space.

AUBIN.

True ; but then the earth does not know herself, but I know her ; her own course she does not know, but I know it ; and her swiftness in it she does not know, but I know it, to a yard and a moment. And so I am the earth's better. Yes, and what are laws over her are service for me ; and the expansiveness of water is my swiftness.

MARHAM.

You have said well and ingeniously, and, Oliver, much to my pleasure ; for the soul is greater than the earth. And I do believe that there are eyes, in which even the first thought of a child is so bright as to eclipse the sun and moon. But these are feelings that are perhaps unsafe for us, except upon our knees, and with our faces in our hands.

AUBIN.

And it is from out of the depth of our humility that the height of our destiny looks grandest. For let me truly feel that in myself I am nothing, and at once, through every inlet of my soul, God comes in and is every thing in me. Weak, very weak, I am, and I would not be otherwise, if only I can keep looking towards righteousness ; — this is what I think sometimes ; and as soon as I feel this, the almightiness of God pours through my spirit like a stream, and I am free, and I am joyful, and I can do all things through Him that strengtheneth me.

MARHAM.

Yes, and what God is in the earth and the sea, that and more than that he is in the soul, — in the humble soul.

AUBIN.

God is the centre of all truth, and so it is to be most largely seen from nighest him.

MARHAM.

To moral and to religious worth, humility is an essential, and it is quite needful for the best uses of the intellect.

AUBIN.

So it is, and many an instance would show it ; but they are not necessary to tell of. If the soul has God within it, then there is in it an affinity with all truth in science, philosophy, art, and religion. God's I am, — God's everlastingly, — God's to grow for ever. There will grow in me the whole wisdom in which this world is made ; and the workings of my mind will be as grand as starry movements some time.

MARHAM.

Oliver, dear Oliver, your words are so high! I do not mean irreverent; but they sound as though they could not be used in prayer, and our thoughts should not be too proud for that, if we can help it.

AUBIN.

Uncle, there have been worshippers whose nature it was to adore God from the tops of lofty towers. It was on the highest hill in Jerusalem the temple was built. It was in a mountain that Moses talked with God. And it was up into a mountain Jesus Christ went to pray, himself alone, one greater time. And it is from the loftier of my contemplations that God feels most adorable. And it is in the thought of what he will make me, that I am most awed by what he is himself, and must be.

MARHAM.

That is a right feeling, Oliver.

AUBIN.

An archangel has perhaps a telescopic eye, that makes a familiar thing of a field like our solar system; he knows the plan of the ages in many a world; he feels principalities and powers like dust beneath him; yet in the magnitude of his mind God is but magnified the more: just as we mortals, going up into a mountain, see the more plainly that it is not on the horizon of the

earth that the dome of the firmament rests, as
children think. From his exaltation, the archangel does but abase himself the more; and he
climbs the higher, but to look the wider, and to
cry the more awfully, — O the depth of the rich-
es both of the wisdom and knowledge of God!
And so again he rises still higher; for it is not
in this world only that he who abases himself is
exalted.

MARHAM.

It is so, and only so, that weakness is made
strong in the world of spirit. O, it is a happy
thing to feel ourselves helpless and naught, for
then the presence of God is felt to wrap us about
so lovingly! Everlasting, infinite, almighty, —
these are words that strengthen us with speaking
them.

AUBIN.

All in all, God is the soul of our souls, and
the life of nature.

MARHAM.

Of all, and through all, and in us all, and the
giver of every good and perfect gift.

AUBIN.

Yes. God is in the frost, and when the savage is starved into a habit of forethought, it is a
lesson from the Father of spirits which he has
had. Astronomy is acquaintance with the laws
of the stars, and those laws are the wisdom and

the almightiness of God ; so that knowledge of them is fellowship with God, in some sense. And the same is true of all natural philosophy ; for it is the philosophy of nature which is wisdom of God in practice ; and so, in attaining the knowledge of it, they are truths from God we get.

MARHAM.

But a very poor knowledge of God.

AUBIN.

So it is, by itself. But I do not say it is knowledge of God, so much as knowledge from him. The soul, or rather knowledge, is quickened within us by heat and cold, day and night, and the necessities of life. It is because the world is what it is, that we are what we are.

MARHAM.

Mentally.

AUBIN.

Yes, and in some moral respects our souls are made by the world about us. There is a likeness between some appearances in nature and moods of our minds.

MARHAM.

I do not understand you, quite. No doubt, we do not always feel the same with nature.

AUBIN.

In the dark, every thing is shut out from us but the omnipresent ; and so in darkness the Godhead wraps us round like a felt presence.

Sometimes a clear night is just what calms me ; and while I am walking in it, high truths rise upon my soul, like stars above the horizon. And moonlight among the trees makes one readier to feel the beauty of holiness. In nature, one view calms the soul, another purifies it, and another sublimes it.

MARHAM.

Night and morning, and sunset, snowy winter, and leafy summer, vary the look of nature, no doubt ; but it is possible, in the sight of the same scene, and at the same time, for one man to feel one way, and another another ; for one looker to be solemnized, and another to be made more hopeful.

AUBIN.

Just as, by looking on the blessed face of Christ, a happy person would rejoice more purely, and a tearful one sorrow more holily, and a sinner feel remorseful, and a righteous man drink righteousness in. And so it is with nature ; and what it makes in us is most blessedly felt by the soul, which is a child of God, through Christ. O, out in the country, sometimes, my soul feels wrapped, as though in the arms of the Great Father. It is as though the wind whispered me divine messages ; and it is as though divine meaning broke upon me from out of the clouds, and the hillsides, and from among the stars. And I know that I am growing and am destined to grow into the spirit of it all, — into the brightness of the sun, and the majesty of night, — into the purity of winter, and the contentment of summer.

MARHAM.

What you speak of, I feel only sometimes, and not every day. Perhaps this is through some fault in me. But they are holy recollections which I have, of having felt as you describe.

AUBIN.

Holy recollections, — so they are. And most trustworthy is what we feel at such times ; for the soul is then in her purer, and therefore truer moods. In summer and winter, day and night, seed-time and harvest, and in the whole order of nature, so perfect, it is as though a persuasive voice were always saying, " Trust me." In corn-fields and orchards, it is as though, from among the yellow corn and out of the tree-tops, it were said to thoughtful listeners, " O, taste and see that the Lord is good ! " And the westerly wind is like a soft whisper from out of the infinite, say-ing, " God is love ; hope thou in him." Then, in the hearing of all these voices, rises in my soul the sweet persuasion, " Dwell thou here with an understanding heart, and die thou shalt with a tri-umphant one." Yes, faith is the easier for the way that nature makes us feel.

MARHAM.

From what you have said, it would seem so.

AUBIN.

Many of the moods of our souls are the deeper for the effect on us of the world outside us. Spiritual feelings have the same words to describe them as many qualities of outward nature have, — pure, open, high, bright, infinite, dark, narrow, gentle, rapid, harmonious, misty, clouded, beautiful. In the soul, there is a midnight and a mid-day ; and there is a spring, there is a summer, an autumn, and there is a winter. Sometimes in the soul there are what are like tempests. And there are seasons in which, in the mind, thought flashes like lightning. I think there are sights in the sky, and states of the air, and scenes among trees, and from hill-tops, which have affected my way of feeling about life, and my fellow-men, and the future.

MARHAM.

Why, Oliver, how can that be ?

AUBIN.

One season there had been a long, hard frost, with an easterly wind, making it be bitterly cold ; but one morning there came such a warm breeze from the south as was delightful to breathe. I walked up and down the lane I lived in, and I drew long, deep breaths. I felt like a prisoner just free. I was as one freshly escaped from evil. I was cheerful, hopeful, and as though the whole world had brightened about me. Now this

was what I must often have felt after frosts, and
after long rain.   And I remember thinking it was
a way of feeling which made it readier for me to
believe in deliverance from misfortune.

MARHAM.

Well, Oliver, after cold, wet weather, on a
warm, clear day, I have myself sometimes felt as
though all hardships and sorrows were easily to
be lived through ; but certainly I never thought a
bright day was intended to make us think so.

AUBIN.

Nature about us is a companionship, which our
souls feel, and were meant to feel ; for there is
to be caught from it a tone so peculiar, as to be
intentional.   Cheerful is what nature would make
us, — not merry, nor melancholy.   Now it is in
cheerfulness that our moral faculties are freest, —
that we most readily trust, and are kind, and con-
trol ourselves.

MARHAM.

What you say is true, I think ; for as far as I
can remember, there are only a very few sights or
sounds in nature that are sad, or ludicrous, or
wildly gay, — only just enough to make it remarkable that the rest are so uniformly cheerful.

AUBIN.

Birds do not sing frolicsome tunes, though they
do sing happily ; the song of the lark is not jovial,
and the nightingale is not a merry songster.   The

bleat of the sheep and the low of the ox are not sad, nor yet mirthful, but serious. Winds, brooks, and rivers do not mourn ; and if in their sound there is any melancholy, it is only in Milton's sense of the word. The tone of nature is what it is, for us sons of God to learn, and for us to be cheerful from it.

MARHAM.

And in nature, what things are not to be called cheerful have, some of them, a moral effect on us ; and some of them make us laugh in a way that we are the better for. Yes, there is much in us which there would not have been, but for birds, and animals, and winds, and trees.

AUBIN.

Last year's birds are dead, many of them ; but many of their songs are lasting on in men who heard them. In my spirit, there are some tones which are the fuller for the birds I have heard sing, — the lark in a morning in spring, the nightingale on a summer's evening, the thrush against a storm, and the robin when the rain was over. In my mind, there is what has come of my being awed by thunderstorms, of hearing the wind in the woods, of feeling the air cool on an August evening, and of sitting on the sea-shore at the flow of the tide.

MARHAM.

Yes, and of sitting still for an hour, on a day so hush as this, and feeling the peace of it.

AUBIN.

If I were none the better for the world I live in, I might fear leaving it, as being useless ; but now I shall leave it for what will better my soul still more. My faith is the more cheerful for what nature makes me feel ; and nature is God about me ; so that the cheerfulness of my faith is partly God's causing, — is what I am to be easy in, and to be sure that God likes.

MARHAM.

Not every one, — and perhaps they are not many who hear the voices of the four seasons, and know what God means us to understand by his so clothing the grass of the field, — but every one that has ears to hear, can hear and understand those blessed words of Christ, — " Because I live, ye shall live also." But I think you said, that what nature means is rightly felt only by those that are spiritual, — that it is they who know best what the woods talk, and what cheerfulness the birds sing. Always the earth is the same, but it may look more divine to us Christians than it did to the heathen ; and perhaps the purer men become in heart, the more plainly they will see God in things about them. But always, and so gloriously, there will be the light of the knowledge of God in the face of Jesus Christ.

AUBIN.

And that light shines through death, and shows

it to be a phantom ; and it shines into the grave, and shows there is no victory in it.

MARHAM.

O, if I could only keep as strong in the faith as I am now ! and then I should die happily.

AUBIN.

. If Jesus Christ had all power over my soul, and were. present with me, and were to lay his hand upon me, I should say, " Lord, do with me what thou wilt." And if the horrors of death compassed me about, and frightful appearances of judgment took shape before my eyes, and if everlasting death gaped against me, I should not fear if I could look into the face of Christ ; for my soul would be calmed, and I should say, " What thou wilt, Lord, — whether it be life or death, — let it be for me what thou wilt, — O, what thou wilt !" And shall I not feel this, and more than this, when I do come to die ? For the Father will be with me. And Jesus said that we ought to be glad of his having himself gone away, because it was to the Father.

MARHAM.

Christ in the flesh reappears no more among us. And it is well, it is surely well ; but to our souls, he is with us to the end of the world. And the thought of him ought to be enough for us, and a happy companionship to die in. Still, I do not wonder at Catholic attempts to feel

Christ in the Mass, and in the sight of paintings of him.

AUBIN.

Well, I do wonder at it, because Christ is to be felt so blessedly within us, after doing his words. And then what Christ was in the flesh, God is in nature. And in the holier of my contemplative moods, it has been as though there were among the trees, and in the air, and in the mere passing of time, a presence like the mind of Christ. It was the feeling of the Father's being with me.

MARHAM.

And with us he is always, and in death we shall not be alone, for he will be with us. Perhaps, towards death, my fancy may get diseased as well as my body, and so the world be sicklied to me, and there be no cheerfulness in the sunshine, nor in human voices, nor in homely comforts. Or perhaps I may become both blind and deaf, and have all sights and sounds shut out from me.

AUBIN.

But the Father is not to be shut out from the soul by any thing else than the soul's own act.

MARHAM.

Lord! leave me not, neither forsake me!

AUBIN.

Nor will he. Nor is it likely that this earth

will be a dungeon to die in, if, to live in, it has been like the presence of God about us, vaguely, perhaps, but devoutly felt.

MARHAM.

If I should grow melancholy, I will remember what happy days I have had ; and I will think it is not the world that is altered, but myself, and not myself, even, so much as my nerves.

AUBIN.

Desponding am I ? It is from my bodily disease, and not from life's being gloomy. For is not the sun shining ? do not boys and girls play ? are not laborers singing at their work, at this very time ? and is not this a marriage-day with many and many a happy man and wife ? Sometimes melancholy is greater than it would otherwise be, through selfishness, through not rejoicing with them that do rejoice. And then, in itself, this earth is what we ought to die out of triumphantly. For in this lower world, has not God's presence been what rightly makes us long for a manifestation of it, higher and still plainer ?

MARHAM.

Adversity I have had ; but much of it has come of my fellow-men. Pain I have had, but much of it has been of my own incurring. Dark days I have had, but then some have been very bright. And then I have had no suffering of any kind but might have been the making of my char-

acter. So that the general impression of life upon me ought to be encouraging and trustful ——

AUBIN.

And a holy confidence in our destiny. Morning after morning, God has gladdened me with
light, so regularly, these many years. And night
after night, he has curtained me round with darkness so peacefully, so blessedly, that I ought not
to shrink from death only because the night of it
is so very dark; for though very dark, it is not
the less divine. Nay, at its coming on, God's
hand moves in it, almost to our feeling.

MARHAM.

Oliver, your words are very soothing, and I
hope rightly so; and, indeed, I think they are;
because, though lofty, they do not embolden or
excite me. And among our thoughts, those
which are grand and calm, both, are almost always the truest. But your voice is soothing, and
when you talk of the grave, you say the word
in such a way as to make it feel like a spacious
home, instead of a narrow house.

AUBIN.

However, it is neither for us Christians, nor for
us living souls. For what is a dead body? It is
a worn-out garment of the soul. It is what is to
be reckoned along with the clothes, the books, the
furniture, the instruments, of a deceased friend.
And then the earth does not open into a grave, of

herself; for it is man who digs that, and peoples it with horror.

MARHAM.

The body returns unto the earth as it was ——

AUBIN.

But the soul rises elsewhere, wise with the knowledge which has come of its earthly dwelling, and sometimes so grown into the spirit of this planetary system as to be like the rich germ of a new world. And such a soul does not rise unheeded out of this earth into the realm of spirits. That is not to be thought, any more than it is likely that new stars rise out of an abyss by chance.

MARHAM.

For every new year, for every fresh state, for boyhood after infancy, for youth after boyhood, for manhood after youth, for my old age, — for every change in life, my soul has been the better, or might have been; and so the last great change will be greatly the better for me, as I ought to believe.

AUBIN.

Rightly reasoned, uncle. Sometimes our fellow-men wrong and grieve us; but it is not in them we trust either for life or against death. If they wrong us, it is because they do not know what they do, — do not even know that they wrong themselves. It is easy to forgive them, —

poor fellow-creatures. But what is not so easy, and yet is necessary for us, and is a duty, is to keep ourselves unembittered by even what ill-treatment we have quite forgiven. Because a soul, for being bitter, is the weaker in its faith both towards God and man, and in an hereafter.

MARHAM.

Ah! if only we did love our enemies, then heaven would be a natural hope with us; for commonly the man who loves most hopes the highest. I will try to be what I ought to be towards my fellow-creatures, and so I shall have joy and peace in believing.

AUBIN.

Yes, uncle. And, O! this world is so beautiful, that it is like a Divine smile about us always; and it is so hopeful, that we ought to die out of it quite willingly and courageously.

CHAPTER XXV.

Sublime is the faith of a lonely soul,
 In pain and trouble cherished ;
Sublime the spirit of hope that lives,
 When earthly hope has perished. — JOHN WILSON.

AUBIN.

THE gloomy, gloomy world ! And so it is to a gloomy man. But it is a bright, bright world to me ; to-day at least it is.

MARHAM.

And a very happy world it would be, if the people in it were as little covetous as you, Oliver.

AUBIN.

Ours, ours, — the world must be ours. Our God's it is ; but for a selfish man, that is not enough, or rather it is nothing. So many millions.of us want to have the world, every one for himself ! And against this there are so many millions of impossibilities !

MARHAM.

And if we had the whole world, there would still be our souls to be saved.

AUBIN.

Which in some countries is not a very easy thing for a man owning only a few miles of land.

The whole world ours, but without God in it! Would any thing tempt us to take the atheistical ownership? You shall have your own way in it; God shall not mind you; and there shall be in it no laws of right, or truth, or love, for you to know of. What you are and do, you shall be and you shall do, but without God; and in your actions there shall be no Divine end answered; and in what you become, there shall be no likeness to God. The world shall be yours, all yours, but yours only, your miserable own.

MARHAM.

What a thought! It is what would spread into a hell worse than Dante's.

AUBIN.

And the opposite of it is heaven, — indeed, the heaven of the Gospel. Ownership in the world I have none, but I have infinite interest in it; for if not my own, it is my God's; and so it is mine in a higher than a legal sense. Yes, this is the beauty, this is the whole sublimity, this is the tender delight of life, — that it is of God's governing.

MARHAM.

What says the Psalmist? The earth is the Lord's, and the fulness thereof.

AUBIN.

And it is mine, not in law, but better still, in God. I have a use of it with which sealed

parchments have nothing to do. There is a tract
of land; the soil is rich; the situation sheltered;
it is well wooded, and well watered, and like
what lie along Yarrow; —

> Fair scenes for childhood's opening bloom,
> For sportive youth to stray in ;
> For manhood to enjoy his strength,
> And age to wear away in.

As I look at such a scene, at the garden, and the
park, at the walks to walk in, the old trees to sit
under, the wide view to be glad at, the meadows
with the cattle in, and the fields perhaps yellow
with corn, I am persuaded of there being in my
circumstances a grandeur of promise greater than
I can guess. For I think to myself, God could
have made the scene of my life like that ; but as
he has not, it is because it is better for me otherwise. Plenty, comfort, and delightfulness are
withheld from me for a purpose. And so I think
to myself, what a happy purpose it must prove.
And from the things which I have not, I persuade
myself of the glories that I am heir to. Or,
rather, this is what I used to do ; for now I have
every comfort I could wish, through your kindness, dear uncle.

MARHAM.

Oliver, my dear Oliver, the kindness is yours.
But do not mention it, for you humble me, — you
do, indeed. For I know there is nothing I can

do for you that can possibly be a return for the profit and pleasure of your conversation. It is only for your body I can do any thing; but, Oliver, you help me to feel myself a soul, a living soul, in a world with God in it.

AUBIN.

A world with almightiness in it; and so a world of infinite promise for us all. For what it is is pain and poverty to what it might be, and therefore to what it will be, or will be followed by; for God is the Lord Almighty and Albrightful.

MARHAM.

Almighty and Albrightful! Whose words are those, for they are not yours, I think, nor this age's?

AUBIN.

They are Wickliffe's. But as I was saying, uncle, I enjoy myself in other people's enjoyments. One of the happiest hours I ever had was at a village, one day, when there was a wedding there. The road between the bride's home and the church was spanned by arches of flowers. The bells rung; and men and women all spoke cheerfully; and the air was so still, as though waiting in the sunshine to listen to the bells. And up through the trees, to the church, came the wedding-party, — the bride in her modesty and grace, and the bridegroom in his joy and his strength. That my marriage-day could ever be a festival for a whole neighbourhood was not for me to think. But the general joy, and the rich dresses, and the scattering of flowers, and the thronging together of all the neighbours, and the peace of the bride and the bridegroom, as they came away from the church, with a blessing on them from their Father in heaven, — the happiness of all this was like my own, through sympathy. It was as though my heart were the larger for feeling it. And I went away from that sweet village with more hope in life, because they were creatures of my own nature who had been made so happy.

MARHAM.

Rejoice with them that do rejoice. And what comes of this commandment is indeed a tender and a holy joy.

AUBIN.

It would not be good for us all to be outwardly happy ; nor would there be room in the world for us all to have every thing we could wish. But there are some few of us whom Nature clothes in all her graces, and houses in all her comforts, and brings out to walk on smooth roads, in love and honor, from all their neighbours. And it is as though it were said to us, "Even out of this earth can you spirits be made thus happy when it is good for you." And then the spirit within us witnesses, if we will let it, — "Even so ; and God be thanked !. But better than happiness itself is the soul's trust that waits for it, — that patiently waits thy giving, Father of spirits ! "

MARHAM.

True, Oliver, true.

AUBIN.

The love there is among dearly loving friends is what will be felt for me when I am known, as I shall be, hereafter. While I am in this right frame of mind, every happy event, everywhere, sounds in the telling like Divine encouragement saying to me, " Thou art not forgotten, my son, and for thee there is a blessing with thy Father in heaven." Already there are the beginnings of Divine justice in our lives, and they and our own sense of justice persuade us that right will be done to that instinct of happiness which is in us, if not in this life, then so surely in another. So that a righteous man in long pain, in poverty, or in sorrow, is a sight before heaven that helps to make immortality certain.

MARHAM.

And when such a man weeps, and we weep with him, we feel so tenderly that God cannot forget the sufferer. Nowhere have I found another life feel so sure as I have in a sick-room, after my having prayed by the bedside of some one dangerously ill.

AUBIN.

From others being dear to us, we know how dear they must be to God. I trust God cares for me ; but that he cares for others I feel strongly, and almost as though I knew it by sight. It is through sympathy with others that we have the sweetest, or some of our sweeter assurances of Divine goodness.

MARHAM.

Have not we ourselves —— but ——

AUBIN.

There was a man that once injured me much, through religious bigotry. Afterwards, misfortune threatened him, and very pitifully, for he was an old man ; but it passed away from him at last, suddenly and very pleasantly. When I learned the news, which I did by letter, at once I knelt and worshipped God ; and then I thanked God for the sweet pleasure I felt. I think I have been more glad in God for what good fortune has happened to others, than for what has befallen myself.

MARHAM.

Why, Oliver, why should you, and how could you have done so ? And was it right ? It is very true that you have never had much happiness ; but when it was granted you at all, I think you ought ——

You do not understand me, uncle. I did not
say that I had been more glad of other men's
happiness than my own ; but that I had been
more glad in God. Because it is long, very long,
before we receive happiness properly. For we
are too apt to take it as though it were our right,
or our merit, or some way our own getting. And
then in the first possession of good fortune there
is the feeling of gratified selfishness ; and that
defiles the purity of joy in God.

Hardly so, Oliver, surely. But your meaning
is right, I think. The earth is full of the goodness of the Lord ; and we ought to think of this,
and not merely of what joy flows out of our own
little fountains, which run dry sometimes, perhaps
through their having been tampered with.

To me, at times, the happier this earth seems,
the surer heaven feels ; and for this reason, I suppose, — that to be grateful to God is to be confident in him. So, along with some poet,

> I think of all the glorious things
>   Which o'er this earth are spread,
> Of mighty peasants and the kings
>   That under it lie dead.

O those memories of the good and great, — how I
love them ! And how much in the world there is

to think of and love ! — green nooks between woody hills, with the sunshine on them, — corn-fields ready for reaping, — the harvest moon at its rising, — men fighting sublimely with the elements at sea, and on land turning them into service, — women in their beauty, and their strange, sweet power, — firesides with families about them, — the laugh of a little child, — the fondness of a Christian father, — the sensation of reading some very good book for the first time, and in man-hood, — and friendships, those true ones that are trusted in the more, the more God is trusted in. In all these things, what delight there is is not chance, but God ; and the more devoutly one feels it to be God, the more it feels like what will last and grow for ever. God in our enjoy-ment ! O, then there is a something of infinity in it ! Yes, God is in our happiness ; and because he has let us know of his being in it, he will be in it for us for ever. For the Father would not have let us know that his gifts to us are from above, and out of an infinite treasury, if he did not intend us more than we have, much more, infinitely more.

MARHAM.

So we will trust.

AUBIN.

And, uncle, so we ought to trust. For why are we made to recollect past pleasures ? Not

for us to regret them ; but so as for us, out of
such remembrances, to hope in heaven the better. And, indeed, our highest thoughts do not
reach what will be the level of our happiness
hereafter. For every instant it will be sublimer
than first hearing the organ in York Minster, and
more tender than lovers' faith, and more joyful
than a birthday with many friends to keep it, and
more earnest than any earthly act of self-sacrifice.
O, how free I shall feel hereafter ! And O the
truths I shall know of, the beauty I shall see, and
the friends I shall have ! At first our everlasting
life will be like a summer's day, so calm, and
beautiful, and long. But it will prove a day that
will last on, and on, 'and on. And when no night
comes, and we do not get weary, and all things
keep on brightening about us, as the eyes of our
understandings open, then, little by little, we shall
begin, in awe and wonder, to feel what it is to be
immortal.

CHAPTER XXVI.

And being but one, she can do all things : and remaining in herself, she maketh all things new : and in all ages entering into holy souls, she maketh them friends of God and prophets For God loveth none but him that dwelleth with wisdom. For she is more beautiful than the sun, and above all the order of the stars : being compared with the light, she is found before it — WISDOM OF SOLOMON.

But understand thou for thyself, and seek out the glory for such as be like thee. For unto you is paradise opened, the tree of life is planted, the time to come is prepared, plenteousness is ready, a city is builded, and rest is allowed, yea, perfect goodness and wisdom. — ESDRAS.

AUBIN.

I DO not think you like hearing of new discoveries, uncle.

MARHAM.

Why, what can have made you think so, Oliver ? For it would be foolish in me to dislike new inventions, or newly discovered principles. But, — perhaps —— Well, I will confess, at first hearing, my feeling is not altogether pleasure in them. I do not know why it is not. Perhaps you can tell me. But you, Oliver, — you rejoice in any new discovery almost as though you had made it yourself.

AUBIN.

So I do, and really for that reason. As regards a machine, the best thing is the invention of

it, the next best is understanding it, and a long
way after this is the money it may be made to
earn. Of all inventions, the best thing is the ingenuity in them ; and what is noblest in all discoveries is the mind with which they were made
out. It is the soul that is the greatness of all human achievements. And these great achievements I love to hear of, for they make me feel
my own greatness, and not presumptuously ; for
in other men's crimes I acknowledge my own
evil liabilities. Human nature is dear to me in
every form of it, — in what is told of great kings,
and in what I have myself learned from a beggar-
woman, — in the prattle of infancy, in the eager
movements of youth, and in the solemn words of
a man ripe and ready for death.

MARHAM.

It is because you either have been, or may
possibly be, in some such situations yourself.

AUBIN.

But then I love human nature as it is to be
read of in Homer's Iliad, in the temples, on the
obelisks, and in the tombs of Egypt, in the apoc-
ryphal books of the Jews, in the Arabian Nights'
Entertainments, in Snorro Sturleson's Sagas of
the Norsemen, in the Chronicles of Jocelin of
Brakelond, in Chaucer's Canterbury Tales, and
in Catlin's account of the American Indians.
Not exactly as Paul meant, yet quite truly, all

over the world, and in all ages, we all have been made to drink into one spirit. If a man is a man in head and heart, and has been so in action besides, then he has an interest in all human things, and a something of right in them. What Beaumont and Fletcher make a man say in one of their plays, I myself feel, and

> When any falls from virtue, I am distract,
> I have an interest in 't.

It is but little I have been, or have had an opportunity of being. Yet when I think of good and great men, sometimes there comes over my mind a strange feeling of fellowship in glory with them. In me, and in them, there is one soul, and I have not lived altogether unworthily of it ; and so in them I recognize my own nature as it is, or else as it may be made by prayer and the Divine grace. The end of Leonidas, and Stephen's martyrdom, are mirrors in which my soul sees her own devotedness. I can conceive, and partly I have lived, the pains and perseverance in which the pyramids of Egypt were built ; and so, in some sense, they are monuments of the laboriousness of my nature. It is my own way of thinking and feeling that is in the better parts of the writings of Fénelon and George Fox ; and so from those books is reflected the character of my mind. The zeal of St. Paul, — Milton's patriotism, — Pascal's purity, — Galileo's sight into

the stars, — the exactness of Cuvier's account of
creatures that perished from this earth more than
a myriad years ago, — what King Alfred was, —
what Washington was, — the mind of the Pilgrim
Fathers, — O, what a cloud of witnesses these
are ! And how they testify the greatness of the
human soul ! With thoughts like these, the more
my soul warms, the more immortal it feels, and
rightly ; for one way I am every thing that I
love ; and, indeed, altogether I am, almost.

MARHAM.

O, if only you could have health and strength !

AUBIN.

And then, dear uncle, I should very likely be
nothing remarkable. Because, for one famous
man, there are a thousand, ay, and ten thousand,
deservers. Excellence is commoner than is
thought, the essence of it is ; only it does
not get expressed, — sometimes out of modesty,
sometimes for want of opportunity, but oftenest
for want of some little knack.

MARHAM.

You think so ? But is not that as though some
better souls had been made for impossible purposes ?

AUBIN.

Purposes impossible in this world, and therefore so highly presumptive of another world.
Often, for one hero, there are a hundred heroic

spirits, only they do not get into action. Because a hero needs five hundred square miles for a stage ; while that space of land is' not meant to be only the theatre for one man to act in, but the native country of ten million people. And so out of a hundred persons who are heroical by nature, one is allowed to be so in action ; and the rest, through sympathy with him, feel themselves, and know themselves, and grow stronger. And every thrill of their souls is prophetic of the high use which God will make of them all hereafter.

MARHAM.

That is well argued, Oliver.

AUBIN.

If a man does earnestly what duty he has to do, then he is any and every character that he truly loves, — he is Howard, the philanthropist, and Sidney, the patriot, and John, the Apostle.

MARHAM.

You cannot mean ——

AUBIN.

That he is those men, or what they really were ; but I mean that he is, and is truly, what they seem to him. As soon as I do thoroughly understand and feel Bacon's Essays, they may be regarded as utterances, — no ! every thing but that. They may then stand as the measure of my wisdom, — no ! not that ; but they may be regarded as the manner in which I should myself

think, if only some little change, some slight freedom, were wrought within my soul. How grand
that engraving from Michael Angelo is! And,
O, what purity, what unearthly beauty, what
heavenly-mindedness, there is in that Madonna of
Correggio! But what I see in these pictures is
what I feel in my own mind; and what I feel
while looking at them is what I am capable of
feeling in other things, — in duty, in virtuous as-
pirations, in my prayers to God, and in my hymns
to him, and in my thoughts of an hereafter.

MARHAM.

Oliver, I think the artist will be more availing
in the world than he has ever been; religiously,
I mean.

AUBIN.

And so I think, uncle. But I do not think
the Puritans were wrong in their age for dashing
out painted windows, and removing pictures from
churches, and pulling down organs, and unfrock-
ing the choristers, and white-washing gilded orna-
ments; because it is possible a worshipper in a
church may be the worse for such things as these;
and, indeed, he will be greatly the worse for them,
unless he is earnest and enlightened. I think,
uncle, I have noticed, that, wherever there is a
great taste for music or painting, character is the
better, or else very much the worse for it. One
or two persons I know, the tone of whose minds

is to me revolting, — made so, as I think, by
their indulgence, — the very word ! — by their
indulgence in the fine arts. A man's moral sense
must be quick, and his reason well trained, or
else, in loving beauty, he will be courting refined
perdition. Still, uncle, I agree with you. And
I think there will come a time when music and
painting, and sculpture and architecture, will be
religious helps, — and more safely used than they
were in Greece, and more successfully than they
have ever been in the Catholic Church, or ever
will be. For truth can be more beautifully expressed than error. And then genius, especially the highest, is religious ; and so it is more
or less religiously darkened, unless purely Christian. Nor are all forms of Christianity indifferent. For the state of mind which Paul argues
for against the Jews is exactly the mood in which
alone genius is creative, — a soul acting out of its
own purified state, and not abiding fearfully by
customs and outward laws. Now when this
Christian spirit becomes common, an artist will
have that for his usual temper, almost, which, as
yet, is only his genial and often very rare mood.
O, yes ! the purely Christian spirit will be the
inspiration of a glorious literature ; and it will
possess the minds of sculptors, painters, archi-
tects, and musicians, and make them priests unto
God.

MARHAM.

All noblest things are religious, — not temples and martyrdoms only, but the best books, pictures, poetry, statues, and music. Very strongly this testifies the truth of religion.

AUBIN.

It is not in prayer only that the soul approaches God, for it is drawn nigher him by all the higher objects it turns to. If a poet will sing his noblest strain, it is into the ear of God he does it ; if an architect will build in his sublimest manner, it is a house for God he makes ; and if a true artist will do his best in music, it is God whom he must have in his mind to glorify, or else to mourn to. And every earnest movement of the mind of man is upwards, and to God, — making us sure of that Divine presence, toward which the soul is meant to be reaching, and in which, hereafter, will be its heaven.

MARHAM.

It must be, and it is, — yes, what you have now said is part of that witness which God has never left himself without in the world and the soul. And, Oliver, you have pointed it out very beautifully.

AUBIN.

And all knowledge, properly held, points to God. Science is in our hands like a Divine gift ; and, rightly thought of, it persuades us of a spiritual world which we are akin to.

MARHAM.

It ought to do, — yes, it ought to do.

AUBIN.

Geologically, botanically, geographically, and every way, the better we know the world, the more familiar it feels, and like a home made for us. This broad and various earth a home for us to live in ! Then we may heartily believe the Maker of it to be our Father Almighty. Uncle, your uneasiness at new knowledge, and my joy in it, is the difference of our two philosophies. You plant yourself upon certain reasons, and you say, " As long as I have these to stand upon, I know that the eye of God must be turned upon me as his child." But some of those reasons alter a little with every new thought, and so you feel as though the foundations under you were uncertain. But my way of thinking is this : — as surely as I live, there is a God ; and my soul claims God as more than her Maker, as being her Father ; and as surely as my soul was meant to feel at all, God is towards me what he feels to be ; and so he must be, and is, the Father of spirits. God is truth ; and so every new truth I learn is fresh likeness in me to God.

MARHAM.

Yes, it is, and no doubt ought to be so thought of, notwithstanding what Solomon says about the sorrowful growth of knowledge.

AUBIN.

In science and in manufactures, new principles, or fresh applications of them, are from the Father of lights, and are meant to assure and reassure us of our near relationship to him. O uncle! there are glad and solemn seasons in which what is called the light of civilization is to my feeling the light of God among men ; and so indeed it is.

MARHAM.

Our knowledge is God's giving, no doubt ; and our uses of it, when innocent, are according to his intentions.

AUBIN.

What is the difference between savage and civilized life ? It is mind. This house and all the articles in it are the results of thought. In every brick about us, there is skill ; in every chair and table, there is intention ; in this couch, there is the idea of the inventor ; and it is not only with colored wool that the floor is carpeted, but also with taste, and with the perseverance and attention of many hours, and many thinkers, — sheep-shearer, wool-comber, yarn-spinner, dyer, designer, and weaver. Why does my shirt differ from green plants in a hemp field ; or this pair of shoes from a yard of ox-hide ? By the ingenuity in them. Why, what way of life we really are living is much more spiritual than we often think it.

MARHAM.

So it is, Oliver ; so it is.

AUBIN.

Man might have been created with the strength of an elephant, and the swiftness of an antelope, and with clothing as strong as what the rhinoceros wears, and as light as the plumage of the bird of paradise, and as gay. In his eye there might have been the glance of the eagle, and the sight of the owl ; and so day and night would have been alike to him. And as in the north the skin of the fox is of one color in summer and another in winter, so the human body might have been made to adapt itself readily to the four seasons and the five zones.

MARHAM.

Man would have been made so if it had been good for him.

AUBIN.

It is good for him ; and he is made so, nearly.

MARHAM.

All the powers which you have been speaking of ——

AUBIN.

Are in the human hand. The hand is a wonderful thing ; and without it, the soul of man would have been always unknown, and never would have known herself; because she could not have exercised herself, could not have quickened, and struggled, and learned. She would not have been known of, although she still would have been a soul ; just as we know now that there is the same and as quick a spirit in the deaf and dumb, as in those that have all the five senses. What delicate touch there is in the finger-ends ! How well the hand is made to grasp ! The hand was not meant to fit into the arm at the wrist more plainly than it is itself fitted to a hammer and to a needle. When the muscles of the hand were made, there was thought of what work the hand would have to do ; and so, as I think, a hammer, an axe, a needle, were as much meant to become continuations of the hand, as the hand was intended to be a prolongation of the arm. The hand was made for tools, as much as to be jointed at the wrist. A carpenter's tools, a miner's implements, and a steam-engine are as much instruments of the soul as the fingers are. And because they can be laid aside, their convenience is so much the greater ; for otherwise they would be oppressively many limbs.

MARHAM.

I am listening, Oliver, and I am wondering.

AUBIN.

Saw, hammer, gimlet, pincers, trowel, — the hand of man is all these things, for it makes them and uses them. In the hand of the first man, there might have been read, as things that would certainly be, — houses, furniture, forges, woollen clothes, shawls of silk, mastery of the horse, ploughs, ships, and railroads.

MARHAM.'

That is quite true, Oliver ; and so, for what you have remarked, we ought to believe the more largely in those Christian promises which sound at first too great for fulfilment ; because we do not know what our souls may admit of.

AUBIN.

Yes, uncle, in our souls there are greater things, grander heights, and more fearful depths, and more glorious issues, than even pride thinks of ; just as in the mind of Adam, and unknown to him, were the beginnings of the tents of the patriarchs, and the art of Tubalcain, and the life of Nimrod, and all the kingdoms of the world.

MARHAM.

From what men are over what they once were, we may well believe in a life of the spirit to follow this life in the flesh.

AUBIN.

St. Bernard reminds his readers that men do not come into the world glittering with jewels or garnished with silks ; but that they are born naked, and poor, and miserable, and wretched, — blushing because they are naked, and weeping because they are born. It is very true, — it is mournfully true, says the old father ; but it is sublimely true,

I think. Let us remember what we are born, and consider how we live, and so we shall feel ourselves greater than we have thought, perhaps.

MARHAM.

Death is spoken of as going the way of all flesh ; but we do not live the way of other creatures ; so, in death, why should we fear going it ?

AUBIN.

Wearing clothes, living in houses, working at trades, — all our way of life, — come of the manner in which the hand is shaped. The soul of man being what it is, his way of living might have been, and no doubt was, foreknown from the make of his hand. An angel might have said to the first human family, — " Work, — do you human creatures work, because you are made for successful work ; for by my foresight I can see rising afar off what you cannot see, nor I tell you of well, — factories, docks, warehouses, corn-mills, observatories, churches, and cities." Man's hand was shaped for the mastery of this world, and this world is being mastered. Now in the soul there is faith, — a faculty with which for man to lay hold of the next world ; and so shall it not, — this faith that we feel, — shall it not be evidence enough for us of things not seen ?

MARHAM.

It ought to be ; and the more we know of ourselves, the better proof it will be felt to be.

AUBIN.

Was Adam's impulse to action a chance ?
Surely not. And was not it true and most trustworthy ? Yes ; for of it have come ploughed
fields, granaries, streets of houses, furniture,
clothing, and outwardly all that we are of what
we were meant to be. Now there are impulses
in us that have a spiritual world for their object.
Then they are to be trusted to ; for cannot we
be sure, — do not we know, — that we are truly,
and not deceitfully, made ? A world to come
we can think of, and we do hope for, and we can
work for ; then it is before us, it is intended for
us, and it is awaiting us as certainly as Memphis,
and Jerusalem, and Rome, and London, waited
men's hands, to begin rising under them. The
shape of man's hand was meant to have for its
object and reward all this civilized life which we
are living ; and just as truly faith has for its end
and recompense a life of the soul, holy, happy,
and everlasting. Nay, in spirit did not St. John
even see for us that great city, New Jerusalem,
coming down from God out of heaven ? And
we, we ourselves, in our peaceful moments, do
not we hear voices gentle and great, and some
of them like the voices of departed friends, —
do we not hear them saying to us, " Come up
hither " ?

20

· MARHAM.

We do, we do. And the nigher we draw to
God, the plainer we hear them.

AUBIN.

Only let us think what kind of a life it is that
we are living, and then eternity is to be lived
for with almost the same assurance that to-morrow is.

CHAPTER XXVII.

He saw through life and death, through good and ill,
  He saw through his own soul.
The marvel of the everlasting will,
  An open scroll,
Before him lay. — TENNYSON.

AUBIN.

O UNCLE, uncle, I do feel so weary to-day!

MARHAM.

It is from the hot day, Oliver. And you have nothing to do. But you are so restless for action.

AUBIN.

But just now I loathe the word. O, I am a-weary, so weary! And why must we be doing, doing, always doing, — why ought we to be? Man made for action!— he is not. For thought and feeling are the great end of life. We are to act so that we may eat, and drink, and get ourselves clothed and housed. But we are not to live for food and houses; but food and houses are to be striven for, for the sake of living; and we are to live for the sake of knowledge and feeling. Action for the mere sake of doing is worthless, for there is no soul in it; and it is even what a man may be the worse for. O, there is sincerity, and greatness, and spiritual growth, in quiet, when it is not indolence !

I cannot understand what you mean, Oliver. You have great aptitude for action, though you have not had much opportunity of showing it. And then you made work for yourself, and did it, many years.

And so now, perhaps, I can talk usefully a little. For, uncle, I am persuaded that a man must have done many a good thing before he is fit to say one.

Why, you make knowledge to be the end of action, and not action to be the proper result of knowledge, as the common judgment is.

I do not say the mind gets informed by action, — bodily action ; but it does get earnestness and strength by it, and that nameless something that gives a man the mastership of his faculties. But I shall strive and work no more. I am in a little boat far below the city of life ; and it is impossible for me to return to where voices are many and loud. I can only be quiet, and think how the stream of time is sweeping me fast into the ocean of eternity.

But you are looking better, Oliver, though you

are not quite so strong this hot weather. And if you should not get well again, it will be the will of God ; and, Oliver, we must submit to it. And I am sure you are resigned, though you may feel it very sad to be withdrawn from active life so soon.

AUBIN.

But, uncle, I do not. But, indeed, I never could get into active life. For it is not often to be entered without help, from such a position in the world as I was early reduced to. Once I was asked what friends I had of any mark ; I confessed I had none at all, and so I lost what would have been a fresh start for me in life. And then occurred to me what I had never thought of before, but what long ago Thomas Decker knew of, when he pondered, —

> Shall I contract myself to wisdom's love ?
> Then I lose riches; and a wise man poor
> Is like a sacred book that 's never read.
> To himself he lives, and to all else seems dead.

The disappointments, and the battle, and the fret of life are over with me ; and perhaps my strength for a walk of twenty miles is over. But the re-membrances of life, and the feelings that have been made in me by living it, — these are not over ; and a great happiness they are, along with this peace which I have now, through you, uncle. My spirit was not calm enough to profit thoroughly by the last six years of my life ; for they were often so very anxious. But now I am living them all over again in thought, and getting the wiser for them, and the more Christian, as I hope. For I can pray, and I can think, though I cannot work, — cannot stir, nor act much.

MARHAM.

Well, I am sorry to say that, myself, I am sometimes distressed at not being able to do what I used to do. And often I have been grieved for you ; I could find you means and friends to enter life with. But perhaps you will be strong enough yet to do something in the world. And this is such an age in the world, too. For now there are so many things doing and likely to be done, and such new prospects are opening in society.

AUBIN.

Yes, among men in yonder town, plans are being canvassed and principles argued ; and in the future, there are to be seen the dim outlines of strange and lofty institutions. This is an age decisive of the world's future for centuries. One true word uttered now is mightier than books were no long while since. And as the world grows lighter with knowledge, new heights of excellence are to be seen, and new paths upwards are to be found ; and fresh pinnacles of glory there are for men to discover, and to make themselves famous by. This is true, uncle. But I am not the man I was a year ago ; for I have other hopes, and other fears, and another view of life, than what I had then. Now the spiritual world is almost more real to me than this bodily life. The infinite and the eternal are become almost my element, and in it this round earth rolls like a phantom. And it would be nothing but a phantom, and the men and women on it would be merely spectres, were it not for God, who is in all things, and is the life and the reality of them.

MARHAM.

And the worth, and the only true happiness of them.

AUBIN.

What labor and haste there are in yonder town ! Action, action, action ! The place is full of it. And it is all for daily bread and other temporary things, though there is an eternal purpose which gets answered in it. Money is what the merchant and the mechanic think of as the end of their labor ; but there is a further end which God designs in it, and which is effected on the men themselves.

MARHAM.

The strength of mind, the decision, the mastery of the faculties, which you spoke of just now ?

AUBIN.

Yes, uncle. And now for what it is that comforts me. From all activity I am not disabled; and not at all am I invalided from the divine end of exertion, though I am from the worldly purpose of it.

It is plain, and yet it never occurred to me, — this twofold use of labor.

This end beyond an end, — this abiding purpose achieved in a temporary way. There is the likeness of it in a plant, which seems to blossom only for the sake of beauty, while inside the flower are forming the seeds of next year's plants. And in many things the way of Providence is like this. Man and woman love one another; and their love is their world; it is all in all to them; and nothing further do they think of; but out of their affection is ordained the birth of children. And when a child is born, there is in the mind of the parents a feeling for it, like what the dove has for its young. But now this fondness proves painful, unless the child grows towards the excellence which its father and mother worship; and so the child's education is certain. Then the child grows a man, and a creature of many wants, which wants the man tries to satisfy; in the trial his mind gets exercised; and so, besides comfort, he gets what he did not attempt, — mental strength, aptitude, knowledge.

MARHAM.

What you have been saying is so only with us human creatures ; and our growth is so peculiar, it is so much that of the spirit, and so long, that it is plain ours is not so much life in itself as a getting ready to live.

AUBIN.

Yonder town' was founded by persons who wanted shelter for their bodies ; but it is dwelt in by men with Bibles, — by living souls. Genius is loving and longs to be loved ; it thirsts to be understood by men and women, and youth, and old age ; therefore, in this craving for sympathy, there is security that genius will be communicative, and so the world be the wiser and the more hopeful for it. — Well, and now men are social by nature, and they will and must live together. But this they cannot do, not even trade together, without honesty and mutual trust. And so even in the necessities of trade, justice and judgment are rooted, — the same principles which, when looked at, are seen to rise heavenwards, and to be the foundations of God's throne.

MARHAM.

And so in life, — the business and the pleasures of. it, — there is often a larger meaning than we think of. And we even learn it without knowing.

AUBIN.

Often and often God makes use of us as his

servants without our knowledge. And we find ourselves richly repaid, without our being able to tell how. And there are some treasures laid up in heaven in our names, that we have never even thought of. O, it will only be by what grandeur will come of it, that we shall know rightly what this life has been with us.

MARHAM.

. It will be so, — it will be so ; and so we ought to be the more earnest in every virtue, as we do not know what great reward it may not lead up to.

AUBIN.

Nor what higher virtue it may not be the beginning of. For us Christians, it is a law to forgive our enemies unto seventy times seven offences. But what is meant for us is that charity which bears, hopes, and endures all things. And so a Christian begins forgiveness as his duty, but goes on with it as his happy nature. — There are many Christian things which must be done or held in faith at first ; but we do not do nor believe them long, before knowing of ourselves that they are right. And then out of that experience our faith grows stronger, and reaches higher still for us. At first, a child loves his father's face, then his voice, then his talk, then wisdom because his father loves it, then wisdom for its own bright sake, and then, better still, he loves it for the sake of God. We human creatures begin with liking

one another for company, then for playing together, then, perhaps, for being of service to one
another, then for our agreeing in temper ; and then
we love one another according to what manner of
spirit we are of, — we love one another's souls ;
and then at last we love the world to come, for
the noble dwellers in it.

MARHAM.

Like a bud opening into blossom, — and beautiful and natural as that, — is the way in which this
bodily manner of existence grows into spiritual life.

AUBIN.

Always when a man lives a good life in his
house, his business, and his dwelling-place, he
gets to feel that there is growing in him a spirit
better than his life's righteousness has been, and
even higher than this world well allows his showing. It is his fitness for the next life, and it is
seen by his friends better than it is felt by himself; and so to all who knew him he is a witness
of the coming of the kingdom of heaven.

AUBIN.

Yes, rightly thought of, every good thing in us
is evidence of our being heirs of God. And if
we do love God, every change that comes over
our souls is felt like an earnest of the kingdom
that is promised us.

AUBIN.

The growth of the willing soul, — how wondrously it goes on! There is God in it. And, O! it is to be trusted in infinitely. Last night I lay awake, and what we have now been talking about occurred to me; and in the first warmth of the thought, I felt myself, O, so blessedly the care of Providence, and so sure of glory to be reached! I felt as an angel may when newly made, and quickening in the smile of the Almighty, and while he is fast growing up the degrees of intelligence, to where there is not darkness enough for a doubt to be in.

CHAPTER XXVIII.

For us the winds do blow,
The earth doth rest, heaven move, and fountains flow.
Nothing we see but means our good,
As our delight, or as our treasure :
The whole is either our cupboard of food,
Or cabinet of pleasure.

The stars have us to bed ;
Night draws the curtain, which the sun withdraws;
Music and light attend our head. — GEORGE HERBERT.

MARHAM.

WHAT are you thinking of, Oliver ? Your cheeks are so glowing, and your eyes so bright, that I am afraid you are too much excited with your thoughts.

AUBIN.

I am trying to recollect something of Coleridge's, but I cannot. But I know the passage begins with saying, that every rank of creatures, as it ascends in the scale of creation, leaves death behind it or under it, and is itself a mute prophecy of the rank next above it. Sometimes water freezes into a resemblance of ferns and leaves, and earth crystallizes into spurs, like plants and trees. And then, among trees and flowers, there is what foretokens the animal world in the

sensitive plant, and in the contractile power of
such river-plants as lengthen or shorten the stalk
with the rise and fall of the water, and in the circumstance of there being male and female trees.
I think it was Goethe who said that the skeletons
of many marine creatures clearly show, that, while
making them, nature was plainly intending a higher race of land-animals.   And then, among these
creatures of the earth, there were things to fore-
show what the better nature of man was to be ;
for the trunk of the elephant is a rude hand ; and
the migratory instinct of the swallow is like strong
reason ; and the faithfulness of the dove is not
unlike the affection of man and wife ; and what the
beavers make to lodge in is an attempt at a home.

MARHAM.

Very ingenious.   Does Coleridge say that ?

AUBIN.

No, uncle.   But now I do remember a part of
what I wanted ; and it is the best thing he ever
wrote, and what ought to be laid up in cedar, as
his nephew thinks.   " Let us carry ourselves
back in spirit to the mysterious week, — the teeming work-days of the Creator, — as they rose in
vision before the eye of the inspired historian of
the generation of the heavens and earth, in the
day that the Lord God made the earth and the
heavens.   And who that had watched their ways
with an understanding heart could, as the vision

evolving still advanced towards him, contemplate the filial and loyal bee ; the home-building, wedded, and divorceless swallow ; and above all, the manifoldly intelligent ant-tribes, with their commonwealth and confederacies, their warriors and miners, the husbandfolk, and the virgin sisters, with the holy instincts of maternal love detached and in selfless purity, and not say to himself, — Behold the shadow of approaching humanity, the sun rising from behind in the kindling morn of creation." Now that is very beautiful, is not it ? It makes me feel as the angels may have done when they saw the young world rounding into beauty, and growing green and peopled, as they looked at it from time to time. It is as though I had been one of the witnesses of the creation ; and I am kindred to those sons of God who did see it, as I know by my being able to feel this way.

MARHAM.

Know it so, Oliver ! how ? Though it is pleasant to think on the stages in creation, improving one on another, till the last, but little lower than that of the angels.

AUBIN.

How the world was once without form and void ; then how it was shaped by the rush of water round it, and the bursting of fire from within it ; then how its bleak surface grew green with vegetation ; then how there sprung up vast trees ; and then, in the forests, how vast creatures began to move, and when their creepıng race had died out, how a better and still a better kind of animals appeared, till at last man was made in the image of the Highest, — of God ——

MARHAM.

With the earth given him to subdue, and every thing in it to use. And so it was for us the earth was made, though at first it was only the pasture of cattle and the hunting-field of the lion. There was progress in the creation from day to day, or rather in one order of creatures over the next order. And so we were the last, because we were to be the highest.

AUBIN.

According to an ascending scale of worth in the creation. It is this delights the soul. First there was made the kingdom of dead minerals, then that of growing plants, then that of active creatures, then that of reasoning activity ; and now there are among us the beginnings of a new creation in Christ Jesus. It is because of her sympathy with it, because of her own progressive character, that my soul thrills to this. And just now I felt as though I saw age beyond age, and height above height, and glory beyond glory, for my soul to pass into.

MARHAM.

I believe in the soul's infinite progress, though I do not think it is to be expected from the manner in which the world grew out of a void into what it now is. Because, if any thing at all is to be inferred from that, it would be, I think, the possibility, some time, of some creatures being made superior to ourselves.

AUBIN.

O, no! but the certainty of social progress, and therefore of individual improvement, and that for ever, probably. It would be as you say, if man differed from the brutes only as they do from trees, and as trees do from marble and iron. For there is nothing in a mineral, which, at its best, could ever become a plant, and vegetable organization perfected to the utmost would never make an animal, and the instincts of all animals in one would not amount to reason. But reason itself is not to be spoken of so, for there is no high place to which it is not competent; and while above us men there are angels and archangels, the difference between them and us is not in nature, but in degree, in what is possible to be outgrown. Yes! there was progress in the geological ages, and it was from one to a higher kind of existence; and now that progressiveness is in the soul of man, and may be in it infinitely; for, by the very nature of the spirit, there is no prin-

21

cipality nor power up to the height of which it
may not grow; and there is no great form, into
the fulness of which it may not spread; and
there is no strength, to the possession of which it
may not get. By the image of God upon me, I
am kindred to the whole family of God; not only
to poets, and saints, and prophets, but to angels,
and to the cherubim and seraphim, and to the
dwellers in the heaven of heavens. Since the
beginning, progression has been the law of the
world. Yes, and to me the recognition of this
truth feels like a troubled joy, and it turns within me to a prophecy of my own infinite destiny.

MARHAM.

God make us and keep us worthy of it ! The
Lord have us in his sight always !

AUBIN.

My being in the eye of God persuades me of
my immortality. For, I think, there cannot but
be an everlastingness in every purpose of an eternal God. My nature will never die out; I will
not fear it will ; for no action of God's ever quite
spends itself, and very probably nothing of his
creating will ever quite perish.

MARHAM.

O, Oliver ! you forget it is written expressly,
that this earth will be dissolved, and the firmament
above it.

AUBIN.

But God is in the earth and will outlive it; and no doubt all that is divine in creation is immortal. The earth will burn up, and the heavens be on fire, and there will be a great void again; and so, perhaps, space be made for the new heavens and the new earth. But in us there will survive a something of the former heavens and the earth that once was; for always there will be in us feelings inspired by them. And our souls will be sublime with the sublimity of perished mountains; and they will be pure with the purity with which morning used to blush in the east; and they will be beautiful with the beauty with which evening lingered in the west; and they will be lovely with the loveliness of moonlight among the trees; and they will be peaceful with the peace into which, on summer evenings, nature often hushed herself.

MARHAM.

You are not talking too much, Oliver, are you? Do not tire yourself; but do go on.

AUBIN.

And the most perishable objects of nature become immortal by having been ways or points through which man and God have touched, in spirit; for spirit immortalizes all things. Animals were created, the later their race, the better, till at last man was made; and now human ages are improvements, one on another. But now also, through man, other animals live to more spiritual purpose ; for man sees, and uses, and thinks of them. And as Bailey says, —

> All animals are living hieroglyphs.
> The dashing dog, and stealthy-stepping cat,
> Hawk, bull, and all that breathe, mean something more
> To the true eye than their shapes show ; for all
> Were made in love, and made to be beloved.

The succession of the five vegetable creations was that of superiority ; and now the last is itself progressive, by its being of more and more use. A tree ripens and drops fruit, and so perhaps is the support of some animal that comes under its boughs ; but it is of better use still, when the fruits of it are gathered by man ; but when the remembrance of the tree is to live in an immortal soul, it is become another thing than what used to grow and rot in an unpeopled world. There was a daisy ploughed up in a field at Ellisdale ; but through Burns's address to it, it lives on and will flourish for ever, —

> Wee, modest, crimson-tipped flower.

Dead is it ? The earthiness of it is ; but not what was the daisy itself, nor even what likeness of his own fate the poet saw in its being ploughed up : —

> Such fate to suffering worth is given,
> Who long with wants and woes has striven,

By human pride or cunning driven
　　　　　To misery's brink,
　, 　Till, wrenched of every stay but Heaven,
　　　　　He, ruined, sink!

And there is one sweet brier that will live as long as the English language, for through the love of Walter Savage Landor it has been spiritualized, and so become an everlasting.

My brier, that smelledst sweet
When gentle spring's first heat
Ran through thy quiet veins.

And, O! in this manner, many are the flowers and trees that live a higher life than can be touched by frost or heat. And if I never were to see a tree again, I could always feel the stillness and the awe and the depth of an American forest; for there is a hymn of Bryant's, the saying of which brings great trees about me, and thick branches over my head, and a feeling of being alone with God. The woods may disappear, but the spirit of them never will now; for it has been felt by a poet, and we can feel for ever what he felt, — how

　　　　　　the sacred influences
That from the stilly twilight of the place,
And from the gray old trunks, that, high in heaven,
Mingled their mossy boughs, and from the sound
Of the invisible breath that swayed at once
All their green tops, stole over him, and bowed
His spirit with the thought of boundless Power
And inaccessible Majesty.

O, but that is sublime ! It is what might have been felt in Lebanon, when it was holier than it is now.

And holier and sublimer all objects grow, with the growing holiness of the beholders. Rivers there are, the Yarrow, the Otter, the Severn, and others, that make unearthly music in their ripplings, since they have been sung of by Wordsworth, and Coleridge, and Milton. And there are birds that died long ago, and yet that are living on still, — the cuckoo of Logan's hearing, the stormy petrel and the horned owl of Barry Cornwall's poems, and the skylark which the Ettrick Shepherd heard singing, —

> O, my love is bonny, and young, and chaste,
> As sweetly she sits in her mossy nest!

Ay, and to the last of life, there is that in nature which there are no words for, but which is to be felt ; and in wild-flowers, there is what the spirit owns and is glad in.

> Once I welcome you more, in life's passionless stage,
> With the visions of youth to revisit my age,
> And I wish you to grow on my tomb.

So felt Campbell ; and so I feel, though I am not old ; yes, I am ; for age is not years, but experience and nearness to death. O, I had forgotten Shelley's poem on the Sensitive Plant !

It is a wonderful poem. In the beginning of it there are flowers, — a garden full of them, that will live for ever. I have now blossoms in my eye, but they will be withered to-morrow; but in my mind's eye, I have flowers that Shelley has shown me, and that are unfading. And why are they? Because some little the meaning of them — what is, as it were, the soul of them — has been shown to my soul. There is the lily, and there is the hyacinth,

> And the rose, like a nymph to the bath addrest,
> Which unveiled the depth of her glowing breast,
> Till, fold after fold, to the fainting air
> The soul of her beauty and love lay bare.

But O the last part of the poem! It is autumn to read it. All through the verses, one feels and breathes September, — yellow, and moist, and decaying, and thoughtful; yes, and even the air of an autumn day is to be felt, — the moisture of it on the skin, but also and for ever the spirit of it in the mind. And so through the immortality of man there is an everlasting purpose even in nature. Forests may vanish, but the awfulness of their depths will be in my spirit for ever; the sea may be dried up from the earth, but never out of my memory; and to all eternity there will be in me what has come of the storms I have heard, and the midnights I have felt, and the brook-sides I have lain upon. But, uncle ——

MARHAM.

I will not interrupt you, Oliver. I was only going to refer to what St. Paul says about all things being discernible by the spiritual man.

AUBIN.

Yes, by the spirit there is a spirit discernible in all things ; and if I am spiritual, then the world is a revelation of God to me ; and there is a spirit looks in upon my spirit from out of the sky, and the earth, and the sea, from out of the sun and the moon, and from out of the rose. It is for the sake of what we men feel in nature, and from it, that this earth has been made. And I have no doubt that there are beings purer than we, who would feel this world round them like a Divine presence; and who would, as it were, see the face of God in every direction they could look ; so wise and beautiful and good all things are really, and so expressively so. Sometimes, after I have been praying, a landscape has seemed to me something so unspeakable, and what I have yearned towards, as though I were being drawn into the bosom of the Father. This religiousness of nature, — how easily and touchingly does Jesus bring it out ! We are with him in Galilee, and we are anxious about ourselves ; so the Master points to the tall, golden flowers about, and says to us, " Consider the lilies, how they grow ; they toil not, neither do they spin : and

yet I say unto you, that even Solomon in all his
glory was not arrayed like one of these. Wherefore, if God so clothe the grass of the field, which
to-day is, and to-morrow is cast into the oven,
shall he not much more clothe you, O ye of little
faith ? " There they fly, a cloud of birds ; and
not one of them shall fall to the ground without
our Father, — not one sparrow shall. And we,
— we are of infinitely more value than many such.
Why, then, are we so fearful, as though there were
no one to care for us, — as though God did not.
Hark ! again the Master speaks ; and we look
up, as he points, and he says, " Behold the fowls
of the air, for they sow not, neither do they reap,
nor gather into barns ; yet your Heavenly Father
feedeth them. Are ye not much better than
they ? " Behold the fowls of the air ! Is not it
as though they were in the air there still ? Is not
it as though they had outlived eighteen hundred
years ? And so they have, in a sense. For
through Christ's looking at them, they became
Christian thoughts ; and they have grown eternal,
through his having felt what a lesson of Providence they were. Spirit as they were at first ;
how all things tend to become spiritual !

MARHAM.

You mean, Oliver, do not you, that ——

AUBIN.

This earth was a Divine idea before it was a

globe; and before becoming earthly shapes,
woods and flowers, hills and rivers and oceans,
were thoughts in the mind of God; and the laws
of the seasons were intentions in it; and that
goodness which God saw in all things on his
making them was what had been a feeling within
himself, first of all. Before being made, all
things that we see were Divine thoughts; and
now they are thoughts in our minds, and will be
for ever, though as objects they will themselves
perish. In this manner does God give himself to
us, — impart knowledge to us, and inspire us
with feeling.

MARHAM.

Your ideas are new to me, Oliver; but I like
them very-much. They make the world feel
what I cannot express.

AUBIN.

Like the bosom of a mother, whose spirit we
have grown into, and in whose arms we can die
cheerfully and full of hope.

MARHAM.

So God grant we may.

AUBIN.

The world God cannot have made in vain, nor
any parts of it, neither clouds, mountains, seas,
nor flowers. It is as a book for us men to read
in, that nature is not in vain.

MARHAM.

You mean that God would not have made the world, but for the human race to live in.

AUBIN.

Yes, I think so, uncle ; and I mean, that, as the world itself is not eternal, therefore we ourselves must be. The Infinite must have an infinite end in what he does. And in the making of this world, we human beings are the infinity. It is our souls which are the everlastingness of God's purpose in this earth. And so we must be, — we are, immortal.

CHAPTER XXIX.

Then woke
Stirrings of deep Divinity within,
And, like the flickerings of a smouldering flame,
Yearnings of a hereafter. Thou it was,
When the world's din and passion's voice was still,
Calling thy wanderer home. — WILLIAMS.

AUBIN.

SHALL I shut the window, uncle ?

MARHAM.

Not for me, Oliver ; for it is quite warm this
afternoon, though the heat of the season is over
now, I think.

AUBIN.

On the hedges, what fresh leaves come out are
pale and hardly green.   And as you stand under
the elms, the inner leaves are turned yellow.
And see in the air, and hanging among the trees,
there is that blue mist that is so peculiar to the
latter weeks of August.   How still it is !   Even
on the poplar, the leaves hang without one stirring.   There is not the least wind.   It is as
though every thing in nature were hushed and still,
to see summer and autumn meet, and part again
almost as soon as met.   There is this meeting of
the seasons at every vine, and under every apple,

and peach, and plum tree. And summer looks at the fruits with her large, glowing eyes, and says, " All these are my ripening " ; and then autumn claps her hands and cries, " But my gathering ! they are for me to gather." And for a few days they dwell in the woods together. At first, autumn has only one or two yellow trees to sit in ; but every day she gets more and more, till, at last, summer has only an oak-tree left her for a throne. Then comes a misty morning, and the oak is not green any longer ; and summer is quite gone, and the whole world is autumn's. And she, — as fast as she gets, she loses it ; and scarcely is summer vanished, before autumn is gone too.

MARHAM.

And such is life, — an appearance for a little time, and hardly for that, it is so vanishing.

AUBIN.

Promise, — promises from day to day, — a repetition of promises ; this is what life feels to me. It is going, — the summer is. O the woods and the hill-sides, the meadows and the gardens, the valley with the river in it, summer morning with its long shadows in the moist grass, and summer evening going away in the west, calm and sublime, like the last words of a blessing ! — O, in all these things, the beauty there has been, — what has it been, and what is it now ? It is God ; and so it is what my soul will be

living in for ever, very soon. As I sat here and
looked at this beautiful scene, — and yet it was
rather as though it were looking into me, than I
at it, — there was a persuasion in me which said,
" This, this wast thou made for." And now I
know something of how a soul may gaze upon
God, and think of nothing else, and want nothing
more for ages ; because the reflection of the
face of God may be, in the depths of the soul, a
joy everlasting ; and will be, for all other delights
will but make God the dearer, and all other
knowledge will but clear our spirits to know him
the better.

MARHAM.

It is a great pleasure, Oliver, to listen to your
anticipations of the future life ; but I cannot quite
feel as you do, for hope is not certainty. Though
sometimes, while hearing you talk, I could forget
that there are such things as hell and reprobation.

AUBIN.

And so could become a perfect Christian.
Do you wonder at me, uncle ? Well, I do believe there is a hell ; but I am not frightened at
its existence, for it is not outside and beyond the
dominions of God. Even hell is not so utterly
unblest as not to be known to God. Painful is
it ? So is this earth very often ; and yet there
has grown in me here such faith as that, to my
eyes, hell itself would not be without a look of

beauty, if the Divine hand pointed me into it, —
to go into it.

MARHAM.

There is a perfect love which casts out fear ;
that is certain ; for so St. ——

AUBIN.

And certain it is, that we might and ought to
feel it, as well as St. Paul. Apostle was he ?
So he was, and chief of sinners once. Religion
is not hopeful enough, and I do not know that it
ever has been in Protestant times ; presumptuous
it has been too often, but very seldom hopeful.
And yet Christians are saved by hope, as St.
Paul says. Yes, hope is light, and strength, and
peace, and virtue, and salvation. And let a soul
be Christian, be a new creature in Christ, and
then it can get for itself high, grand evidence out
of hope. A life to come we hope for, and so we
shall see it.

MARHAM.

I trust so.

AUBIN.

I could be sure so, if it were only because I
can hope it.

MARHAM.

Sure of a thing because you hope it !

AUBIN.

Yes, uncle, though you smile at the notion.
For how have we come by hope ? Have angels

visited us all, one by one, and endowed us with
the feeling?   Or were we despairers once, and
did we through some magic get ourselves made
hopeful?   Has hopefulness come of any forbidden
tree that we have eaten of?   No, no!   It is our
nature.   And through making us hope for immortality, God has made us a promise of it.

MARHAM.

But it is not to be thought that all things will
be ours, because we hope them.

AUBIN.

No, not all things, and not many things; and
therefore certainly that one.   I might hope that
Venus might be the first world for me to live in
after death; I might hope for some one particular
star to be my throne; and in such things as those,
hope would not even be expectation, and still less
would it be certainty.   When we trust in the future, what hopefulness is in us is the inspiration of
God; but what particular objects we wish are
fixed on, perhaps, by our self-will.

MARHAM.

That is a wise distinction, Oliver.

AUBIN.

Hope is an instinct of there being infinite good
in our destiny; now, as that good is not earthly,
it must be heavenly; and so, if faith is the evidence of things not seen, hope is the certainty of
them.

MARHAM.

As being an inspiration and promise of God in us, you mean.

AUBIN.

Yes. For promise of God to us it is. And so I think that, in life, not to be cheerful is to blaspheme against God.

MARHAM.

Hope is more of a virtue than is often thought, and it is perhaps only not the greatest; for St. Paul counts hope along with faith and love.

AUBIN.

There are many evils which are more than half cured by hope. Hope brings good things about us, not so as to be handled, but so as to be owned and rejoiced in. Hope prophesies to us. Hope makes us free of the universe. I am a pilgrim, and life is what I have to travel over; and, O! I have many dangers and many wants; but hope is my all in all, nearly. Hope is light, and courage, and a staff; and when I sit down, it is a friend to talk with; and when I suffer, it is an angel to stand by and strengthen me; and when I have wandered away in sin, and repented and returned to the right path, then from hope I get my peace of mind again, and newness of virtue.

MARHAM.

Hope renews you in virtue, do you say?

22

Yes, because hoping for goodness is all but getting it.

So it is.

And then the longing of the soul would be long, long misery, but for hope. O, how my soul used to yearn after I could not tell what ! Strange feeling it was ! Sorrow, joy, love, worship, — it was all these, — an infinite longing. It was what would have felt wealth like poverty, and what no sceptre would have pleased, — a longing, an infinite longing, to which the whole world felt little and nothing. I used to think it was discontentment, and yet I could not tell how it could be. But now I know it was not.

It is the way youth often feels.

And rightly ; for that feeling is no discontent, but it is the soul prophesying to herself her greatness that is to be.

But almost always this feeling dies away.

Die away it does not, though too commonly it is quenched ; but it is not the less natural for that, nor the less meaning. For if this sublime yearn-

ing of the spirit is often quenched, so is conscience, so is love, and so is reverence.

MARHAM.

And quite as often, perhaps ; for of these
affections, there is in multitudes a much greater
seeming than life. O, but it is sad to think how
many souls I have known grow torpid ! In youth,
they were loving, and thoughtful, and devout.
Every great and beautiful truth was welcome to
them, and their souls ———

AUBIN.

Were like homes of the Holy Spirit, perhaps ?

MARHAM.

Almost as open, and clean, and cheerful, as
though they were. But now they are the lurking-
places of cunning, and the dwelling-places of
selfishness and pride. O, how the soul can allow
herself to be darkened and polluted ! It comes
of her false service. For there is the world
about her, and she worships some things in it with
powers that ought only to have God for their
object.

AUBIN.

Yes, and this youthful yearning of the spirit is
an earnestness, which often the man uses for selfish purposes. And so through this feeling, that
ought to have made him free of the world, he
becomes its slave. This yearning in him he
thinks to gratify with money, or luxury, or fame ;

but he cannot. More, more, — it wants more ; it wants more than the whole world. And so, with all his gains, the man but gets the more covetous, and not the more contented. For this craving of his soul has in it a something infinite, and is not for the ownership of the earth at all, but for the beauty of it, and what there is of God in it.

MARHAM.

I think your explanation of the feeling is right ; but why does it rise in youth first, for in childhood it is not felt ?

AUBIN.

Because it is not till childhood is over, that the soul is a soul, — grown, I mean, into any knowledge of itself or its wants. O, I remember, at first, what a mystery this infinite want in me was ! Sublime, and sad, and loving, — it was so strange ! It tortured me, because I thought it was a fault ; but now it does not, for I know its meaning. It is my soul, that is come of age, making her claim upon the infinite in her right as a child of God.

MARHAM.

Hark ! Yes, it is the clock striking.

AUBIN.

From over every town, east to west, the clocks are striking the hour. One, two, three, four, five, six ! And the Christian meaning of

the sound is, " Thus far on through Time."
And the hopeful thought it makes in us is, " And
so much nigher to Eternity and Heaven."

MARHAM.

So we will hope.

AUBIN.

And out of pure hearts, confidence in the future
cannot be too great. Because, what is hope ?
It is what is most worthy of belief, by its very
nature. For in hoping rightly, all that is best in
us yearns together for the infinite, — love and
reverence, and conscience, and the feeling of the
beautiful.

CHAPTER XXX.

The wave that dances to the breast
　Of earth can ne'er be stayed;
The star that glitters in the crest
　Of morning needs must fade.

But there shall flow another tide,
　So let me hope, and far
Over the outstretched waters wide
　Shall shine another star.

In every change of man's estate
　Are lights and guides allowed;
The fiery pillar will not wait,
　But, parting, sends the cloud.

Nor mourn I the less manly part
　Of life to leave behind;
My loss is but the lighter heart,
　My gain, the graver mind. — HENRY TAYLOR.

AUBIN.

DEATH, — the Greeks were afraid of the very word; they would not use it if they could help it; nor would the Romans, though less sensitive. And we, — we Christians speak it like an unnatural word. And yet the thing itself, when it happens, will be quite a matter of course; and for us Christians, there will be no sting in it; and all the bitterness of it will be found to have been drunk by us long ago. For our life is an act of dying; and we die just as fast as we live. The pleasures of boyhood, holidays and half-holidays, climbing trees, rolling down green hill-sides, looking for birdsnests, playing with snow, chasing one another, especially in the twilight, sporting in the water, and swimming, — all this I have been dead to long, long. Many a purpose of station and fame, that was once life of my life, I am dead to. Every month I die to some old object, or hope, or delight; and every midnight do I die to a yesterday.

MARHAM.

Ay, in the midst of life we are in death; we are; and it is most true.

AUBIN.

But not most melancholy, nor as much so as your tone, uncle. For if life is so very like death, then death cannot be so very unlike life.

MARHAM.

What is that? how is that?

AUBIN.

It is quite a triumph, is not it? — detecting the nothingness of death, this way. I will show you how it is. Our daily death ——

MARHAM.

Why, Oliver, what an expression, — our daily death! But it is a true one. And if we lived in the feeling of it, we should not be afraid of death long. If only men did die daily, then they would not die at all. But this they will not do.

But yet, whether we think it or not, we become dead to many and many an object. This is our mortality.

AUBIN.

And no such very sad thing. You cannot leap over gates, and across ditches, and up to the boughs of trees, as you used to do. It is no time with you now to undress yourself on the bank of a river and jump into it, careless about the depth ; you cannot run a mile in seven minutes ——

MARHAM.

No, I am sure I cannot.

AUBIN.

Well, but do you want to do it, or any of those other things ? No, you do not, — no more than you covet a condor's wings, or Nero's old palace, or Samson's strength, or any other impossibility. Then where is the grief, or any reason for it ? Grievous it would be, very, if there were an impulse in you to run eight miles an hour, and you could not achieve four ; or if, at sight of a gate, you always wished to leap over it and could not. But as you do not wish any of these boyish things, inability to do them is nothing to lament. The sorrow, if there is any, is in your having grown not to care about what were the pleasures of your childhood, and some of your youthful objects. Now there are those to whom boyish sports are a delight at fifty years of age, —

men who are happy for hours together in blowing soap-bubbles, and chasing butterflies. But then who are they ?

MARHAM.

Poor idiots, certainly. But there are things of quite another class from what you have mentioned, which you and I have become uninterested in.

AUBIN.

Have grown indifferent to. And grown into this indifference we have, and not decayed into it. Many childish delights, and many youthful joys, a man has no pleasure in ; for he has grown thoughtful, and so in thoughtless things he is no longer pleased. And is this, then, melancholy ? No, uncle, no ! I am free of the hall where the Muses live. They talk to me divinely about the arts and sciences, about what the ages were that are past, and about what the ages to come will be like. One Muse thrills me with her voice, in singing, and then one of her sisters entrances me with music, and from time to time they give me nectar to drink. Mortal as I am, I drink the drink of immortals. This is what I do, and often. So that it is no decay of nature, when I am out in the fields, if I am not eager after wild fruits, like a boy. Childish games have no interest for us now ; but it is because of our interest in life, — the great game of the passions. Many things I do not feel about

as I did at-fifteen ; but it is because since then I
have thought the same things as John Milton, and
sat under a tree with Plato and his friends, and
heard them discourse together. True, the earth
is not to me what it was. It is no broad play-
ground now ; but it is something better still, for
it feels under my feet like the floor of a temple
not made with hands. Fellow-creatures met by
chance I cannot now be merry with for an hour,
and then miss for ever without caring ; but this
is because between me and God the fleshly veil
is worn so thin that light shines through, and
souls look solemn in it.

MARHAM.

Go on, Oliver. You have more to say, have
not you ?

AUBIN.

There are youthful pleasures an old man has
no relish for ; and this grieves him for other reasons than I have said, perhaps. He, — I may say
you, — you remember, uncle, your sports as a
little child. They would be no pleasure to you
now, if you were to try them, — that you know ;
and so perhaps you are pained, as though you
had lost some old and happy feelings by time's
having changed your nature. But it is not so.
As an old man, your soul is not of another kind,
but only greater than it was when you used to
clasp your mother's knees. There is no inno-

cent happiness that a man ever grows strange to. You do not incline to bowl a hoop yourself; but in showing little Arthur how to do it this morning, and in watching him, and walking after him, and now and then touching the hoop yourself, I very much mistook appearances, if you were not quite as much delighted as the child.

MARHAM.

So I was, — that I was, good little fellow! He is a wonderfully quick child; is not he?

AUBIN.

Very; and very good-tempered.

MARHAM.

Ay, he begged me to promise him another lesson to-morrow, which I did; and you must come and help. But, running after little Arthur's hoop, I have got away from your line of argument; but it was you who started me.

AUBIN.

So it was; and I have seen that you delight in a hoop now as much as you ever did; only it is through the fingers of your grandson.

MARHAM.

You have me, you have me, — you have the old man!

AUBIN.

No, I have not, — not the old man. Your body may be old, but you yourself, — your spirit is as young as it ever was; it is both old and

young.   When a person is said to be twenty, or
forty, or sixty, what is meant? This chiefly,
that he has the feelings of those years.   O, beautiful is what old age is sometimes, and nearly always might be, — the last years of a Christian, a
man who has lived in the use of his best feelings,
who has worshipped God as heartily as he has
loved his dearest friend, and who has loved every
one of his neighbours like himself!

MARHAM.

The recollections of such a man are a happiness to have.

AUBIN.

Always through his sympathies he can delight
himself, and be growing in goodness.   There is
his youngest son, in love with a sweet lady ; and
through his child he himself loves again like a
youth.   Here is an infant comes to him and holds
him by the hand, and he speaks to the little creature ; and because he talks with it lovingly, his
own heart in his breast grows young again.
Plough he cannot, nor sow, nor attend to farm-
ing in any way ; but he can, and does, love his
neighbour as himself; and so in the fields close
by, the growing crops are a great interest to him ;
and down in the meadows by the river-side, the
grass refreshes his eyes, it is so green ; and its
being so rich delights him on the owner's account.
It is so, uncle, is not it ?   It is so with you, I
mean.

MARHAM.

Do you think so, Oliver ? Well, perhaps it is.

AUBIN.

An old man may have ill-health, but so has a young man. And very beautiful in its season old age often is, — the last state of a man who is wise in life, having lived, it all ; who loves God and man, and man the more reverently because of God's loving him. And he is a man, too, whose heart is open to all his fellow-creatures, and kept open by the force of the prayers that come out of it, for his family, and friends, and all men.

MARHAM.

It is — it is — it is prayer is the life of the soul.

AUBIN.

The oak-tree in the middle of yonder field is an emblem of a good old man. There it stands, the growth of many, many years ; inside it is the little stalk which opened out of an acorn, and the sapling which for years used to bend backward and forward with the wind ; and in its trunk are what were its outside rings at twenty, fifty, and a hundred years old. It stands aloft now, a full grown oak, — an object beautiful to look at, and that is wisdom to think of. Once that tree might have perished by any one of a hundred accidents, — by a careless foot, or a drought, or a snail, or a hungry sheep. But it was to grow to what it is.

In the shade of it the cattle lie ; in its leafy arms birds build their nests and sing ; among its branches the wind gets itself a voice ; somewhere in it the squirrel has a home, and all over the boughs are growing what will be his winter's store.

MARHAM.

But what is the likeness between this tree and old age ?

AUBIN.

Just as in the middle of that oak there is the sapling of two hundred years ago, in a good old man there is the heart of his childhood. An aged Christian is not an old man only ; he is of all ages ; for he has in him the heart of a little child, and a boy's way of thinking, and the feelings of a youth, and the judgment of a man ; he has in him a son's fondness, a husband's tender affection, and a father's love ; and confidence, esteem, enthusiasm, — all that is best in our nature is strong in him ; for though many of his dear objects are taken hence, his feelings for them are the same as ever. And through his ready sympathy, there is no love in the house that he does not thrill to, and no joy in parlour or kitchen that he does not rejoice in, and no hope in any inmate's bosom that he does not hope in. And if his neighbours prosper around him, or grow more virtuous, it is to his feeling as though he were himself the better.

MARHAM.

I like to hear you, Oliver ; go on.

AUBIN.

Outgrow much, no doubt, old age does. But mind, — it outgrows some things, but it does not dwindle down from any. And besides that, its way of growth is the same as what makes little children be such as the kingdom of heaven is of. For always out of the heart are the issues of life. Yonder oak is no longer an acorn moistening just under the ground ;. nor a little plant in the turf, kept from scorching by the tall grass ; still, high as its top is, and wide as it spreads, the tree flourishes in the same way the sapling grew ; and its roots are under the grass, and are kept moist by it ; yes, and the heart of the oak — the very middle of it — is just over the spot where the acorn opened. Old age grows up to the height of thoughts not of this world ; but then its roots are the same as ever, — its sympathies do not fail it, and the dews of heavenly grace are never withheld from falling on it. It is always autumnal, but then it is always shedding ripe fruits ; and even the look of it is what every beholder is the better for feeling.

MARHAM.

O, if I thought the tree of my own old age like that, I should sit under it in peace, and, perhaps, — ay, perhaps with pride. For pride is a weed that will grow in shade as well as sunshine, in streets, and houses, and upon tombs, and everywhere.

AUBIN.

That is one of the fruits of your wisdom, my dear uncle. Excuse my interrupting you, uncle.

MARHAM.

I am old, Oliver, but I am happy ; and I ought to be happier than I am. God pardon me for not being so! Few old people have such comforts as I have ; and how desolate many of them are, — childless, friendless, and infirm ! I am sure, often I am wretched, when I think what their feelings must be.

AUBIN.

Those feelings, as far as they cannot be eased by man, are meant by God, and therefore meant for good. And then they can pray ——

MARHAM.

Yes, they can, they can ! There is no burden of the spirit but is lightened by kneeling under it. Little by little, the bitterest feelings are sweetened by the mention of them in prayer. And agony itself stops swelling, if it can only cry sincerely, My God, my God !

AUBIN.

There is a degree of distress, in which all human anodynes fail, and friendly words fail, and the best of reading fails ; but prayer never fails.

MARHAM.

Never, — never, — never. But still, to look at a bereaved and joyless old man is a melancholy sight.

AUBIN.

Very melancholy; because a quite joyless must be a quite unchristian man.

MARHAM.

You do not understand me, Oliver. What I mean is, that it is distressing to see a man spend years, as Solomon says so touchingly, which have no pleasure in them. It is as though it were out of the course of nature. No, that is not what I mean.

AUBIN.

I know what you feel exactly. And now I will tell you what I feel. I see an old man, a widower, perhaps, bereaved of his children, very weak, and almost sleepless. In the cup of life, there are only a few dregs for his drinking. It is so. And what then? Why, the cup will be the sooner ready for him to dip in the living fountains of water, which the Lamb from the midst of the throne will lead him to. Courage, thou poor sufferer! No, not poor, — but happy I ought to have said. For in thy face there is what answers to something in another world. Yes, good old man! It is as though it were known to thee, by some instinct, that Christ is just about rising

23

from his throne to say, " Come, thou blessed of my Father."

MARHAM.

Ámen, Lord Jesus, amen !

AUBIN.

Whom the Lord loves, he chastens. But when a sufferer is chastened toward the end of life, and, indeed, till the very end of his mortal life, it is because God loves him immortally. It must be, and it cannot be otherwise. No ! it cannot be any other way than that. So that my pain, — what little I have, — my pain shall be counted all joy. And I will reckon it so. And cannot I easily ? I ought to do, if I only recollect myself a little. Why should I ever have been so impatient for happiness ? Why should I wish for more than I have now ? Am I afraid of my share being given away ? Cannot I wait awhile ? Thousands of years I had to wait before being born ; so that to wait a short while before being blessed is a very little thing, — very. Ay, ages on ages the stars had been twinkling by night, and the sun shining by day, before my reason was lighted up. And as yet I have it only in an earthen vessel, — a lamp of crumbling dust, that is wearing away fast. Well, let it wear away. For when the flame in it escapes, it will become fire before the Lord ; and it will be like a light set in a golden candlestick for ever ; and it will be mine, — mine everlastingly. And it will nowhere be eclipsed, — no ! not among the radiances of the angels ; for it will have from my life a color of its own ; and from God it will have a beauty of its own, and a glory of its own. Wonderful, very wonderful, this is, and yet it is certain, that, from among all the inhabitants of this earth, no two minds are similar altogether. And at the end of the world, of all the souls native to it, there will be no two alike. Every one of us will have a character of his own ; and every saint will have a glory of his own. And myself, what I am to be, I am becoming. Yes, what I am to be everlastingly, I am growing to be now, — now, in this present time so little thought of, — this time which the sun rises and sets in, and the clock strikes in, and I wake and sleep in. Courage, then ! For what goes on in my spirit now will show itself ages hence. They could never be to another person — my pains and thoughts — what they are to me, — not exactly. What I shall be in eternity, I shall be by my endurance now and my hopefulness. My trials I might bear with murmurs, and so I should get to doubt God ; or by hardening my heart against the feeling of them, and so I should become a stoic ; or by fiercely defying fate, and so I should grow atheistical. But I endeavour to suffer Christianly. What I am to be hereafter, I must be becoming now ; and so I am, indeed. For, day by day, I am growing fixedly into the attitude which I bear my sorrows in ; and from under them, my look heavenwards, whatever it is, is becoming eternal with me. And then it is not as though any trouble could be spared me, and I not be other than what I am to be. O my destiny ! God keep me growing towards it ! My crown of glory ! Lord, make me worthy of it !

MARHAM.

For some time I have not been able to catch all your words, Oliver.

AUBIN.

I thought some time I might be going into a furnace of affliction, and I was talking with myself about it. And I was saying, " Body ! thou must burn away here, and for thee there is no help possible. But, soul ! out of this furnace, this straitened and fiery place, thou shalt escape, —

And thou shalt walk in soft, white light, with kings and priests abroad,
And thou shalt summer high in bliss upon the hills of God."

MARHAM.

Whose lines are those ?

AUBIN.

They are Thomas Aird's, and a beautiful couplet. I often say them to myself ; and always when I do, it is as though it were an August

afternoon, and I had lived for ages, while my
spirit in me feels so calm, yet earnest, and as
though it were growing into great thoughts. Yes!
and what is there I may not hope for? For I am
like Melchisedek of old; and I am king and priest
both; for so to God Christ has made me be.
Prayer is the sacrifice I have to offer; and morning and evening, day and night, it is welcome, for
the Father seeks to have it. My passions are
the subjects of my kingly rule, and my throne is
the Gospel; and from the height of it I judge the
men, and things, and the affairs about me. My
soul, my soul! be thou faithful in judgment, and
thou shalt grow up to the companionship of King
Alfred, and St. Louis, and George Washington.

And thou shalt walk in soft, white light, with kings and priests
 abroad,
And thou shalt summer high in bliss upon the hills of God.

CHAPTER XXXI.

Transition into the divine is ever woful, yet it is life.
                                        BETTINA ARNIM.

He that lives fourscore years is but like one
That stays here for a friend : when death comes, then
Away he goes, and is ne'er seen again. — THOMAS MIDDLETON.

MARHAM.

I HAVE been thinking, Oliver, of what we talked about yesterday. What you said has done me good, though I wish I could remember it better. My memory is not what it was, I think. Well, I must be patient. I am an old man, and so patience ought to be my special business. There is not much else for me ; there is no work for me in the world. My share in life I have had, and there is no further part for me in the struggles and successes of it. Now I have to study to be quiet, and wait for my dismissal ——

AUBIN.

Your admission, uncle. And it is a sublime waiting. Blackly the gates of the grave frown against us, outside them ; but from the inside they will be beautiful, for they will be seen through light that is not of the sun, nor the moon, but older ; yes, and newer, too, for what is eternal is always young.

MARHAM.

More trust is what I want. But it will grow in me, perhaps, with the patience that old age forces. For I must be patient; and more and more I shall have to be. For with an old man friends die fast, hopes come to nothing, the world lessens in interest, and things that were once a passion are not cared about.

AUBIN.

Is it beginning to be so with you, uncle? Then why is it? There is an answer, and a happy one. It is because you are growing up to a higher order of things than what are of this earth. For what this world has to teach you, you have learned.

MARHAM.

O, no, no!

AUBIN.

All the wisdom and freshness of the world you have not exhausted. But what each man's nature is capable of is commonly imbibed in three-score years and ten, though perhaps an angel might profit in this world for ages; just as a daisy is perfect with one year's growth, while in the same soil an oak will be deepening with its roots, and rising with its head, for two centuries or more. Do you feel as though you might some time, perhaps, be weary of life, — be thinking that there is nothing new in it, and no more to be known from it ? Weary of it you will never be, uncle, for you will be patient, and always you will think that life, even as endurance only, will prove to be a privilege, and a rare one, perhaps ; for they are not many who live to exercise the patience of fourscore years. The patience of eighty years did I say ? I ought to have said the blessedness of them ; for with a God to be glad in, the believing soul must always be happy, or else be just about being the happier for suffering.

MARHAM.

Yes, and so I hope for more faith than I have. I want it. In my last days, I fear feeling to have no pleasure in them ; for it ought not to be so with me, as a Christian.

AUBIN.

Nor will it be, if you keep looking for the great hope, and the appearing of our Lord Jesus Christ. Childhood, youth, manhood, marriage, friendship, trading, study, pleasure, and sorrow, — you have got the good of them all ; and some of them you might have tired of, if they had lasted with you long, but now they feel like the first lessons introductory to a wondrous book that has to be opened yet.

MARHAM.

O, the very thought an old man ought to wait with !

AUBIN.

Feelings and motives in hearts of flesh you know the working of, various as it may be; so now you are ready for the knowledge of souls in some other than this fleshly estate. In the hum of the town that is near us, a youth hears what inspirits him; but you do not, for you have heard it so long. And your heart, as it gets purer, craves a holiness that is not of this world; and so the city of God is the easier for you to see with your eyes of faith; and the less you are of this world, the more plainly are the voices to be heard which call to you from above to go up thither.

MARHAM.

And up there, O that I may go! For thither they have ascended whose lives were parts of my life, and in whose deaths I died myself, — died deaths that have had no resurrections yet; but they will have; for every affection of mine will live again, or rather will be joy again in the sight of dear, recovered friends. But in this meanwhile I do not see them; and others are being taken after them.

AUBIN.

Yes, one by one ———

MARHAM.

And faster and faster ———

AUBIN.

There are being assembled in the other world

all your kindred, both after the flesh and after the spirit ; and with their going hence, this world is to you less and less like an abiding-place.

MARHAM.

As you know, Oliver, my friends have died fast lately.

AUBIN.

And become spirits, and friends of yours gone into bliss. And with every longing after them, you grow more akin to heaven. And so, out of the very decay of this life, there grows in you the spirit of another life.

MARHAM.

Once I saw a large tree so hollow as to be little better than a case of bark ; still it was living. But inside the tree, and overtopping it, grew a sapling so strong and green. And the hull of the old tree was a fence round the young one ; though, indeed, they were both one tree, for they had the same root, and it was only the stem renewing itself. A very curious and pretty sight it was. And it pleased me, as being a happy emblem of myself. And I said, " My life is rooted in God fast and everlasting, and though outwardly I may perish, there is within me a life to be renewed to all eternity."

AUBIN.

Such a tree I myself saw near Dieventer in Holland, with an old man and a little child near it. A very old man he was. He must be dead before this, and his grandchild be growing up into his place in the world. *Dead* is a word that must be used ; so that I wish all wrong meaning could be kept out of it. For there is a sense in which that old man is not dead, and never will be, though departed he is, no doubt. Through one minute's look at him, he lives on in my memory ; and does not he, then, surely live on in the universe that produced and supported him ? O, surely, surely ! Since I saw what I have been speaking of, I have never once recollected it till this minute, and it is as though I saw it now. Even without my knowledge, that scene has lived on in me six years. Now my soul is like a thought in God ; so I will never fear dying out of the Divine mind. Last night it occurred to me that to be remembered of God is to live in him. And so it is, I have no doubt, though to-day I do not understand how. For there are some truths which at one time are quite plain, though at another they seem obscure. This is according to what mood we are in. Just as the stars shine more or less brightly with the state of the atmosphere.

MARHAM.

There cannot be any forgetfulness in God, and all things live in him according to their nature, the robin for its two or three years, the lark for its seven or eight, and the raven for its century.

AUBIN.

In God the fountains rise, and the rivers run, and the oceans ebb and flow; and shall not my spirit continue to be a spirit in him? But in death there is the loss of the body; and in health, is not there a losing of the body and a re-gaining of other flesh every minute? And then, has a river the same water running in it any two hours together? A fountain is a fountain, in God, for a hundred, a thousand, and many thou-sand years; so I will not fear but my soul will be a soul in him for ages of ages, as the Greek has it, or, in our English phrase, for ever.

CHAPTER XXXII.

Virtue thus
Sets forth and magnifies herself; thus feeds
A calm, and beautiful, and silent fire,
From the encumbrances of mortal life,
From error, disappointment, nay, from guilt.

WORDSWORTH.

AUBIN.

As I got up from my bedside prayer this morning, I said, " I am ; and because I am what I am, I am immortal." Do you not feel the force of this ? Nor do I now, though I did this morning, but perhaps with my heart more than my head, and that, perhaps, was more sensitive just after prayer than it is now.

MARHAM.

I am well persuaded that after earnest prayer the mind is clearest, and the will is freest, and the judgment is wisest, and that then thoughts come to us most nearly like Divine messages. And after kneeling to God, our first few steps are almost certainly in the way of eternal life. It is after having drawn nigh to God, that our feelings are most nearly like Divine guidance. So that the thought you had this morning may be quite true, though you may not be able to tell how it is.

AUBIN.

Uncle, there is a state of mind between prayer and reasoning, in which the windows of heaven are partly open above us, and while we are looking upwards, we have at the same time some sight of things about us ; and in the light of God, they look in a way which is not to be doubted, though not to be proved, nor even spoken of, easily.

MARHAM.

God is with us nigher than we suppose ; and he is in many of the workings of our souls, — a power that we do not think of.

AUBIN.

I have some thoughts, on the first coming of which into my mind I clasped my hands and said, " O, not of my own thinking are these, but thy glorious sending, O my soul's God, thou God of truth ! " And sometimes I have had such beauty in my soul, that I could not but believe it a something out of heaven. And some seasons have felt to me, O, so unearthly, so unlike what the tongue can vouch for, that I am sure of there being a heaven nigh me, and of its spirit reaching into my spirit at times. These are experiences that I do not distrust, for they are akin to what our Saviour says of his doctrine being to be known to be of God by the doing of it. The Christian heaven, — does any disciple wish to be

sure of its existence? He can know it for himself. There is even a sixpence that will let him
into what will be blessed certainty for him ; but it
must be his last coin, and he must halve it with a
worse sufferer than himself ; and then for a while
he will be inside the golden gates, and under him
the earth will be like holy ground, and there will
be the feeling of a glory round his head, and there
will be the thronging round him of a presence like
that of angels, and in his ears there will be the
delight of a Divine voice, saying, " My son, my
son, in thee I am well pleased."

MARHAM.

O, very precious such experiences are ; and
they might be commoner with us than they are.
For God is to be, and indeed is, felt in every
mood that is godlike. But it is the loving soul
that believes most easily, and knows most largely
what the Divine purposes are.

AUBIN.

I have moments, in which immortality feels too
great a thing for us men, — incredibly great.
And for joy sometimes, and sometimes for fear,
I cannot assure myself of my ever being to walk
alongside the river of life. I remember once
feeling in this way, and I sat down on a bank to
think. And I saw minnows, and other happy
little things, that dart about in brooks ; and I said
to myself, that they had not been too little for

God's making. And with looking at them, I got
to love them. And then I felt the more tenderly
God's love of myself, — that love which insects
live in, as well as angels. Then I said to myself,
"Let God do with me what he will, any thing
he will ; and whatever it be, it will be either
heaven itself or some beginning of it." Nothing
of God's making can a man love rightly, without
being the surer of God's loving himself, — neither
the moon, nor the stars, nor a rock, nor a tree,
nor a flower, nor a bird. And not the least
grateful of my thanksgivings have been hymns,
that have come of themselves on to my lips, while
I have been listening to the birds of an evening.
Only let us love what God loves, and then his
love of ourselves will feel certain, and the sight
of his face we shall be sure of ; and immortality,
and heaven, and the freedom of the universe, be
as easy for us to believe in, as a father's giving
good gifts to his children.

MARHAM.

How should we know any thing rightly about
God, without loving him ? It is only with the
heart that we can believe unto salvation.

AUBIN.

Infinite power, wisdom infinite, infinite love,
infinite life, — the God of infinities we would
gladly offer ourselves up to, all of us, willing
sacrifices. But many of us shrink from some

small offering when we .are led up to the altar, if it is in an obscure corner of the world, or lowly in look. For, at first, our wish is to perform grand service before many witnesses; but this is not what God wants often, and so it is seldom a person is called to it; but what he does wish is the sincerity of the soul. And when a soul does become all his own, it is lit up from within with such Divine light as glorifies every thing else. Duty is an angel, reverently beloved, that walks beside the man, with solemn steps; and common life is a path, shining before him more and more; and the future is a mist which he will pass through, and so be nigher God; and if to-day the world feels round him like a temple for worship in, then to-morrow there will be a further world for him to pass on into, and it will be the holy of holies; so his fervor trusts.

MARHAM.

Virtue known and praised by a whole town has its reward, perhaps, in popularity; but they are the good deeds, done by one hand unknown to the other, and they are the prayers prayed in secret, that have the special promise of reward by our Father in heaven. The only virtue that speaks of a reward at all plainly is what says least about it, and it is what can lose money, and forego opportunities, and be misunderstood by

24

friends, and be alone in the world, happy enough in only hoping for heaven.

AUBIN.

The hopefulness of human nature is infinite, and in a good heart it is unquenchable ; and it is evidence of heirship to what is not of this world.

MARHAM.

But, Oliver, what are our fears ? for sometimes our hearts are as though they could misgive us about a world to come.

AUBIN.

Fears are angel-thoughts in black, telling the same grand message of another life as our hopes do ; only they are mourners the while for what unworthiness is in us.

MARHAM.

Such a life as yours was for that long time would have made almost any body else heart-sick for the rest of his years. But I do think with you calamity must have been all joy.

AUBIN.

It is a joy to think of, but it was not to bear ; and I mourned under it more than was right. For I fancied a life was being bowed into the dust, that otherwise would have been of some height in the world. Once, from being well off, I was made poor, through offence being taken at what I did religiously, and which you know of. Those persecutors are now dear remembrances of mine, because, but for my forgiveness of them, I could not be so sure as I am of my being myself forgiven by God. They knew not what they did ; and most of them — five or six — would say so now.

But they did you good, Oliver, when you did not think it, nor they either. For what blows were struck against you, God directed to the sculpturing out of a feature in your character, that would otherwise have been less noble than it is.

And, uncle, I have a tender interest in the men who made me endure grief for what was my conscience toward God ; because this is said in the Scriptures to be fellowship with Christ's sufferings. This is a world in which we are being tempted together, and some of us perfected together, — all of us, if we will. Much of what I am, I am become by the wrongs I have done, and got pardoned, — griefs which I caused my parents and teachers, my school-fellows, and one or two fellow-students. Yes, among us men, these three things are a large part of our virtue, — to endure, to forgive, and ourselves to get pardon. And so my enemies, through repenting towards me, become other and perhaps better than they would have been but for wronging me. Christ died for the world ; and we have fellowship with his sufferings, when we endure and forgive persecutors; for through a right spirit toward them, earlier or later, they will be changed. Yes, to endure wrongfully and forgivingly is to be bruised for other men, and in the end to have them healed with our stripes. Let a man suffer with Christ, and he will know of his being to reign with him; for there will rise in his soul such a strange, strong persuasion of it. So, uncle, I have forgiven my enemies, and I love them; at least I trust I do. They made me suffer much and unjustly; but it was because I had been calumniated to them by their passions.

MARHAM.

That was five years ago; and at that time, Oliver, I should not myself have understood you rightly; I should have been unjust to you, I am afraid.

AUBIN.

You might have been cold towards me, but, my dear uncle, you would never have been false nor unfair. But those words I ought not to use; they would not betoken me much the better for having had all manner of evil said and done against me falsely. And this is a thing that I ought to be blessed for having had happen to me. O uncle, what I once hoped to do, and how I have failed of it! But I think I did my best; and no one can do more than that. We do what we can in this eartb, and we cannot achieve more. Our human ability has its bounds far short of controlling the planets, and infinitely short of regulating destiny. We work according to our means ; and perhaps we are thwarted by the enmity of the world or by Mammon ; but these are God's enemies as well as ours, and they fight against him more than against us. If what is godlike in us brings trouble on us, it is God's concern more than ours, — the Master's more than his servants'. There is not a righteous failure anywhere but compromises Divine Providence, and is what God will see to.

MARHAM.

We Christians work for God, and not for ourselves ; and when we fail even utterly, it is only to find our cause retrieved in heaven.

AUBIN.

O, we should expect to live again, — at least I should, — if it were only to hear sentence given on such righteous causes as have been cried down in this world. If I were no Christian, I should yet think in my flesh to hear God speak, though it were only to justify to men what had been the lives of Socrates, and Barneveldt, and Madame Roland. Good, and just, and great, and devout, was De Barneveldt ; and before the sword went through his neck, his last words were, " O God, what then is man ? " This was more than two hundred years ago.　The words went up from off a scaffold into the air, and they have not been answered yet; but they will be some time, if there is any truth in the truth, or any meaning in conscience.　This is what I should have thought, without being a Christian.　But now I know of a day in which the world will be judged in righteousness; and there is not a man but, one way or another, makes me surer of it.

MARHAM.

I like what you said just now about our suffering from one another.　And it is so great a pleasure to hear it from you, after your having been so misunderstood, and —— 　　　　　　　　.

AUBIN.

That my world did not know what I was in it, is nothing; for think of the years that went over before Jesus Christ was known; and, indeed, is he known yet?　And in a world in which Christ suffered for his goodness, and was an outcast, without a place to lay his head in, it would be almost a fearful thing to be altogether comfortable; so I have sometimes thought, and so I should still feel, only that my happiness has come through Christ, — through your Christian love, uncle Stephen.　At ease in a world in which my Lord was such a sufferer!　I hope, if I had been, I should have made occasions of self-sacrifice.

MARHAM.

Why, Oliver, your poverty did come ——

AUBIN.

Only of what I could not help doing for my conscience.

MARHAM.

And it was Christ in you, — your conscience was ; for if it had not been, you would not have acted as you have done more than once. And you have made religion of your sorrows, and so you have become what I am so glad of.

AUBIN.

And happier than I should have been otherwise. For a man who knows how to sorrow rightly knows how to be glad with a holy joy ; and when he is happiest, it is as though there were a something of God throbbing in his bosom. It is as souls that we are happiest ; and so suffering makes for happiness, because it helps to make the soul. O, what good sorrow does us often ! To many a one, while he is happy, the outer world feels eternal ; but as soon as he is sorrowful, all worldly existence is only a film, because God and his soul feel so close.

MARHAM.

Like as a father pities his suffering child, and embraces it for it to feel his love the better, so the Lord makes himself felt with his sorrowing creatures.

AUBIN.

While I am happy in myself, there is a God

plain to my eyes in the broad green turf, in the branching tree, and in the flowing stream ; and it overarches me in the firmament, which is not only blue, but a holy joy to look at ; and from the sky at night, it watches me with ten million eyes ; and sometimes it makes me clasp my hands and say, " O Lord, our Lord, how·excellent is thy name in all the earth ! " This is when I am in joy ; but when I am in grief, and in want of some loving assurance from God, I do not think of outward things, — fruits ripening on trees, or wheatears waving yellow ‑and thick against harvest ; and the stars vanish from between me and God, and so almost does my body, and I have quite another feeling of him than what nature can give ; and through my grief, God is nigher me than through his own glory in creation. For it is whom the Lord loves that he chastens. In affliction, I am with God almost spirit with spirit ; and then there forms within my soul that consciousness of adoption which cries, " Father ! Father ! " O, yes ! we belong to the world we cry to more than to this one we suffer in.

MARHAM.

For we are not in the flesh, but in the spirit, if so be that the spirit of God dwell in us ; as St. Paul says, before writing of that spirit of adoption whereby we cry, Abba, Father !

AUBIN.

That cry is not formed in the throat, nor does it come any way of nerves and veins; it is not of the body; and so it witnesses a life not of the body, — more than witnesses, for it is the thing itself. I am one with God through the earnestness of prayer, — the Father! Father! that I cry in my agony. I feel myself in God, and God in me, and the world is nothing to me, neither life nor death; for I am as though I were past and through them all, and as though I had almost entered on the sight of God, — the Beatific Vision, the Divine Ecstasy. Now, as I think, these spiritual states, unearthly as they are, are to be regarded as promising a disembodied life; just as, while I was an infant, my ears and eyes were prophetic of what was to be a world of sight and sound for me to live in.

MARHAM.

But, Oliver, there are those for whom sorrow is not only a dark night, but bewilderment; and so they lose hope; what would you say to them?

AUBIN.

Your sacrifice is burning on the altar, and around you the temple of life is filled with smoke, and no light comes in through the windows, and the very walls you cannot see; but you know where you are; for as long as you suffer, you are nigh the altar. That you know, and by that knowledge hold fast. Be quiet, fear not ; and be you sure that when your sacrifice is over, one after the other, the windows that open into the infinite — faith and hope — will show themselves ; and the air about you will be the clearer and the sweeter for having been so darkened awhile.

MARHAM.

It ought always to be enough for us to be sure of God's being with us. But, Oliver, there have been times when I have not believed as I ought to have done ; and perhaps it may be so with me again, for sometimes misgivings come into the mind the oftener for being resisted.

AUBIN.

And so they always do, I think. But I would have you think as I do, dear uncle. As I am now, a little trouble would darken my spirit, so as that hope could not shine into it at all ; but I look over the earth, and up at the clouds, and into infinity beyond ; and then I remember that I can shut it all out, with only my hand on my eyes : and so I am quiet, even when it seems as though the whole firmament of truth were hidden from me ; for this may happen through only a very little cloud of doubt.

MARHAM.

When doubts are over, we are the better for having been under them. And this is what we ought to remember. And when in trouble, we ought to think how much the better we shall be for it, some time.

AUBIN.

Sorrow sobers us, and makes the mind genial. And in sorrow we love and trust our friends more tenderly, and the dead become dearer to us. And just as the stars shine out in the night, so there are blessed faces that look at us in our grief, though before their features were fading from our recollections. Suffering! Let no man dread it too much, because it is good for him, and it will help to make him sure of his being immortal. It is not in the bright, happy day, but only in the solemn night, that other worlds are to be seen shining in their long, long distances. And it is in sorrow, — the night of the soul, — that we see farthest, and know ourselves natives of infinity, and sons and daughters of the Most High.

MARHAM.

Yes, Oliver, there is use in old age, and it is well that this life should commonly end with illness.

AUBIN.

It is nothing to me, now, what men think of me. But what I am to God is every thing. Pain simplifies the character; and I think what little I have had has wrung more than one little hypocrisy out of me. It has been worth my being ill, only for this. Sometimes I feel as though I would not have one fault or weakness unknown to you, uncle. And I do think, in the kindly atmosphere of home, that a character will always grow the faster and the healthier for being exposed all round, — for having every foible known to those who will kindly allow for it. I never did care much, I hope, but now I do not care at all, to be esteemed even as what I am; and so I think and feel, and talk with persons more freely, and perhaps more pleasantly, than I used to do. Smooth, and paint, and varnish the trunk and boughs of the oak, and the majesty of it will be less hurt than the grandeur of the soul is by its attempting to look what it is not, either in knowledge, or feeling, or manners. O, I remember once there came into my mind a thought as though out of heaven, and I said to myself, " What I am I am, and I will not pretend to be more "; and suddenly I felt as though I were right with every law of the universe, and as though there were a way certain for me up to the fatherly presence of Him who said of himself, " I am that I am."

MARHAM.

Oliver, from what unexpected things I have heard from you many times, I could well believe that there are few things in this present life but do rightly witness to the life that is to come.

AUBIN.

Annoyances, distractions, troubles, wrongs! In enduring them, the persuasion rises in us of our not being born for such things only. For by them the soul's sense of order is wronged; and by that very feeling, she knows herself meant for another element than the stormy one of this world. And now and then, amid her distresses, in a more than usually perfect way, the soul has the peace of God rise in her, and she witnesses to herself, "This peace is not of this world; and if not of this world, then it must be of another, and I myself must be of it too." And when a wrong is done us, and we bear with it, and are grieved for the evil-doers, sometimes it is as though the angels of heaven were looking at us, and as though there were an instinct in the soul, that actions higher than this world reach a sympathy beyond it. And so they do. And so, under injustice, we Christians can rejoice and be exceeding glad on account of our great reward in heaven.

MARHAM.

Badness shows the certain existence of goodness, as being its natural reverse. And the world is never so out of tune, but some strain of heaven is to be heard in it by the ear that is spiritual.

AUBIN.

Nearly always, uncle, music makes me feel myself what I am not, but what I must think I am to be ; for as a boy I knew something of what my manhood would be, by the manly feelings I had now and then. In listening to music, it is as though there were stirring in me the beginnings of another manner of life than what is possible to be lived in the flesh, or be thought of either, — but certainly freer and more earnest.

MARHAM.

I have felt the same, or rather what you speak of ; for what you understand to be the meaning of it, I had certainly never thought of before. But is it really a thought, or only a fancy of yours ?

AUBIN.

It is a belief of mine, but of course a very slight one. And, indeed, I think our nature affords many more tokens of being immortal than are commonly minded. This world's feeling so mean and poor argues us born for what is higher.

MARHAM.

And so we are ; for we are heirs of God, and joint heirs with Christ.

AUBIN.

It sounds profanely, that horses have been stabled, and cooking-fires been lit, in cathedrals. But the thought of God is a holier temple than a minster is, and sometimes we live in it worse than soldiers in a church; for really discontentment is blasphemy, and an ill look against another is a curse. O, sometimes it feels to me quite profane that I should be living; and I draw in my breath slowly, as though unworthy of God's air; and it is to me as though the brightest life of man would be but a dark track on the shining floor of heaven.

MARHAM.

Ah, yes! what is our goodness? what is our virtue? Nothing, nothing!

AUBIN.

Not only men, but even their thoughts, by being humble, get exalted. This world is nothing; and so it may well be to me, if I am heir to a Father in heaven, and to some one of his many mansions. At times, the brightest virtue of man is dim to me; and why? It is because the eyes of my understanding are opening, against I have sight of God. This world is mean to me, only because I have eyes not of this world; because I am growing a new creature in Christ.

MARHAM.

You seem to me to rely so confidently, Oliver ——

AUBIN.

On the same kind of argument as the author of the Epistle to the Hebrews makes use of, when he writes, that a man comes to God only through

first believing in his existence. Could we have
called upon God if he had not wished it ? For
could not he have made us so as to have had no
feeling of him, and no want of him ? That I can
pray, " Lord, help me ! " is a proof that he will
help me. Because a prayer can be prayed at all,
there is certainly a Divine ear to hear it. It is
because I can call upon God in the day of trouble,
that I may be sure there is help for me, somewhere or somehow, under Providence. Here is
a parent, who is all anxiety and love for his child.
And what his child is to him, he feels as though
he himself might be to God. By his nature, by
the way he is made to feel, his own trust in God
is the stronger for his child's trust in himself.
My God, my God, help me as a father ! — when
a man prays so, is it' no more than if he had
wished well to himself ? It is not merely that the
man is allowed to pray, but he is made to do it ;
and his heart in him is made in such a way that
he prays out of it the more believingly for his being
a father.

MARHAM.

That I quite think, Oliver.

AUBIN.

It is not by chance, but by design, that a man's
becoming a father makes him pray the more believingly. And so you think, uncle. And I think
myself that every way of feeling is to be trusted
to, that grows out of a Christian heart.

MARHAM.

Yes, out of a heart that really is Christian.

AUBIN.

The purer in heart I become, the more I want to see God.

MARHAM.

A blessed want; for Christ has promised it shall be satisfied.

AUBIN.

And through Christ in me, I am sure of it. My soul yearns to God; then it will be taken into the bosom of the Father, some time. God is love, God is truth; and he would not have let me long for his face, if he had meant me never to see it.

MARHAM.

No, he would not; for if we are made to hunger, it is so that we may eat; or if to thirst, it is because drink is to be had, and because it is good for us.

AUBIN.

The universe is juster than my justice, and better than my best thoughts, and will work to a more blessed end than even my love can hope, so that safely I may trust in it, all I can, and unboundedly.

MARHAM.

A mother may forget her child, but God cannot forget us.

25

AUBIN.

No, never. And when a child dies, and a mother feels as though, if gone for ever, the universe might have perished with it, is not it as though the truth of the universe were pledged to her for her seeing her child again? I think so. And by the beauty of every star that shines, by every thing good in this world, and by all that God has done in our knowledge, and by every thing right we know of him, that mother will have her child again.

MARHAM.

Yes, she will. And we shall all of us have our hopes, — such of them as are pure. For nothing of God's giving dies from us into the great grave of the world, without there being to be a resurrection for it, in some more glorious form. For nothing can fall from us, and be forgotten before God.

AUBIN.

If I had ever known a stone the law of gravitation did not hold good by, then I might fear for myself proving the one soul which God might forget. But it is God's being in it, that holds the earth together; and there is not a grain of sand but feels him, nor a thought of mine but is a witness of him. For could I remember, could I think, without faculties? and they are not of my own maintaining in me. Because if it were not for God, my soul would dissipate at once. So that my very fear of being forgotten is a proof that I am not.

MARHAM.

Well, so it is. There is no one who would not easily believe in a life to come, if this present life were the wonderful thing to him it ought to be.

AUBIN.

Sometimes it does seem to me so wonderful that I should be alive ! It quite startles me for the moment ; and I cannot help saying to myself that I am, — I am, — I am. It is so strange that the world should be, and I be in it, and walking about it, that it is as though voices from above might call to me, " Thou ! thou art alive, — alive out of nothing. And thou ! what, what art thou doing now ? " This hand of mine ! it is curious, very curious, more curiously made than I know. Whether a brute knows any thing of himself or not, I cannot tell ; but this I do know, that I am myself fearfully and wonderfully made. And this fearfulness and wonder ! my God ! it is thyself ; it is what I have my being in. When I clench my hand, it is through power of thy lending, O God ! — power that thou knowest of, and that I am to answer for the use of. By what I am, Lord God ! what I am to be is nothing so strange. I was born of my mother, and she of her mother, but not without God ; for one hair of their heads they had not themselves the power to make white or black. And besides, Eve was not born of herself, nor did she spring out of the dust, nor did she get made by chance, nor did Adam. Sometimes, if I could doubt my existence, I should ; for it does seem so strange, that for all eternity I should not have been, and now, this year, that I should be. Ay, when I think of it, the miracle is in my being at all, and not in my being to be again.

CHAPTER XXXIII.

But enough is said to make a speculative man see, that if God should join the soul of a lately dead man, even whilst his corpse should lie entire m his winding-sheet here, unto a body made of earth taken from some mountain in America, it were most true and certain, that the body he should then live by were the same identical body he lived with before his death and late resurrection. It is evident that sameness, thisness and thatness, belongeth not to matter by itself, for a general indifference runneth through it all, but only as it is distinguished and individuated by the form.

KENELM DIGBY.

AUBIN.

I DO not think embalming a body is right.

MARHAM.

Why not ? For is not it natural to attempt it ?

AUBIN.

But then who are they to whom it is natural ? The old worshippers of Isis and Osiris, rather than us Christians. It is according to nature for a dead body to rot and vanish ; and so we ought to let it, for no one can attempt to mend the ways of nature and not maim himself some way.

MARHAM.

But how in embalming a human body ?

AUBIN.

In his feelings about death and the dead. In any thing to violate nature is to wrong one's self.

MARHAM.

I know it will be no matter to me what becomes of my body, any more than of my clothes ; yet I feel as though it would be pleasanter, if I knew why my body must dissolve.

AUBIN.

It would have been an awful thing if the human body had continued fresh after death, and only with the breath out. We could not then have buried a body, nor hidden it away, without brutalizing ourselves. And besides, it would have made us feel at last as though we were only bodies ; and death would have been a worse terror to us than he is. And then, uncle, I am sure that wrong feeling about dead bodies vitiates faith in immortality. Besides, if I died to-morrow, why should my corpse be felt about so strangely, when it would be only one of several bodies that I have had and worn out. For it is said that in the human frame every particle is changed in seven years. But now how begins the gravestone? "Here lieth the body of John Smith." But more truly it would say, "Here lies the last of the bodies of John Smith," or "Here lies the body from which John Smith departed," or "Here lies the body which John Smith had the day when he departed this life." Either one of these forms is truer than what the stonecutter uses, and, as well as being more correct, is happier to think of.

MARHAM.

And if truer, then better every way. I should not see much of the sublimity of a mountain, if while looking at it I had a mote in my eye ; but the grave-mound of a friend is a greater matter than the Alps are to some of my feelings ; so in those feelings I would not have any thing false, if possible. As rightly as I can, let me think and feel in regard to my friend's disappearance.

AUBIN.

In some countries, a corpse is not to be touched for fear of being made unclean by it, while in some others it is tended almost as though alive. There have been countries in which the dead have been lodged more grandly than the living ; and in some places, they are hurried out of sight indecently quick.

MARHAM.

It is custom, chiefly ; else I was going to say that carelessness about the remains of the dead would argue but little kindly feeling one with another, among the living.

AUBIN.

I feel solemnly among the old walls and arches of what was once a church ; and shall I feel less reverently beside what was once a saintly man to look at ? Mere flesh and bones, — dust returning unto dust, — is it ? What, then, are the remains of Fountain Abbey, of Rievaulx Abbey, and at

Castleacre ?. Stones and lime ; and with poor
workmanship in them compared with the make of
a human body.   The body of a departed saint is
dead, so it is ; but it is the ruins of what was
once a temple of the Holy Ghost.   It is a dis-
used temple ; in it, loving wishes no longer form
and rise to God like incense ; the light of reason
in it is put out ; the book of remembrance in it is
shut, and there is no more reading from it ; divine service in it is over, and an eternal Amen
has been said to it by Fate ; and at the soul's
going forth from her temple, there was joy, though
elsewhere than among men.

MARHAM.

Yes, we are temples of God ; or rather our
persons are, as long as our souls are in them.   It
is the indwelling spirit that makes flesh and blood
be a temple.   We will remember this, and so
not think more of the temple than of what sancti-
fies it.

AUBIN.

On York Minster there are always repairs going on, and it is the same with the human temple.
From what it was ten years ago, every particle
of my body has been changed ; but it is not so
with my soul.   Four times over has my body
been changed ; and when it is changed at last, it
will only be seven years more swiftly than before.
And after all, we shall not quit the world more

suddenly than we entered it. It is more than ten
years since there was in my body any thing of
the limbs I used to run with as a boy ; but I
have the thoughts I had then, and very likely
every one of them, though not to be called up at
will. Now is not this proof enough of spiritual
existence ? It is what Dr. Johnson did not know
of, perhaps, when he would have liked to have
seen a spirit. A strange wish !

MARHAM.

He was confident in there being a world of
spirits ; but he had never seen it, and so ——

AUBIN.

Nor have I ever seen my own head ; but that
I have it, I am sure. But you will say I can
handle it with my hands. And so I can ; but
then I have to depend on the correctness of what
feeling is in my hands, and that is what I cannot
be certain of. In every thing, for the correctness of what knowledge we get, even through
our eyes and ears, we have to trust the truth of
our make, and so at last of our Maker. My bodily faculties I have used as trustworthy ; and at
least as much I will trust what spiritual feelings I
have been made with. And I think there are
thoughts which I should sooner and more rightly
trust than either my eyes or my fingers. I should
not believe in another world, for seeing a crowd
of ghosts, at all more firmly than I do now. For

then I should have to credit my eyesight ; and
since trust I must, I can quite as surely trust
what witness of the spirit there is' in my spirit.
When I go down on my knees, sometimes there
is that from within me which calls aloud, " Father ! Father ! "   And always that cry is answered, because that yearning of the spirit changes
into its own answer, into a mingled feeling of
awe, and faith, and love ; and it is as though I
were wrapped round with a cloud, and were spoken to from above, " My son, my son, in whom
I am pleased ! "

MARHAM.

There is much truth in what you said once,
Oliver, that if a man feels like Christ, he will get
to think like him more and more.   And we get
to feel like Christ by doing his commandments.

AUBIN.

A man has doubts that weaken his faith ; then
let him fix on some one fault of his own and mend
it, and there will be one doubt the less in him,
most likely.   Or he cannot hope much, he is so
mournful ; then let him be some worse sufferer's
hope, and he will soon have heaven a dear
thought with him.   Only let a disciple live as
Christ lived, and he will easily believe in living
again, as Christ does.   And in this way he may
believe and almost know himself to be a living
soul, as well as a body that can be touched.

MARHAM.

Yes, and let a man live the life of the spirit, and he will the more easily think of himself outliving the life of his body.

AUBIN.

Uncle, when a body becomes dust, there is not a grain of it that does not feel the laws of attraction and gravitation.

MARHAM.

And so the soul is not to be feared for ; for if through God every particle of the body is drawn into use, then here are a thousand and a million instances of the certain way in which the soul must be drawn into life.

AUBIN.

Yes, spirit to spirit we go, like to like, children to our Father, and godlike to God's self. In God I live, and move, and have my being ; and in him I shall weaken, and faint, and have my death. This is certain. But, indeed, I am always dying. No two days is my body the same, and no two minutes. By my breathing and my heart beating, my body is decaying and renewing every moment, my bones and even my eyes ; and it is not of my own will, but of God ; and so will my death be. My body will fail me only to leave me on the bosom of the Father, and to let me feel it more warmly than ever. Four bodies I have worn out ; and parting with this

fifth one whole will be what will be called my
death, but what will be really my life, — my newness of life.

MARHAM.

Four bodies, one after another, you have had,
and I ten or more. It is quite true, I suppose.
And it is knowledge along with which embalming
would not have become a practice, nor such
tombs have been built as are in Lycia.

AUBIN.

In a mausoleum or a grand tomb, so much is
made of the body that one thinks of it too much,
as though it had been the whole man. For my
own body I would not have a leaden coffin, nor
a tomb, nor a bricked grave ; but I would have
it laid in the mould. For now it is hot and cold
with the air, and well and ill with the weather,
and the way the wind blows ; and so the way of
nature let it go when I am gone, — ashes to
ashes, and dust to dust.

MARHAM.

But, my dear Oliver ——

AUBIN.

This frame of mine, — it is mine through eating, and drinking, and breathing. This body
of mine is out of wheat-fields and gardens ; it
has come to me out of the ground, through the
roots of herbs and trees, and in wholesome air
from the forests of Norway, and the woody mid-

dle of Australia, and the banian-trees of Asia.
There is in my veins what has been in a rainbow,
perhaps, and very certainly what is from the rice-
fields of the East Indies, and from the cane-brakes
of the West Indies, and from out of the sea.
Wonderful is the way our souls take flesh, and
have their earthly being. It is well known to us,
and so is not much to' think of; else even life
after death would be an easier thought than it is
sometimes.

MARHAM.

We men may well hope to live again; as we,
and we alone, are let know what wonderful way
we are living already.

AUBIN.

It is better not to think so much of the bodies
of the dead as the Egyptians did in embalming
them, and as the Arabians did in making rock
tombs for them, and as the Romans and other
nations did in their various funereal customs. I
would not wish to have my body laid under the
floor of a church; but in the earth let it be laid,
and let the grass grow over it, and under that
green mantle of her spreading, let Nature be free
to take again into herself what has been my body;
into grass let it go, and up the roots, and into the
green boughs of trees; and in vapor let it rise
from the ground, and into the clouds.

CHAPTER XXXIV.

O, though oft depressed and lonely,
  All my fears are laid aside,
If I but remember only
  Such as these have lived and died!
                    LONGFELLOW.

AUBIN.

I WOULD not allow of any creed in the Church
but the Bible ; and it should be heresy for one
minister to use a word of it against another, except lovingly.   O, but there would then be the
peace of God among Christians, and very soon,
perhaps, throughout the world !

MARHAM.

In Eton church, under the arms of Sir Henry
Wotton, it is said, in Latin, that underneath lies
the author of the maxim, that a great flow of argument is what runs to a disease in the Church.
And then the reader is told to ask for his name
elsewhere.

AUBIN.

His epitaph is not in such good taste as Walton's life of him.   How few good epitaphs there
are ! = I have seen somewhere, that on the tomb
of one Count Algarotti, a philosopher at Pisa, is
what he himself ordered should be cut, — Here

lies Algarotti, but not all of him. A word or two more would have made it religious, and the best epitaph I know of. Of all the monumental inscriptions in Ely cathedral, there is not one that is good, I think; but I did not read the more modern ones.

MARHAM.

You must have been very fastidious when you were there, Oliver; for some good ones you must have seen, because so many dignitaries of the Church have always lived at Ely, — men of learning, and leisure, and often, no doubt, of poetical, as well as devout feeling. And then, if I remember rightly, the tablets in the cathedral, and the inscriptions on tombs, are very numerous.

AUBIN.

So they are; telling what stalls, rectories, deaneries, wives, children, learning, virtues, and years, the clergy of that rich soil have had; and what have been the lives of several officers of the Right Honorable the Corporation of the Great Level of the Fens.

MARHAM.

Such persons are gratefully remembered in those marshes, I dare say.

AUBIN.

So it would seem; for an epitaph says that one deceased was very dearly remembered in Thorny Level, in the Isle of Ely, and in Deep-

ing Fens, in Lincolnshire, on account of his ability in draining fenny and marsh lands. Another
inscription says, — "Under this marble rests what
there was of earth in Thomas Benyon, a clergy-
man. Us survivors he taught how to die, on the
twenty-fifth of February, in the year of our salvation sixteen hundred and eighty-nine." Now
that is well, but it is followed by another line or
two, not quite so good. I wonder why it is that
funeral inscriptions are almost always so poorly
written, so universally wanting in taste.

MARHAM.

It is nothing surprising, Oliver. For such inscriptions are commonly written by men blind
with tears, and with unsteady hands. And there
is a distress that is not rare, and that quite dis-
ables the mind for correct thinking, and especially
for tasteful expression ; for taste comes of mental
harmony ; and so there is no wonder it is wanting
on tombstones, which are written on in a troubled
spirit almost always.

AUBIN.

Uncle, you are right. And I am rather
ashamed of myself for what gravestones I have
smiled at ; for I was thoughtless ; as I ought to
have known that epitaphs are the utterances of
mourners, and are nearly all of them what would
sound very natural, if heard from quivering lips,
and with a stop here and there to keep a sob

down. I remember having seen, at Chowbent, a tablet to the memory of Dr. John Taylor, the divine, and from which he appears to have died in his sleep ; and this was what he used to wish might be his earthly end, — so the sexton of the chapel said

MARHAM.

Archbishop Leighton used to say, that if he might choose a place to die in, it should be an inn, so as to escape seeing his friends weep ; and he did die at' the Bell, on a visit to London. He thought, by dying at an inn, he should feel the more like a pilgrim starting on the last part of his journey home.

AUBIN.

Spenser makes a wanderer be told, that death is itself an inn : —

> Death is an equal doom
> To good and bad, the common inn of rest;
> But after death the trial is to come,
> When best shall be to them that lived best.

In his last illness, Pascal was troubled at his' having more comforts than some other sufferers, and he wished to be carried to a hospital to die. He was religiously mistaken in wearing a girdle of spikes, — at least we will hope he was ; but without any doubt, he was a Christain in earnest. His pains were very great for a long while, but especially towards the end of his life ; but they

26

were what he could almost take his ease in, for, as he said to his sister, it was a happiness to him to be in such a state as to have nothing to do but to submit humbly and calmly.

MARHAM.

In the life of Dr. John Donne, he is said, his last fortnight, to have been so happy as to have had nothing to do but to die.

AUBIN.

The good men of his age died more deliberately than is often done now. As soon as they knew themselves mortally ill, they finished their earthly business, sent for their friends to have a few last words with them, said, perhaps, how and where they would wish to be buried; and then they could watch the great eclipse of life, and, with the darkness growing on them, could wonder and worship in quiet.

MARHAM.

Bishop Ken had even his shroud made in readiness for his death, and he used to carry it about with him when he travelled; and he put it on in his last illness, and died in it.

AUBIN.

His brother-in-law, Izaak Walton, was not so ascetic, but was quite as good a man, I think; and I think would not have put a shroud on, but would rather have died in a meadow on a summer afternoon. I remember the last stanza of a poem

which he made, as he sat on the grass under a
sycamore-tree, and perhaps with a book on his
knees, and a dog nigh him. He says, I could
wish many things, but most, to —

> with my Bryan and a book,
> Loiter long days near Shawford brook ; —
> There sit by him and eat my meat ;
> There see the sun both rise and set ;
> There bid good morning to next day ;
> There meditate my time away ;
> And angle on, and beg to have
> A quiet passage to a welcome grave.

Dear old Izaak ! By feeling those lines of his,
one is better fit for death than by putting a
shroud on. Walton thanked God for flowers,
and showers, and meat, and content, and leisure
to go a-fishing. And I thank God for my knowing of him ; for he has done me good by his
books and cheerful piety.

MARHAM.

Walter Pope and Izaak Walton would have
liked one another, I should think. Walter Pope
wrote a poem called the Old Man's Wish. I
remember a verse of it : —

> May I govern my passions with absolute sway,
> Grow wiser and better as life wears away,
> Without gout or stone, by a gentle decay, —
> A gentle — a gentle — a gentle decay !

You would not think those lines had ever been
Latin ; but they were once, and were translated
by Vincent Bourne.

AUBIN.

I like them, uncle, very much. And I like the way John Keats wished to die; it is what he felt while he was listening to the nightingale once, and I suppose in the dark.

> Darkling I listen; and for many a time
> I have been half in love with easeful Death, —
> Called him soft names in many a mused rhyme,
> To take into the air my quiet breath:
> Now more than ever seems it rich to die,
> To cease upon the midnight with no pain,
> While thou art pouring forth thy soul abroad
> In such an ecstasy.

He died where there are more nightingales than there are here; and we will hope he felt at the last what he said himself, that disappointments and anxieties are the subtile food on which to feel how quiet death is. Uncle, I will repeat to you the last lines of what is supposed to have been Nicoll's last poem : —

> Death is upon me, yet I fear not now.
> Open my chamber window, — let me look
> Upon the silent vales, the sunny glow
> That fills each alley, close, and copsewood nook.
> I know them, love them, mourn not them to leave;
> Existence and its change my spirit cannot grieve!

Brave Robert Nicoll! for when he was thus resigned to death, he had a dear wife and a useful employment, and had just struggled through poverty up to the sight of a high and bright path in society.

MARHAM.

You read me, yesterday, a sonnet of Bryant's. I should like to hear it again. He wishes in it to be in his old age like the month October, and to die like it.

AUBIN.

I will read it, uncle ; and this is a right day for. it, is not it ?

Ay, thou art welcome, heaven's delicious breath!
  When woods begin to wear the crimson leaf,
  And suns grow meek, and the meek suns grow brief,
And the year smiles as it draws near its death:
Wind of the sunny south! O, still delay
  In the gay woods, and in the golden air,
  Like to a good old age released from care,
Journeying, in long serenity, away.
In such a bright, late quiet, would that I
  Might wear out life like thee, 'mid bowers and brooks,
  And, dearer yet, the sunshine of kind looks,
And music of kind voices ever nigh ;
And when my last sand twinkles in the glass,
Pass silently from men, as thou dost pass.

Friends with him, — he would wish to have friends with him at the last. And so would I. He would wish to have kind voices within his hearing, and he is right ; for, O, the magic, the comfort, the unutterable, the tranquillizing power, there is in the human voice ! I could wish myself to be able to hear to the last, and never to be too weak to read. Some men have died with books in their hands ; and I think Petrarch did.

And Bailey says there is that to be written yet,
which good old men shall read, and then,

Closing the book, shall utter lowlily, —
"Death! thou art infinite; it is life is little."

Ah! some such book once I hoped to attempt
writing.   But the trial was not to be allowed me.

MARHAM.

Yes, Oliver, in part it was to be, and is.   For
no old man would have been more grateful for the
book than I am for your talk.   We have been
talking about how some men have wished to die ;
but how one would like to know what thoughts
they had at the last, — those poets and philosophers that are dead !

AUBIN.

A man like Tasso, for instance.

MARHAM.

Yes.

AUBIN.

Uncle, I have a piece by me that I wrote two
years ago.   It is called the Last Vision of Tasso.
Towards the end of his life, the poet imagined
himself visited by a spirit.   His friend, the Mar-
quis Manso, says he once heard a most lofty con-
verse ; but, as it seemed to him, it was Torquato,
at one time questioning, and at another replying.
Though, as the listener says, the discourse was
marvellously conducted, both in the sublimity of
the topics, and in a certain unwonted manner of

talking, that exalted him into an ecstasy with hearing it.

MARHAM.

I should very much like to see what you have written, Oliver. For there is in it, I have no doubt, a good deal of what you have felt yourself.

CHAPTER XXXV.

I can behold how merit lies in ashes;
How darkness, circled round with brightest glories,
Its hollow head upreareth;
How in the wise man's room the fool is sitting,
And virtue grieves all wretched and forsaken;
How hateful vice and vile demerit scoff her,
And drive her trembling from the home of fortune;
The bad tree blossoming, and by lightning stricken
The noble stem. This can I see, still hoping.

And therefore will I hail the better future,
Which in me lives, which I behold within me;
Thither to meet the young day will I hasten,
Following the star to which my fate I 've trusted.
When I the dust from off my feet have shaken,
Then will I, too, soft branches round me waving,
Lie down in happy quiet!
For One I know amid the stars is circling,
And from their bright choir draweth strains harmonious.

F. VON ZEDLITZ.

TASSO.

How the time has gone! Still I have not been asleep; at least, I think I have not. And yet now the light shines on the other side of the room. Ah, sun! very beautiful sun! Thou art not wearing old yet, but in thy light I have grown old before my time. No! it was not in thy light that that happened to me, for it was in the dungeon at Ferrara. Seven years! Ay, they madden me to think of. And I was mad; I was.

But on which side of the hospital door I first
grew frenzied I will not say, and I will try not to
think. That God knows and will judge upon, —
he will, he will. Nay, but I pray thee, God!
pardon the matter, and pardon me. For I will
not ask thee to judge between me and him, —
him that was my master. God forgive him the
wrong he did me! I do, — that is I hope I do.
Only yesterday they gave me the sacrament, and
twice since then I have been bitter against Alfon-
so, and thought God would judge him. Ay, I
should not have thought that without I had wished it. May God, merciful and compassionate,
pardon me! I will confess this sin while it is
fresh; I will do it this evening. Why, it is
nearly evening now! Ah! one, two, three, five
swallows! O you blessed creatures! For you
have the spring to come before you, and you
bring the summer from behind you; and with
you it is always a glad earth. This very minute,
you are flying up and down, and across the Ti-
ber, and in and out of the Coliseum; and some
of you, the while, are resting yourselves on tree-
tops and on churches. And you see the Capi-
tol, and can fly to it so easily! but now I shall
never reach it. I shall die without my crown.
I have hoped for it for years, and now I shall
miss of it by this sickness. Poor Torquato! I
did think once, that Virgil might perhaps have

some time called thee brother. But that is past hope. For now that I could work, I am dying; and now that I have just got the means of living, my lifetime is over; and now that the hand of tyranny is off me, the heavier hand of death is on me. O, what I might have been! But that will soon be stifled in the dust of what I am about to be. Once I hoped before this to have ascended up on high, and been one of the greater lights in the firmament of thought for ever. But I have not risen, and I shall die out like a marsh-light extinguished in rain, — I, Torquato Tasso. I am heart-sick. I am not afraid of death; but can I trust him quite? Me, my uncles, my mother's brothers, have defrauded; to me, friends have been false; and me, my patron imprisoned. There have been times — I remember them — in which the face of every man was that of an enemy against me. I knew how people felt towards me; and so, by my walking down the streets of Ferrara, my soul has been, as it were, pierced through and through with swords. Then I have been cheated by the very years of my life; for fifty of them have spent out of my strength what ought to have been the health of threescore and ten. After whispering me all my life, and drawing me on to be her crowned poet, fame has deluded me. To me, my own faculties have not always been true. What is there has been true

to me ? My relatives, my friends, the public, my
patrons, fame, — yea! and my genius, — these
all have been false to me. To me, all things in
life have been treacherous ; and so why should
death be true ? Of all things, why should only
death be true to me ? Me it will be sure to
mock, some way or other. But it may be, — it
is, — it must be, — O, it is I myself am the mock-
ery, and the falsehood, and the delusion. My
mind is a mirror with a flaw in it, and things cannot be true to it ; they cannot look right in it.
·O the strangeness of my make ! Ah, well ! but
there is this now. Life is bright to all other
men, but to me it is gloomy, and always has
been ; and so perhaps what is painful to others in
death will be pleasant to me. And so it will
be ; for I feel my spirit invited into death ; but
other men have their souls shrink from it, ay, and
from the very shadow and the thought of it. I
knew it, — my soul is not as other souls are.
But — Fool, fool, that I have been ! Again,
again, — O this destiny of mine ! — again must I
be an exception to the whole world, and for the
worse. Others feel towards death as an enemy ;
but it is to find him their friend. So says what
must be believed. But I do not fear death, and
so he will prove terrible to me. Fearful and
false he will be to me. But I will not think it,
and, indeed, I ought not, because it is not for me

to think any thing positively, because I was phrenetic once, I know. And this misgiving about
death may be mere frenzy, and I suspect it is ;
— yes, and I will believe so, I will think so. I
have been mad with misery once, and so God
help me ! My experience of life has been horrible ; at least I think it has. And, indeed, I cannot be sure what it has been at all ; for this life
is a half-sentence ; and the end of it is not to be
read in this world, and so one cannot tell how it
will read. My existence as yet, my deeds, my
attempts, and my sufferings, are like the four half-
lines that Virgil wrote against the palace of Au-
gustus ; for it is what is to come after them that
will make their meaning ; and what that is I cannot tell yet. Again, O holy and blessed appearance ! yet again before I die ! O, unworthy of
it I am ! I am unworthy the sight. For only
just now I have allowed my soul to cloud and
darken with distrust, and my lips are still moist
with the breath of words murmured in discontent
about what my earthly lot has been, when indeed
I know only what my life has seemed, while
what it will prove to have been is not for me
even to guess.

SPIRIT.

Often the yellowness of disease, and the white-
ness of hunger, and the transparency of consumption, are the illuminated beginning of what reads

on into a patent of immortality for man ; and
there are many in heaven, for whom in that writing the first is a red letter, having been colored.
so with the blood of their martyrdom.

TASSO.

For my poet's work I have not had a hod-
man's pay, — I have not, I have not. For
many, many years, men gladdened themselves
with my fancies, but not one of them ever rejoiced me. To houses without number my books
have been like a theatre, in which the inhabitants
have amused themselves at will ; and like a library, in which from time to time they have informed themselves with thought and feeling ; and like
a tower of refuge for them against enemies, for in
reading my verses they have forgotten their woes.
To many hundreds I have been all this ; but
what have they been to me ? Neglect, envy, and
malice. Gates do not shut out anxieties ; but I
have shut out cares from many a man's mind
many a time ; from many a prince's mind I have ;
and often I have been let want the food and lodg-
ing of a door-keeper. My miseries do not grieve
me to remember. But that I could not be understood, could not be loved, — it is this distresses me. For till just now, they had all been
ungrateful to me, — all my acquaintance, and my
readers, and my countrymen.

SPIRIT.

And have not they all been ungrateful to God ? Have you never thought of that, — never thought that in that respect you are standing towards the world in the same way as God ? And then, in this world, the greater a man is, the more he is misprized at first. Has it not been so nearly always ? Was it not so with the philosophers, and the poets, and the prophets of old time ?

TASSO.

Yes, yes ! I see them, the great ones. With the eyes of the spirit, I see them. And they pass in company before me, — the thinkers of the world, and the sufferers of it. And there is one seems to reproach me, and another pities me, because I have grudged entire brotherhood with them. That high and solemn fellowship of yours I have sinned against. O ye members of it, brothers of my spirit, pity me and pardon me ! pardon me, for I have been selfish. Round your brows there is a halo, and on mine I have hoped to wear the same ; while from your pathway of thorns on this earth I have shrunk and wished to turn aside. O ye glorified sufferers of this world, forgive me !

SPIRIT.

And is not there known in this earth a name which is above every name, and have you not known how that name was first received ? And among men, always, has not God over all been most forgotten of all? Your countrymen have been ungrateful to you for your bright and beautiful thoughts; but have they, many of them, been grateful to God for sunshine and starlight? You have been forgotten, Torquato, and so has the goodness of God been. But the Lord is slow to anger, and it is of his mercy the world is not consumed.

TASSO.

O wrétch that I have been, and profane, to have breathed God's air and made it into murmurs against his Providence! Ah! I should have borne with my fellow-men the better, had I thought of God's forbearing me. Yes, and now I see in life a man cannot be discontented, unless against God. O God! pardon my thoughtlessness, for it has been great and wicked. But indeed I could not always think aright; for I was in want, in great want sometimes, and indeed often.

SPIRIT.

You have wanted bread in St. Anne's hospital often, and often in villages and towns.

TASSO.

Ah! you know that, you do know that! I am glad you do. It was hard with me; was it not?

SPIRIT.

Suffering is perfection to the Christian, and to the poet it is wisdom and glory.

TASSO.

When I asked the world for bread, there was given me a stone, often.

SPIRIT.

So often, that out of those stones you have built for yourself a monument in the world on which to have your name inscribed for ever.

TASSO.

O, now for that assurance the blessed God be thanked ! for it means — does it not ? — that men hereafter will hold me dear. I do not care for honor now ; but I do wish to be loved, and it is what my soul craves. I have never known a man I do not long to have love me. But men have not known me often ; they have thought they have, but they have not, and so they have not liked me much. Though some have loved me without knowing me ; the poor have. Yes, they have been kind to me many times, — often, — always, almost. In the Apennines, I have heard them sing verses of mine more than once. There is not a cottage there, but I could wish my name to live in. For the people there have hard hands, and are brown in the face with the sun ; but they have love in their eyes, and they have voices that do not deceive. I have been often healed of my melancholy, for a time, by a peasant's hand laid on my shoulder, or by his wife's looking in my face. For once I was much with cottagers, dependent on them for food and shelter. That was when I was an outcast from court and city, and wandering over Italy afoot. O my wasted manhood! ·But it was by others it was wasted, not by me. Was my genius only my concern ? It was intrusted to me ; but it ought to have been fostered by others ; but it was not. And I, — I did what I could with it ; and I could not do more. In anxiety about a meal from day to day, I spent thought which the whole world ought to have been the better for for ever. For years I had to walk in the darkness of poverty, and so I had to use like a lantern the genius that might have risen on all Italy like a sun, had I been treated rightly at that court of Ferrara.

SPIRIT.

By your ill usage there, the world is the worse, perhaps, but not you, Torquato. For do not you remember in your youth what your pride was as a courtier, and your ambition of place ? It was well for you that you failed of your wishes, or you would have become vain, and so your genius would have failed you. There was a time when you were near valuing men for their power more than their goodness, and for their honors more than for the way they got them. And so your love of man was changing into lust of grandeur. And as a poet, what would you have been without love ?

and without love, what would you be as a Christian, to die? Your heart was hardening; but
sorrow softened it, and kept it soft; and in the
company of the poor, it was moulded anew and
better. And so now your feelings are youthfully
fresh, and poetically pure, and as strong as ever.
It was well the court, and life at it, became hateful to you; for what your feelings were becoming
once, do you not remember now, Torquato?

TASSO.

Remember! remember! I remember! And
it is a horror, all of it. My relatives, my ac-
quaintances, and my patrons used me so ill for so
long, that I have been sick of life. And there
have been moments in which immortality has felt
to me like a weary thought. God will forgive
me this, because my spirit was diseased and
could feel nothing healthily. For it was at a
time when I wanted sympathy, and bread, and
some little provision against old age; and out of
so many thousand persons, there was no one to
offer me these things.

SPIRIT.

You suffered by that; and so did your neglect-
ers, and worse than yourself; for they missed
becoming famous, and they failed of being Christian by not helping you. A cup of cold water
given to a Christian is not without a reward.
But he that gets the love of a Christian poet wins

more than a throne, and what kingdoms would
not buy.

TASSO.

O God ! that some others had judged like that.
And I should have been happy then. But she
that was my life would still have died, — perhaps
she would ; but that would not have frenzied me ;
it would have made me a mourner all my days ;
but that sorrow I should have felt like God's
hand upon me, like a loving touch. But that her
brother's tyranny debarred me of Leonora, and
imprisoned me from the sight of her, — this was
what maddened me. And I was mad ; for years
I was. O those many lost years, the best of my
life that ought to have been, and the brightest of
my genius that should have been ! Why, O,
why were they darkened so ? Are there many
such minds as mine in Italy ? Is there now, or
fifteen years since was there, another Torquato
Tasso in Ferrara, or in Rome, in Florence, in
Milan, or in Venice ? From among a million, I
was to write the Jerusalem Delivered ; and from
among a million, I was to be phrenetic. First
one thing happened to me, and then another, and
then I was hated, and then there was nobody I
could trust ; and so I went mad. And it was at
a time when the laurel was in leaf out of which
my poet's crown might have been wreathed.
But it was not to be. The laurel-leaves would

have withered on my brow, it grew so hot.   And
it was as though a voice had come out against
me, — "Frenzy for thee, Torquato, instead of
fame."   My mind might have been the home of
splendors, and the birthplace of glories for men ;
but it became confusion, a lurking-place for sus-
picions, a horror of darkness, and an atmosphere
of infinite melancholy.   Like deadly mist off the
Campagna, and more thickly than that, must my
sins have gone up to heaven, for them in their
falling to have rained into my soul, as it were,
fire and brimstone, burning, and blackening, and
wasting it.   Is it over yet ? is it all over ? Is
the air clear between me and heaven ? and is
there no cloud that may drench my soul in destruction yet !   Me God made a poet; and
he lit up in my mind a light which other men
have not ; and perhaps it was to light me to other
duties than theirs ; and I have not gone after
them.   And so I have sinned worse than other
men.   And my miseries have been my punishment ; but not all of it, perhaps.   There is more
to come yet, and the heaviest part, perhaps.   O
my God ! my God ! then do not thou let me
remember the past, but in mercy make me forget it.

SPIRIT.

Was it for his crimes St. Paul suffered the
loss of all things ?   Was it under God's ven-

geance Stephen died crushed and bleeding on the ground ?   And the army of martyrs, — were they sinners above all other men ?

TASSO.

O, but I have been perverse ! Loving chastisements I have called the sufferings of others ; but I have been impatient under my own, as though they were heavy vengeance on me.   But indeed my sorrows have been, some of them, what do not often happen.

SPIRIT.

And in your genius you have had the use of a light that is not often given in the world's darkness.

TASSO.

It was losing that awhile which has been my greatest loss, and now it is my most painful remembrance ; for I shudder at my mind's having darkened, perhaps, with its own sinfulness, or in God's anger, perhaps.

SPIRIT.

It was in neither ; but it was for good, — the good of others chiefly, but also for your own.   It was for good ; and it was good.   Over the eyelids of her child asleep in the daylight, a mother draws the coverlet ; and it is in her love.   But over the eyes of your waking understanding, when the veil was drawn, it was done in love that is infinite.   Be you sure of it.   A spectacle to men

were you ? You were, and such as no other man
could have been. Was your madness a strange
thing to hear of ? It was ; and men minded it ;
and by thinking of it, they, some of them, felt
anew the mysteriousness of their being. Irreligious men heard of you, and were thrilled ; and
they felt again those roots of the spirit of which
the Godhead is the soil ; and so their souls re-
vived. Does not the Lord say that all souls are
his ? And so they are, and your soul shows it.
And how souls do not live of themselves, but in
God, has been more believingly felt by many, for
their having seen darkness come and go across
your mind, you yourself helpless against it. A
star or two may be obscured, and men not heed
it ; but over all Italy your mind was like a sun,
and at the eclipse of it men thought of God.

TASSO.

Speak on, speak on. My God ! my God ! I
thank thee.

SPIRIT.

You have suffered, Torquato, and greatly, and
as few ever suffer. But the thought of that
should calm, and not trouble you. For have you
written nothing, said nothing, done nothing wrong?
You can remember — cannot you ? — a hundred
things, for the least of which you would be glad
to suffer for days and weeks if only it might
be undone, and be as though it had never been.

But this is what could not be. And, indeed, like night, evil has its use in this world; though alas for them by whom much of it comes! Do not understand your great afflictions as meaning that you have been much worse than other men; but rather than that, let your many sorrows assure you that you are not of those who have sinned against men more largely than suffered with them.

TASSO.

God! against thee it was my ignorance that repined; and thou wilt pardon it, wilt thou not? O merciful One! wilt thou not? Nay, but it is of thy mercy there has been vouchsafed to me this knowledge of thy Providence. And this mercy of thine is an earnest of forgiveness : so I feel it. Lord! my spirit yearns to thee now in trust and love.

SPIRIT.

And the more tenderly so for what your sorrows have been.

TASSO.

O that I had felt years ago what I feel now! And why did not I? Why had I not this knowledge against the time of my affliction?

SPIRIT.

You could not have had it against your sufferings, because it was to come through them. For there is a wisdom that in this world only comes with sorrow. And in virtue there is what only a mourner is so blessed as to reach. Of all the souls you have known, Torquato, have not the afflicted been the gentlest, and those that have sorrowed most been the most firmly believing? And by whom have the best words in this world been spoken? As you know, by those who had under foot the ashes of their living martyrdoms.

TASSO.

Glory to them! for round them the world roared and glowed like a furnace of affliction; and, asbestos-like, their souls were but whitened in the fire. And, my God! glory to thee in the highest! Glory to thee, with my whole glad heart! My God! my God! how strong my spirit grows with thanking thee! Now I can hope, now I can trust; and I will, world without end, do with me what God will.

SPIRIT.

God does nothing but what the soul may trust in.

TASSO.

And what my soul shall trust in now, though the stars darken at it, and the moon turn like blood. But, indeed, worse appearances than these I have outlived, and worse, perhaps, than I shall ever know again. Abandoned of men I have been; and I have almost feared I was abandoned of God. My soul has craved for another soul to know it, and not been known; I prayed

for peace, long, long before it came to me ; and,
flat on the ground, I have wept like an only and
an orphan child, till, in my wretchedness, the cold
earth under me has felt like the bosom of a dead
mother.

SPIRIT.

But there was on you then the eye of your Father in heaven ; and now you will be the happier,
the longer that eye rests on you ; for to feel it is
to have the soul brighten with its light, and warm
with its love, and gladden with the infinite blessedness that is in it.

TASSO.

O, it is all glorious with God, — the future is.
And the past will not be so painful to me, now
that you have pitied it.

SPIRIT.

Then it may be a blessed thing for you to think
of ; for, Torquato, God has pitied it.

TASSO.

O. God ! Thou blessed, blessed God !

SPIRIT.

In pain, man feels himself a soul ; and through
agony, when rightly borne, he gets to know himself akin to spiritual greatness. Out of the ground
the food of the body is got with the sweat of the
brow. And the bread that came down from
heaven, — is it not man's through the blood of
Jesus Christ ?

[1] TASSO.

Through the precious blood of Christ.

SPIRIT.

And mortality never has immortal truth grow in it, but in pain. The spirit gains on the body in pain ; and it is in pain that men die out of this world into the other. The books of the prophecies are the treasures of the world now ; but of the prophets themselves, there was not one but was persecuted. There is not a noble feeling but began with some one who had died to the world in agony before his living in the spirit. And there is not a gentle thought but is tender with some one's sorrow. Yes ! and any time, on any matter, when the word of the Lord comes, seldom does it get spoken, but through the self-sacrifice of some believing soul.

TASSO.

O, you are a spirit from on high, and your words sublime me. And, as you said, these things of earth have been looked into from heaven, and been pitied.

SPIRIT.

And been gloried in, too. Of the millions of souls that are ushered into this earth, the birth of every one is a joy in heaven, though with trembling, on account of its being made subject to vanity. But there is a warmer interest in those greater souls that are born, only one or two

in a generation; for their greatness is great capacity, and that of woe as well as bliss, and of sin
as well as goodness; and then, in their wrestles
with doubt and despair, they can be but little
helped by others. Over one sinner ending his
sinfulness, there is joy in heaven; and there is
more than that over one with whom mortality is
ending, — some greater soul, that has been more
greatly tried, — a man, after all his wrongs, with
a heart of love, and eyes of faith, — and, besides,
who has the peace of God in his mind, and on
his lips words that men are the better for. You
look doubtingly; but it is of yourself that I have
been speaking, Torquato.

TASSO.

Of me! O, of me!

SPIRIT.

Have you never considered what the way of
Providence is with the souls of men, though you
are yourself one of its greater agents? Life is a
lesson from God; but the meaning of it is what
men have to be taught by one another, the child
by its parent, and the young man by his elders.
Nature is God about you. It is a great truth;
but most men see only as much of it as is shown
them. And who are they that show it? The
poets who are raised up from time to time. As,
age after age, men have their understandings en-
larged, there are those born who can speak the

greater thoughts that are wanted, and who, by
saying what they feel themselves, make others
feel more nobly.   These are the interpreters of
God to man ; and some of them have been known
as theologians, and some as philosophers, and
some as poets, and some as prophets.   And,
Torquato, you yourself are one among them.
Yes, among souls, your spiritual estate is become
like a principality and a power.

TASSO.

I become a power among spirits !   Then it is
by suffering I have grown strong.   And God be
thanked I did suffer.   O ye years of agony !   By
you I was set apart from among men ; but it was
for my consecration.   My baptism of fire ! blessed for ever and ever be the season of it !   What !
Do I — Can it be ?   It is.   Yes, it is you, Leonora.   My life, my love !   Your hand, Leonora ; give me your hand.   O, I cannot feel it !
But your presence I do feel ; into my soul I feel
it, — and so strangely, so blessedly !   But why
have not I known you before, though always my
spirit has trembled in me ?   Tell me, dearest Leonora, why have not I known you sooner ?

SPIRIT.

You would not have known me now, but for
your greater faith.   The more God is believed
in, the better his ministers are known.   You have
understood pain and misfortune as having been

sent to you from God ; and so all other messengers are easy for you to recognize. And so it is
that I have been known to you, Torquato, — my
Torquato.

TASSO.

Gone ! She is gone ; and how suddenly !
Gone into heaven she is, for I saw her enter ; and
as she went in, she smiled and pointed with her
hand. And as I looked, I saw spirits standing
together, — cherubim and seraphim, the spirits
of love and of understanding, — and some with
palms in their hands, like martyrs. And there
was one like Dante ; and still his look is thoughtful, but happy also, and like the face of one who
sees into some mystery of God, how joyful it is.
The brightness in which those spirits stood together was like twilight to the infinite splendor
beyond. It was as though they were waiting
there for some soul freshly coming out of this
dark earth. And it was for me perhaps, — O,
perhaps for me ! Come over me, death ! thou
delicious change ! For thou art immortality, and
heaven, and sight of Leonora. Ay, she, — O,
she has gone through this change that is changing
me ! And through her, death is grown sweet ;
for it is to where she is that my spirit is being
drawn. Ah, Leonora ! I do not see her. But
she is in God, and so am I, and my death will be
through God. Yes ! blessed be the God who is

in her, and in me, and in our love for one another! He is in all things, and in death. And so, as the eyes of a believer open, all things grow beautiful, very beautiful, and death becomes divine.

CHAPTER XXXVI.

"O dreary life!" we cry, "O dreary life!"
And still the generations of the birds
Sing through our sighing, and the flocks and herds
Serenely live while we are keeping strife
With Heaven's true purpose in us, as a knife
Against which we may struggle.   Ocean girds
Unslackened the dry land: savannah swards
Unweary sweep: hills watch, unworn; and rife,
Meek leaves drop yearly from the forest-trees,
To show above the unwasted stars that pass
In their old glory.   O thou God of old!
Grant me some smaller grace than comes to these; —
But so much patience as a blade of grass
Grows by, contented, through the heat and cold.

E. B. BROWNING.

AUBIN.

O THIS westerly wind and sunshine!   How the white clouds drive, and the poplar-leaves glance and rustle!   Every breath is health this morning.   So lofty and so blue the sky is, and such fresh thoughts one has in looking up at it. It is poetry and religion to be in the open air to-day; is it not?   It is as though God were abroad.   What am I saying?   As though the Divinity were not omnipresent, and present always and everywhere alike!   I mean, this morning feels as Eden may have felt, when, in the cool of the day, Adam became sensible of the Lord God's presence among the trees.

MARHAM.

It is a very pleasant morning. I looked for you in the garden, Oliver.

AUBIN.

In autumn I do not much like the sight of a garden.

MARHAM.

It is melancholy ; it certainly is.

AUBIN.

The melancholy of the woods I like ; but in the blighted prettiness of a garden there is no promise of a revival. But the woods look so grandly in decay, that it is as though they knew of their being to be green again. So when I saw how the dahlias were blackened with the frost, and how one flower hung its head, and another was dropped on to the ground, I came through the garden, and I have been sitting in the field here and meditating.

MARHAM.

What about ?

AUBIN.

Sit on the bench here, and I will tell you, uncle. But I must remember first, which I do not think I can very well.

MARHAM.

O, you have been dreaming, Oliver ; and pleasantly, I hope.

AUBIN.

No, I have not been dreaming, but only feeling. I have been feeling like a portion of the scene about me, and as though my being were blended with that of the trees and the fields ; so that the leaves fell as though through my spirit ; and it was not as though I heard with my ears the robin sing, but* as though he sung within me. And I felt just as the trees and hedges and grass might feel together, if they could know of their life's subsiding into a wintry pause.

MARHAM.

Yellow, and then naked, and then as green again as ever ! I ought not to have seen this in the woods seventy times, without myself growing old the more cheerfully. It is a day for thinking, this is ; and every autumn, for a few days, it is as though there were a power in the air making us be thoughtful.

AUBIN.

The spirit of the season is on us, and it is as though from every thing about us we were whispered, " Now know yourselves." And a very seasonable warning it is, after the contentment that summer has given us, in health, and warmth, and plenty, and light. Summer would make us self-sufficient ; but autumn says to us, that we are mortal : very mildly she speaks ; but if she is not minded, then the voice of winter is the more terrific, when he comes roaring out of the north. And if a man dies at the coming of winter, he dies the more mournful if he has not talked quietly with the autumn just gone.

MARHAM.

Poor man! But we do not any of us feel as we ought, that here we have no continuing city.

AUBIN.

Except on a day like this.

MARHAM.

Ay, this is an old man's day.

AUBIN.

And an invalid's.

MARHAM.

The leaves are fading about us, and so the more submissively do we ourselves fade as a leaf.

AUBIN.

Yes, our feelings are soothed by nature about us; and then, as soon as they are calmed, they grow hopeful of themselves, and our walk among the dead leaves becomes triumphant, and we say that we know that our Redeemer lives.

MARHAM.

Among the works of God our feelings get soothed, and grow prophetic of immortality; but not so among the works of men, not so in towns. In a town every thing is so noisy and bustling; and it is as though there were not much thought in it fit for an old man to have, and not much feeling about it that he can well share in.

AUBIN.

Yet men grow old in towns, and faster than in the country, perhaps. And in a large city, the clock never strikes twice in the hearing of the same population ; for within the hour, a child has been born and some soul has been taken. O, in the sight of God who sees it all, how the population of a city must be ever changing ! In one home there is a babe just born, and in the next house is stretched the cold length of a corpse. Always there is one generation going, and another coming. So that in a city the inhabitants may be as many as ever, but they are never the same, even for a few hours. Year by year, and hour by hour, the population renews itself ; the son in the place of the father, and youth out of decay. Now, in an aged heart, is there no sympathy with this ? Nay, in this life of a city, ever fresh and strong, is not there something like the immortality of the soul ? is not there what shows how the inward spirit may renew itself through the very perishing of the outward form ? For in some cities, energy, wisdom, frankness, friendliness, and little peculiarities of mind, are the same from age to age, while the men, and the buildings, and the streets, are changing every day.

MARHAM.

Your faith is like an evergreen, for it is always so fresh ; and in the smoke of a city it does not fail, but even there it smells of the country.

AUBIN.

Why, uncle, you are quite figurative.

MARHAM.

Am I, Oliver, am I? Well, then, more exactly, your faith seems to me like ivy, which not
only mantles human homes and keeps them
warm, and makes them beautiful, but which
climbs round old castles, and lives on their walls,
making it seem as though the very stones are
not so dead but that life is to be had out of them.

AUBIN.

Well, uncle, well!

MARHAM.

Ivy is the beauty of old ruins; and your faith
is not unlike it, for it springs up so strongly from
amidst fallen hopes. But just now you said you
did not like the sight of a garden in autumn; why
do not you?

AUBIN.

Because it is only melancholy. For within
the fence of a garden, decay is not wide enough
to be sublime. But in the fields and woods, it is.
There, decay is so vast as to be grand. And
at any sublime sight, the soul feels herself immortal. For whether purely, or justly, or kindly, or
devoutly, the more we feel, the more certainly
immortal we feel. And in such experiences
there is what is worth regard, ay, and thanksgiving, — special thanks to God. For often our

holiest efforts are discouraged ; and while making some of our loftiest attempts, it is as though we were spoken to by God ; and as though he said to us, " Fear not ; for it is into my bosom you are striving ; be nothing chilled." And then, for a few moments, there is the warmth of immortality about our souls.

MARHAM.

So that we feel best what we are to be, when we are what we ought to be. A gust of wind ! Down come the leaves !

> Like leaves on trees the race of man is found,
> Now green in youth, now withering on the ground.
> So generations in their course decay,
> So perish these, when those have passed away.

And long, long ago perished Homer and his listeners.

AUBIN.

Perished ? Not he ! For, to our knowledge, the very words of his mouth are living. And his Iliad is brotherhood for Homer with men of all nations and times.

MARHAM.

Ay, and with ourselves. The leaves fall about us just as he heard them fall ; and the same thoughts come into our minds as did into his with the sound ; and we think how, from the tree of life, human existences are for ever being loosened and shed like leaves.

AUBIN.

How the air smells of dead leaves! Decay, decay, everywhere decay! All things, everywhere, look exhausted. So that to-day feels like a day out of some Greek Olympiad, or as though it had been kept for us out of some Egyptian cycle, or Chaldean year. For all things do feel so old!

MARHAM.

To you, do they, Oliver? It is the melancholy of the season, and the reverie that comes of the warm, still day. You had been sitting here some time when I found you. What had you been thinking of? Your thoughts were ——

AUBIN.

They were with the men of old time, with the population of Nineveh and Babylon, and the builders of the Pyramids, and the dwellers of Enoch, the first city. I have been thinking how this earth has been sailed upon by the Phœnicians, been travelled about by Abraham and his camels, been traversed and fought on by Roman armies, been swept over by Goths and Huns from the North, and always from east to west been the pathway of civilization.

MARHAM.

It is a curious thought, what this earth has been in different ages of it, — the pasture-ground of the patriarchs, the quarry of Egyptian builders, and the battle-field of the Romans.

AUBIN.

Once this earth was the floor of the bridal bower of Adam and Eve, and many nights 'that was all it was to all mankind. But now it is the cornfield, and the meadow, and the garden, and the hearth of many million families. And it is become besides the graveyard of nations. Graveyard, did I say? Well, so it is; and it is the birthplace of souls as well.

MARHAM.

So it is; so it is! Yes, it is! I am wondering what it is, Oliver, that makes what you say be so very persuasive of an hereafter. I cannot tell whether it is your voice, or what it is.

AUBIN.

Uncle, we will thank God that — But come how it may — Dear uncle, what I mean is, that into a mind not superstitious, whatever way faith comes, it cannot but come rightly. And I would say this; that there is a state of mind — and I think it is a reasonable and a right state of mind — in which nearly every human circumstance is suggestive of immortality, — even those matters, I mean, that are thought the gloomiest. And so the universality of death is to me the certainty of life after it.

MARHAM.

But from some poets one might learn that the uniformity of death is the frightfulness of it.

AUBIN.

Ay, death makes no exceptions. Righteousness is cut down uncrowned; honesty perishes without having proved the best policy; men that called on God die unanswered; and many a disciple dies, with many a Christian promise not kept to him. Now these are the things that make existence feel unfinished at death. And so it is that many things that are untoward in this life point toward another.

MARHAM.

They do; so they do. Down come the leaves again! O, what a shower of them!

AUBIN.

And so, because we men fall like them, we cannot rot like them. Good men die as early as the bad; and if one bad man dies the sooner for his vice, there is a good man dies the earlier for his virtue, for his self-denial, and his poverty; for poverty is not the less killing for having been nobly incurred. Good and bad look alike in death, and so death itself cannot be what it looks.

MARHAM.

If death makes good and bad be alike, then it is only a seeming, or else for a very little while; that is your meaning, is not it?

AUBIN.

Death is not what it looks; cannot be and must not be believed so.

MARHAM.

Cannot be and must not be ! And saying so, do we know what we do say ? Because death is God's càusing. And as regards Providence, what must or must not be is not 'for man to say.

AUBIN.

Out of his self-will it is not. As to death, man cannot speak out of his own knowledge ; but he can and may out of the spirit of God. For in good men, the Spirit itself does bear witness with their spirits.

MARHAM.

In the saints of God it does.

AUBIN.

And in all disciples, according as they are more or less Christian. In yourself, uncle, there is the witness of the Spirit : there is, I know, for sometimes I hear it speaking in your voice. Uncle, there are persons dead, about whom I have feelings which I dare not distrust. Once I was in the death-chamber of a sufferer for righteousness' sake, — a man that had died in his virtue. My feelings were of awe and triumph ; and while in the room, every breath was like inspiration in me, and I said, " I know that his Redeemer liveth."

MARHAM.

A friend of yours, was not he ?

AUBIN.

Yes, uncle. The day he was buried was just

such a day as this. He was buried under an
elm-tree, and the leaves fell on to the coffin and
into the grave softly, and so fast! It was as
though nature were grieving over him. And,
indeed, he was a man whose love the very trees
might miss. For in his eyes they were more than
wood and leaves; and what Moses saw in one
bush, he saw something of in every forest and
shrub. And for him, there was not a tree but
had burning in it the presence of God.

MARHAM.

That manner of sight I should be sure he had
from you. A good man, a very good man, he
was; so I have heard you say.

AUBIN.

And so he was: and he died in his goodness,
and almost through it. And at his grave-side,
my thoughts asked, "Why was this? for cannot
goodness be so good as that none should be the
worse for it any way?" There was no answer
made me but silence; though for a thinker that is
enough. And as I turned away from the grave,
there was in me what was like the Divine voice
asking, "About what I am designing to do with
you mortals, why art thou doubtful? for hast thou
not known me?" And then I said to myself,
"Ay, why at all do I doubt God? For justice
and goodness in me are his inspiration, and they
prophesy of what his Providence will do. Yes,

and God will be better than my goodness, and so
my friend will prove happier than my hopes."
And so I grew cheerful, and left him

. Where his fathers sleep in their hillocks green.

A beautiful line, is not it? It is the Swedish
Tegner's.

MARHAM.

And you have no exception to make to it;
have not you? I have none myself. But always
you will have it, that the real man is what no
graveyard ever gets; for you so earnestly distin-
guish between body and soul. But, indeed, it is
a very forcible line, and you may well like it.

AUBIN.

It makes one feel as though in the grave there
were sleepers, but not dead bodies; and as though
the earth were warm about them, and conscious
of having them lie in her bosom.

MARHAM.

Mother-earth! That fond phrase of the
Greeks! Mother-earth!

AUBIN.

Ay! and cannot one imagine her crying to the
Father of spirits, for pity on the dead bodies in
her bosom, — children that have lost their breath,
but her children still? And now if such a voice
from earth to heaven could reasonably be, then
always it is as though it really were crying. And

there is in the mind of God the feeling that such a cry would make ; for God not only answers prayer, but anticipates it. So that, from among her sister planets, whatever this earth could rightly pray for for her children, already God is granting them, or else he is intending.

MARHAM.

My prayer is pure ; O earth, cover not thou my blood ! — So Job says, and then begs the earth not to silence his cry. In thè Scriptures there are many passages which are as though the earth could think and feel.

AUBIN.

And as though she could speak. And, O, if she could, if she could ! And if she did, for all the sufferers in her ! If only men's sighs lived on the air, we could not bear the sound. But it is as though God did hear what man would not bear to hear ; for to his nature it is possible, and to his almightiness it would be endurable, and in the ear of his foreknowledge it would be a sublime sound : for as he listens from everlasting to everlasting, it is as though voices that are anguish one moment are crying aloud with all angels the next. But, indeed, with God, past, present, and future are one ; and to his eyes, in the sowing of tears, there is ripe at once the golden harvest of joy.

MARHAM.

Ay, we will think of what our destiny looks to God ; and that shall comfort us.

AUBIN.

It ought to. And then we are members of a family. And so we will think what the human race must be in the eyes of God, — dying, dying, dying everywhere, — spirits that have called upon him, souls that have talked with him, men that have felt themselves his children. And in death do they all dissipate into nothing ? About this earth are stretched the arms of God ; and as he clasps it to himself, is it only an urn filling with human dust ? O, no ! God is infinite, and there must be infinity in every purpose of his ; and man is the only creature through whom that infinity can be answered in this world. A world made for nothing ! That is not to be thought of. And made for nothing it will have been, without man is immortal. In all probability, and in all certainty, this earth will perish, and so will every daisy, and oak-tree, and animal, and bird, and fish ; and all will be as though this world had never been, unless there is a survivorship of souls.

MARHAM.

And that there will be. Blessed be God !

AUBIN.

Ay, and through our souls, through what we have had to do with it, through what it has been to us, through our memories, the earth itself is eternal, and so, again, has not been made in vain. Either this world is a folly, or man is immortal. Man's future life is the wisdom of the universe; and so doubt it we must not, and we cannot.

MARHAM.

Oliver, dear Oliver, your words are too positive. I do not mean that they are not most blessedly true. But perhaps, as to what the Divine purpose in the world must be, we should not be confident, but only confidently trustful.

AUBIN.

Uncle, you are right. Still it is pleasant, — the way in which the end of the world points on to the immortality of man.

MARHAM.

So it is.

AUBIN.

So as for herself not to have been made in vain, the earth asks another life for men, and one to outlast her own.

MARHAM.

And it is theirs; for it is promised them.

AUBIN.

So many things are such witnesses of human immortality; even sin is, and in letters that are like red iron in the dark. Often into a sinner there is burnt what convinces him that his soul may be changed, but can never, never die.

MARHAM.

Awful, very awful proof of an hereafter! and yet most of us can guess at it, out of our own experience.

AUBIN.

So we can. In the very abasement of our nature, we are consciously immortal, and so we are in our highest moods.

MARHAM.

But in them we may be deceived; for they are our proudest.

AUBIN.

I was thinking of those only that are our purest.

MARHAM.

Right. And it is certain that, whether visible or not, all souls must have in them foretokens of their infinite continuance.

AUBIN.

Especially towards death; some souls, as it were, plainly going home, in going out of this world. And there are some who die, and are followed by their works, and not only by them, but by their righteous sufferings, — witnesses that cry aloud, along with the souls of the martyrs under the altar, "How long, O Lord, holy and true, dost thou not judge?" But judgment there will be, and the day of it is appointed; so we can be patient, and be earnest in getting ready for it.

MARHAM.

Oliver, what are those verses you repeated last night, when looking out of the window?

AUBIN.

What I remember of a translation from Uhland. They are expressive of impatience for death; and yet I like them. They are what an old man might well say, looking up at the stars on an autumu night, with the leaves falling about him.

> O golden legends writ in the skies!
>   I turn towards you with longing soul,
> And list to the awful harmonies
>   Of the spheres, as on they roll.
>
> O blessed rest! O royal night!
>   Wherefore seemeth the time so long,
> Till I see yon stars in their fullest light,
>   And list to their loudest song.

In the day we do not see the stars, but night brings us in sight of them; and that night of nights, the night of death, will carry us up to them, and through them, and beyond them, and into the bosom of the Father, as we may well believe.

MARHAM.

Amen! amen!

CHAPTER XXXVII.

And is this all that man can claim ?
Is this our longing's final aim ?
To be like all things round, — no more
Than pebbles cast on Time's gray shore ?

Can man no' more than beast aspire
To know his being's awful Sire ?
And, born and lost on Nature's breast,
No blessing seek but there to rest ?

JOHN STERLING.

MARHAM.

I HAVE been reading at the window here, and I think, Oliver, in two books at once, perhaps. For my eyes have been straying, now and then, from this book of grace to the book of nature, outside. And, Oliver, I have been thinking, that it is only from my reading in the Scriptures that I find myself encouraged to draw nigh to God. In the book of nature there is little I can read to encourage me ; or I should rather say, perhaps, there is very little encouragement there which I can read of myself. For I cannot doubt that to Jesus all nature was like the smile of God ; and to the Psalmist it would appear, sometimes, to have been like God become plain about them. But they are only the true children of God, on whom nature does not frown as' well as smile.

29

There have been times when almost I could have wondered, that, with the heavens to spread himself through, God should care about having a human heart for his temple. Oliver, I cannot wonder that some men have felt their own nothingness so painfully, as to have had misgivings too strong for their faith sometimes. The nothingness of man before the vastness of nature, — it is only a wise faith that can bear it, with the weight with which it sometimes weighs on some minds. And there has been an unbelief, which has justified itself by asking scornfully what David would have asked with mingled feelings of humbleness, awe, and trust, — What is man, any man, that God should regard him, while there are stars shining in the heavens, and while there are the sun and moon of his making?

AUBIN.

Uncle, the stars do not glorify God, except through the mind of man. The sun and moon praise God only with such rays as can enter the temple of a man's soul.

MARHAM.

I do not understand you, Oliver; at least, I think I do not.

AUBIN.

There is no such thing as sound, outside of the ear. A noise is made by the air being made to vibrate; but the vibrations of the air become sound only by their striking on the drum of the ear.

MARHAM.

Yes ; that is so, I suppose.

AUBIN.

And not in a bird's or a dog's, but only in a man's ear, is Handel's Messiah the sublime music which it is.

MARHAM.

Well, that is true.

AUBIN.

And now what was the world before it could shape itself in the intelligent mind of man ? And before there was any ear at all, what was the world, all round ? what else but silence ? Brooks ran on noiseless beds, and rivers went over noiseless falls, and seas ebbed and flowed in silence. Breezes played without a whisper ; and winds, high winds, blew over plains and through forests, and not a sound did they make. The world was a silent world, before the ear was made for hearing. And over the earth there was no beauty, till the human eye opened on it.

MARHAM.

Do you mean, in the same way as music is not music, except in a human ear ?

AUBIN.

Yes, and for the same reason as the world was a silent world before the ear was fashioned for the air to vibrate on. And in this way it is only through man that the stars glorify God. The sun and moon praise God through me. My soul is the priest that nature worships through. The mountains are dumb, till what feelings they make in me speak out. The valleys rejoice before God, only through what joy they make me glad with. And the roar of the sea is a deep-toned anthem, only while my soul is like a temple for it to sound through.

MARHAM.

Yes ! now I understand you.

AUBIN.

The mountains are high, but they are not to belittle me : and they are to humble me, only the same wholesome way by which, myself, I feel all the lowlier for my own high thoughts. Nor are the stars to discourage me with their splendor ; as though, in their brightness, I could be minded of God only a little. For glorious as they are, they glorify God only by the thoughts they make me think of him. And it is by their rays entering into my worship that the sun and moon praise God. Day and night, in forests, and in the depths of the sea, over plains, on the sides of mountains, and up the regions of the air, God sees hŏw good are all things of his making. But it is in the temple of man's soul, that he listens for how they worship him.

MARHAM.

And to the door of that temple comes the Holy
Spirit, too, at frequent seasons. A high thought,
Oliver, and yet not a proud one·! For it is very
sad, and it is awful to think, how there are
souls God listens for praises in, while worship in
them there is none; how, as temples, they are
foul with sin, and dark with ignorance, and are
profaned, day and night, with the hateful voice of
folly speaking in them, and with the riot of the
passions.

AUBIN.

O, like the sacred quiet of a church is the
peace which nature would make in the soul at
times! Out of woods and off lakes, and from
over fields and meadows, there are thoughts,
which might come into a man's mind, bright as
angels out of heaven. Yes, and for all men there
are high seasons, when influences from nature
might enter the soul and make in it a holy presence like that of angels met together, and a feeling of praise sublime and various, like that of
assembled multitudes, and a fervency of love to
God, that knows him draw nigh, O, so nigh to
the soul it is in! And now this worship, — if
there is none in the soul, because it is wicked,
then what a fearful thing its wickedness is! Only
through my mind can things round me glorify
God ; and how dreadful a matter it is, if my mind

is so that it hardens itself against tender influences, and shuts itself against devout thoughts !

MARHAM.

It is ; it is very dreadful. Of earth and water, of day and night, of the four seasons, of the sun and moon and stars, — of all these in their worship I am a priest unto God. And if I am unholy, if I am a faithless priest, then my sin, — my sin, — it is as wide as the world, and it reaches to the sky. But what is this which I am saying ? Sin is against God. And this is all awful considerations in one.

AUBIN.

So it is. Yet, uncle, as you say, it is a dreadful thought, — that of a man's so imbruting in heart, as to become insensible to the atmosphere of worship he is living in.

MARHAM.

Ah, Oliver, too much it is as though the world were only for our waking and sleeping in ; as though the earth existed only for us to gather, and store, and eat the fruits of it.

AUBIN.

While really there are uses of it, which are not accomplished in our stomachs.

MARHAM.

Nor in our purses, Oliver, nor in the fleshly mind.

AUBIN.

Nor altogether and at once in even the holiest soul. For the uses of the world will be unending.

MARHAM.

And so not a moment of our lives, nor one circumstance of them, is in vain. And this is great comfort to know of. What hours I spent at school still last on in my mind. What books I read many years ago still teach me, in some secret way. And my inclinations now bend the way they do, from my resolutions of many years ago. And as you said one day, Oliver, so it is. There is an eternal purpose in the world, which gets answered in us ourselves, — in the gratitude to God, which autumn strengthens in us ; in the reverence of the Creator, which sun, moon, and stars make in us ; in the awe, with which mortality pervades us ; and in the beauty, with which fair scenes imbue our souls.

AUBIN.

My thought, uncle ; and you remember it as being so ! But the good expression of it, uncle, is your own, certainly. And it is as though the thought were fresh to me. But, uncle, I was meaning to say, that I think there are other uses of the world to us than we know of. I think it is likely there are uses to us of the world that now is, which will begin to be felt, first one and then another, only in the world that is to come.

MARHAM.

Oliver, I am not sure that I understand you quite as clearly as I do commonly.

AUBIN.

Hereafter there will be uses of this world which will begin in us, through our memories. I think there is no day so poor, but it is enriching me for ever. Hereafter it will prove, perhaps, that often, and in the simplest way, great wonders are entering my mind without my knowing of them.

MARHAM.

I think, Oliver, you can explain your thought a little more clearly.

AUBIN.

For the world about us, we shall be the better in more ways than we know of. Of the sounds we hear, and the objects we see, and of the matters that happen to us, even the commonest, more will come than we suppose. Winter and summer, whether I am well or ill, of every day I live, there is an everlasting result in me; and so there is of every action I do; and so there is of every sensation I have, as I think. And I have so many thousand sensations in a day, and so many million in a year! And never is one of them over for ever, as I think. Possibly I may feel them all over again; and certainly there will be a something of them last on in me, for ever and ever. They will be a fountain of thought and feeling in me, for ages.

MARHAM.

Yes ; matters that are nothing to us now may be very wonderful to us as spirits.

AUBIN.

A rock may be itself but a mass of sandy grains, and yet be the fountain of a stream, bright to look at, and sweet to drink, and a hundred miles long in its course, and green and flowery all along its banks. And from the recollections growing in us, there is to be a stream of profit, I have no doubt. As a child, the feeling I had for my father was the beginning of what I felt towards God. And there is many a feeling made in us now by strangers to us, by our benefactors, and by our friends and relatives, that will hereafter and in infinity be the beginnings of new, and dear, and sublime emotions in us. And all objects about us are turning to spiritual seed in our minds, with our hearing and seeing them.

MARHAM.

And God makes the good soil of the human mind be infinitely and very variously fruitful. What seed is sown in it now will grow to a glorious harvest hereafter, underneath the new heavens.

AUBIN.

In some age or other, I shall say of some heavenly marvel, perhaps, " It is wonderful, wonderful ! And yet in the earth it was hinted to me, by the tones of the wind, and the way the clouds went over my head." I think, perhaps every sight in the world that now is may avail us in the world that is to come. On the golden floor of heaven, it may be the better for me that I have noticed even the worm's way in and out of the earth. It may be that some of our little observations now will open into wonderful knowledge hereafter. A plant comes out of the ground a little bud. It opens and grows, and blossoms, and seeds, and then dies. Now, there is much more in this than I know of yet ; much, very much more. Yes, yes ! If I knew all that is to be learned from a daisy even, I should be less of a stranger to God than I am. But I shall know it some time. All about me, tree unto tree is uttering speech, and flower unto flower is showing knowledge. But it is in a language that I do not well understand; but which I shall remember ; and so which I shall learn the whole meaning of hereafter.

MARHAM.

See, Oliver ! Look at yonder rose-bush, and see the flowers under it. Flowers, sweet flowers !

AUBIN.

Gentle words they are, that come out of the earth ; and they tell us, out of the depths, the same thing the stars witness from the heights above, that everywhere life is beautiful. Flowers are pretty to look at now ; but hereafter they will be recollections, that will blossom in us again, and turn to seeds of new thought. For, as I think, there is nothing I have ever seen or heard which I shall not remember, — not a gnat in the sunshine, nor a water-fly on a pool, nor a swallow in the air. I have wondered over a little bird coming out of an egg-shell for a little life of four or five years, and over a sparrow as having been created to become the prey of some hawk, and over the way of a snail, as being made instinctive for it, and over the waking of a torpid worm in spring. Now, some time or other, these wonderings of mine will turn to strange, unearthly knowledge, and be the beginnings of fresh ways of feeling in me, and even perhaps of worship.

MARHAM.

Yes, in our memories, there is more storing up than we can tell. And God is so wonderful, that what is nothing as a sight, or an event, may prove very precious as a recollection, Oliver. As you have been saying, yourself.

AUBIN.

Sometimes I remember little matters of ten and twenty years ago, how I plucked a flower somewhere, or how I heard a bird sing, or how I had a person speak to me. Perhaps I have not remembered these things once before; yet the recollections of them come into my mind quite perfect; and trivial as they are, and because they are so trivial, they are awful almost. For I cannot help feeling that, strange as this memory is, the purpose of it must be stranger still. The other day I recollected something, not only the action itself, and exactly how I did it, but how the air felt the while, the way the sun shone, and a hay-field smelled, how two or three trees stood, and how a foxglove looked that was nigh me. What thousands and millions of recollections there must be in us! And every now and then one of them becomes known to us; and it shows us what spiritual depths are growing in us, what mines of memory.

MARHAM.

Even our idle words, whatever they may be, will have to be accounted for in the day of judgment. So, it is very likely, there are lasting on in our memories all the sights we have ever seen, the actions we have ever done, the thoughts we have ever had, the words we have ever heard, the books we have ever read, and the prayers that ever we have prayed.

AUBIN.

And, uncle, to the soul, all these recollections will be of use, some time or other, but in what way, and to what strange purpose, we cannot tell, nor even guess. And no wonder! For in their earliest days, what did the dwellers of the earth know of what uses were under the soil ? Nor would they have guessed them, even had they been shown what beds of clay, sand, stone, and coal were down under the green turf. They never would have thought of there being beautiful and comfortable dwellings to be shaped out of clay and stone; nor would they ever have thought of there being heat and light in a black mineral. And so, perhaps, even in our darker recollections, there will prove hereafter to be some pure and bright use ; and in the millions and millions of remembrances we are getting, there are strange joys preparing in us, and new manifestations of the understanding.

MARHAM.

And now, Oliver, I understand you. The more I think of life, the more wonderful it feels. But it is with God and immortality, it is wonderful.

AUBIN.

A plant draws earth and water into itself, and

so blossoms. And out of this world our human nature is drawing to itself millions of experiences ; while it is above, in heaven, that it will flower.

CHAPTER XXXVIII.

Two worlds are ours; 't is only sin
   Forbids us to descry,
The mystic heaven and earth within,
   Plain as the sea and sky.

Thou who hast given me eyes to see
   And love this sight so fair,
Give me a heart to find out Thee,
   And read Thee everywhere. — KEBLE.

MARHAM.

A FINE evening, Oliver ; clear and bright is it ?
I am glad of it. And now again it is evening ;
indeed, it is night ; night again ! A little while
ago I was not ; a very little while more and again
I shall not be. In history a lifetime is a mere
handbreadth, and before God it is as nothing. In
the past, any age of it, where was I ? Where was
I when Abraham departed out of Haran ? Where
was I while young Plato listened to Socrates, and
while the book of Ecclesiasticus was being med-
itated ? and when Britain was first heard of at
Rome, as an island beyond Gallia ? And in the
year nineteen hundred where shall I be in this
world ? Where shall I be when the great men of
the future shall talk together ; and when they have
been founded and have risen, — those better insti-

tutions, that are to be ? Ah, those stars ! they will be shining on, after I myself have been vanished hence, long, long. Time lasts on, and on, and on. In its course the patriarchs went down ; so did the prophet Samuel, so did Babylon and Nineveh, so did Pericles and the other famous men of Athens, so did Julius Cæsar, so did Rome, so did King Alfred, so did our fathers, so have all men done, so are we doing, and so all men will do.

AUBIN.

We are born and we draw a breath ; some a longer, some a shorter breath. We are born, we draw just a breath, and then we die.

MARHAM.

The stars ! They shine on us, they shone in the past. They shone on David, and made him wonder ; and they shone on a woman he knew well, on Rizpah, as she sat, by night as well as day, all harvest-time, watching by seven dead bodies. Those stars shone on Rizpah, as she sat in sackcloth on a rock, with dead bodies nigh her. And now they shine on the bare rock. But they do shine still. Still those stars shine as they ever did. O, what a strange, strange feeling this makes in me !

AUBIN.

It is the immortal instinct of our nature conscious of a misgiving. It is the same as when

we feel ourselves mortal, knowing the while of
our immortality.

MARHAM.

With some poets, it would seem to have been
as though their hearts had failed them at sight of
the stars.

AUBIN.

The stars are not meant to wither us with their
rays, but only to make us feel what a nothing our
duration is to theirs, — what a nothing our bodily
life is. · And thus it is only spiritual life we can
think of as being life at all.

MARHAM.

Yes, Oliver, it is only the life of the soul that
is life at all.

AUBIN.

And then how does life feel evanescent? to
what faculty is it so? This life is fleeting, sadly
short to our feelings, — to the feeling of the infinite, to the instinct of immortality, that is in us.
Ah, then, there is, — there is in us an instinct of
an hereafter.

MARHAM.

With a few words of faith, how the weak soul
gets refreshed, as though with a breath of heavenly air! Oliver, I think the world does not look
the same to us that it did to the heathen. Nor
can it now look the same to believers and to un-
believers. For when a man is in Christ, the eyes

of his understanding are opened in another manner than is known to one without Christ in the
world. And, Oliver, I must not forget our conversation this afternoon ; and, indeed, I am not
likely to do so soon.

AUBIN.

Uncle, you will excuse me ; but I was a little
surprised, — no, not surprised, at what you were
saying just now. But the strain of what you said
was new to me from you, uncle.

MARHAM.

Why, to tell the truth, I have just now been
musing over a chart of history, and talking with
myself not wisely. The stars ! See them !
They are aloft in their places, so calm, so still,
so pure ! The noises of this earth do not reach
up one mile towards them. A little way from the
surface of it, this earth is bounded all round with
silence. Our clamors are all shut in upon ourselves.

AUBIN.

How we triumph and murmur, and laugh and
cry, here ! And all about objects that are so little judged of from on high. Patience, quiet, is
what is preached to us from the stars. Our cries
do not reach them, but their speech does extend
to us. Their rays reach us. And what is the
feeling they make in us ? It is calm and solemn ;
and always it is the same. Though a man does

not feel it, when he is fretful or angry. But let him cease from earthly anxieties, and then he will hear the language of the stars. At times the Son of God had not where to lay his head in this earth ; but he did not therefore believe himself the less heavenly. And let a man feel the quiet of the stars, their great and sublime calm ; then let him think of their solemn calm as being what his own soul calms with, and he will feel himself so highly related, that he will not mind much what house or what circumstances he has to live in here for a little while.

MARHAM.

Your understanding of what the stars say is quite as true as what I was saying just now, and far better to believe. Yet, Oliver, it is a strange, solemn consideration, that we must die, and those stars continue shining on for ages, and for long, long ages, perhaps. ,

AUBIN.

And what of that ? Many a clock will outlast me for years, and perhaps for centuries ; and it will tell the hours, when myself I shall be told of, on earth, no more. They will shine on my grave, — the stars will ; but me myself they will not out- last. Sun, moon, and stars are the marvellous clockwork by which time has been indicated for me, and will continue to be. For the time of my death there is a look the sky will have, though I do not know what. But perhaps the sky will be blue, and with the sun quite bright in it; or it will be cloudy, perhaps; or, perhaps, all golden in the west; or perhaps starry, the whole round of it. And if I am to die while the stars are shining, then there is a way getting ready, which they will all be standing in the while; perhaps with one planet in the east, and another in the west, and a certain constellation at the zenith. And when every star has found his place, then I shall ascend into mine.

MARHAM.

Going up from belief in God to the sight of him! I think, Oliver, that perhaps God will be seen hereafter, through those same faculties by which now we believe in him.

AUBIN.

Myself I quite think so, uncle. And in the same way I think that there are many of the experiences of common life which will turn hereafter to immortal uses.

MARHAM.

As you made me understand so well this afternoon. In this world we live for the next, and in the next we shall be the better for having lived in this. Somehow, in the believing soul, the ends of the world that now is lengthen on into the beginnings of the world that is to come. Christ is in heaven, at the right hand of God, and he is in our hearts the hope of glory. We live mortal lives for immortal good. And this is such a world, and really it is so mysterious, that there is not one of its commonest ways but perhaps is sublimer to walk on than we at all think.

AUBIN.

At night, when we walk about and see at all, it is by the light of other worlds. Though we do not often think of this. And it is the same in life. There is many a matter concerning us that is little thought of, but yet which is ours, as it were, from out of the infinite. Yes, our lives are to be felt as being very great even in their nothingness.

MARHAM.

And as you say, Oliver, they feel so mortal to us because ourselves we are not mortal at all, but immortal.

AUBIN.

Yes, and rightly thought of ; even our mortal lives are as wonderful as immortality. Is the next life a mystery ? So it is ; but then how mysterious even now life is. Food is not all that a man lives by. There is some way by which food has to turn to strength in him ; and that way is something else than his own will. I am hungry, I sit down to a meal, and I enjoy it. And the next day, from what I ate and drank for my pleasure, there is blood in my veins, and moisture on my skin, and new flesh making in all my limbs. And this is not my doing or willing. For I do not even know how my nails grow from under the skin of my fingers. I can well believe in my being to live hereafter ; how, indeed, I am to live I do not know ; but, then, neither do I know how I do live now. When I am asleep, my lungs keep breathing, my heart keeps beating, my stomach keeps digesting, and my whole body keeps making anew. And in the morning, when I look in the glass, it is as though I see myself a new creature ; and really, for the wonder of it, it is all the same as though another body had grown about me in my sleep. This living from day to day is astonishing when it is thought of ; and we are let feel the miracle of it, so, perhaps, that our being to live again may not be too wonderful for our belief.

MARHAM.

Yes, I think it may be so, Oliver. Myself, I have thought that I have believed the better in the life to come, for feeling how mysterious is the life that now is.

AUBIN.

Almost any right feeling about this present life helps to rectify our feelings about the future life. All our best moods feel immortal. Does ever a brave man lay down his life, and feel it merely a mortal one ? I think not. For the good soul in

him will not let itself be thought of so. A heart
has only to be noble, and of itself it will fill with
faith. No martyr ever went the way of duty and
felt the shadow of death upon it. The shadow
of death is darkest in the valley, which men walk
in easily, and is never felt at all on a steep place,
like Calvary. Truth is everlasting, and so is
every lover of it ; and so he feels himself almost
always. " To die is nothing to being false. I
feel death like nothing at all ; and so it is nothing
in itself most likely." In battle, let it be for his
country that a man stands up ; and his brave,
noble soul makes him feel that there is in him
a life, that is no more to be touched by can-
non-balls than God is, or than the kingdom of
heaven is.

MARHAM.

Let us love God, and then of our being to live
on in him we shall not doubt. It is our love of
God that is the soul, the strength, of our faith in an
hereafter. There are so many things that would
seem against us and not for us, only that we love
God ! So very many painful things !

AUBIN.

Darkness is of use as well as daylight ; and so
are the doubts that cloud our minds as well as the
certainties that light them up. So many thousand
things about us are painful to look at and know
of ! But what sadness they cause in us is good

for us, and is a feeling which it is wholesome for us to walk about in for a while.

MARHAM.

I think, Oliver, that the more one feels what this world is precisely, the surer one is of its being to be explained in a way not known of yet, — a way that will justify want and agony even to goodness itself. And thus so many objects about us, that are sad to look at now, will turn in the future to recollections wonderful, and perhaps blessed, as you said this afternoon. Yes, Oliver, to the eyes of faith how all things change, and sad things look solemn, and dark things look brightening, and bright things look brighter! And then, too, there are times, not those of our most virtuous moods certainly, when our best thoughts feel empty, and when events move us only to despair.

AUBIN.

Just as a house is a home only to what domestic feeling is in a man, so very largely this world is God's world only to what godly feelings are in us. And it is only to my Christian feeling that the world feels ——

MARHAM.

What inspires you with courage, and hope, and trust ?

AUBIN.

Yes, uncle. There have been times when to

me nature has been meaningless ; and there have
been men to whom it has been disheartening.
And well I remember the time at which nature
began in my eyes to grow good with the goodness of God. It was like as when a white cloud
grows golden with the rising sun. And now to
my trustful, Christian heart, nature is so that
whatever is in harmony with it I can be well contented to become, even though it might possibly
prove to be nothing. In many a beautiful scene,
on a summer's day, it is as though it were said to
me, " Feel now how blessed are the Divine
hands, into which it will be thine sometime to
commend thy spirit." And now, to-night, is not
it as though God had darkened the world for me
to feel him the better in it ? And what are those
stars but the thousand eyes of God's love watching me ? And the soft west wind, — is it not
what my soul might well go forth upon calmly and
hopefully ?

MARHAM.

The life of all things else is our life.

AUBIN.

And what the sun rises in and sets in, our souls
may well be trusted to last on in. The morrow
of the world is a purpose in the mind of God,
and so is the great to-morrow of my soul. And
I can be well contented to have my life subside
on the bosom of him in whom the day died away

this evening so beautifully, and in whom it will begin again in the morning so grandly.

MARHAM.

Almost all things encourage the faith of a thoughtful and believing mind. It is easy to believe that the souls of the righteous will shine on through death, since they have, for the life of their lives, that God in whom sun and moon and stars last on through change, and eclipse, and ages.

AUBIN.

My soul will live on in God, through death, like a thought that lasts on in the mind through sleep, and forgetfulness, and threescore years and ten perhaps.

MARHAM.

Yes, I live in God, and shall eternally. It is his hand upholds me now ; and death will be but an uplifting of me into his bosom.

CHAPTER XXXIX.

And may it not be hoped, that, placed by age
In like removal, tranquil though severe,
We are not so removed for utter loss,
But for some favor, suited to our need?
What more than that the severing should confer
Fresh power to commune with the invisible world,
And hear the mighty stream of tendency
Uttering, for elevation of our thought,
A clear, sonorous voice, inaudible
To the vast multitude, whose doom it is
To run the giddy round of vain delight,
Or fret and labor on the plain below?

WORDSWORTH.

MARHAM.

VERY much I like it. But I am another man than I was when I was there thirty years ago. And the people there are almost all other than I used to know. The land slopes as it used to do, upwards to the brow of a hill, and down towards a brook. The brook runs on, stony at the bottom in one place, and gravelly in another; and the grass alongside it is long and green, and with flowers in it. Prettily grow the foxglove and the water-lily. And all day long, while the daisies are looking up at the sun, the brook flows on, and here and there it gurgles; and so it does in the dark, all the night through, and while

the daisies are shut. The water runs there, and
the grass grows there, and the flowers blossom
there, and smell there ; and the sun shines there,
and midnight is dark there, and there all things
are as they used to be. Only the men that were
there once are not there now.

AUBIN.

And how did you feel ? You had old thoughts
come back to you, and old feelings. How did
life feel to you there ?

MARHAM.

Oliver, it felt to me there what it does to me
too often, perhaps. What is it to live ? It is
to grow older. It is to have more pain, or else
more fear of pain. It is to have some friends
grow cold, and others die. It is to learn more
and more reasons, every year, for being willing
to die.

AUBIN.

So it is ; and not lamentably so either. For
to live thoughtfully is to advance in life, and feel
ourselves being laid hold of by the powers of
the world to come.

MARHAM.

A grand phrase is that of St. Paul's.

AUBIN.

So it is. And, uncle, did not you feel more
faith, as well as more resignation, when you found
yourself an old man, where you used to live as
a youth ?

MARHAM.

I hope, I trust, I did feel myself better persuaded of an hereafter than I was when I was a
young man. But I cannot be sure how far the
peace I felt there was that of the spirit, and not
merely that of the fineness of the day.

AUBIN.

Worthy of trust though ; however it may have
been made in you, I think.

MARHAM.

'Perhaps so. For I think there is a religiousness 'in the calm of a beautiful day, and that it
is what an irreligious man has no feeling of.

AUBIN.

A fine day is universal harmony. There is
nothing out of place with the sunshine on it,
and hardly any thing even of man's making but
seems to stand right. And in the soft, warm,
still air, all sounds are musical ; the screams and
calls of children, the crowing of the cock, 'the
singing of the lark, the chattering of the jay, the
ring of the anvil as the smith works at 'it, 'the
lowing of the cows in the meadow, and the caw-
ing of the rooks high up in the air, the song of
the 'wren in the hedge, 'the bark of the dog by
his kennel, and the rattle on the distant railway.
I have been in what I thought was an altogether
ugly neighbourhood. But there came a fine day ;
and it was just as though it were said to me,

" See now how easily beautiful all things are."
And so when we feel ourselves immortal, then
all things round us are right, stormy weather as
well as spring-time, people that cannot understand us as well as those that do, hard things
as well as pleasant things, sweet women and
resolute men, children in their innocence, and
bad men in their badness, as far at least as their
badness is our trial.

MARHAM.

How is it, Oliver, that sometimes in misfortune an old man will sorrow more than he did
in his youth, and yet his faith be as strong as it
ever was ?

AUBIN.

I think, because, though sorrows do not often
last on in us all through life, yet they may re-
vive in us for a time. Indeed, the same misfortune is not the same trouble always. For when
a young man mourns, it is for his one grief.
But when an old man is frightened, it is with a
fearfulness which has grown in him from the
losses and bereavements and pains of a whole
lifetime. When an old man weeps for any thing,
a hundred old sorrows weep from his eyes, many
an old friend lies dead before him, and many a
piece of ill news sounds in his ears afresh. But
still in it all, if he is a Christian, he feels something of the peace of God ; and, O, so sweetly

it feels ! And it is to him as though dead friends lay, one in one chamber, and another in another; and as though one misfortune threatened him, and another mourned to him, only to make him feel the quiet of heaven, how great and sweet it is.

How much Christianity has done for old age ! I think that, of thirty epithets the Romans used to describe old age with, there were only two or three but what were sad or contemptuous. But indeed it is hard even for a Christian not to feel rather sadly over old age, when it becomes decay of the faculties. An old man may remember things of seventy years ago : yet still it is mortifying for him, when he finds himself beginning to forget little things of yesterday. Now, Oliver, what would you say to such a person ?

You say, your memory fails you for common things. But now this is not a thing for you to grieve about. For why should you be remembering much more of the little things of this little life, when you are so nigh the great things of a life that will be infinite ? News, things that happen daily, — these we are to know of, for the sake of the wisdom they help to make in us. But at fourscore years, a man is little the better for recollecting well the countless events of a day ; because whatever wisdom they can teach or inure him to, he must have learned already. And so it is not so much memory that is failing with you, as the earthly purpose of it that is signifying itself fulfilled.

MARHAM.

Thank you, Oliver. What you have said is ingenious, and I trust that it is true, for it is very comforting.

AUBIN.

So many ways, tenderly and solemnly, does old age, as I think, suggest there being certainly a blessed world to come. When old, a man loves God more than when young; and loves him in a more childlike way, — loves him with more wonder, from greater depths, and up greater heights of thought. And this love of himself will God draw back from? Will he draw himself up into his immortality, and leave his human creature yearning after him in vain? No; he never will. This love, of his own making in the soul, will he withdraw from? O, no! And the many things that soften an old man's heart, — what are they, but God's way of making it love himself the better! And in the failure of memory for the little things of to-day and yesterday, and in the weakening of such faculties as are more peculiarly earthly in their use, is not it as though God were loosening the soul for its freer coming to himself? A flower dropping its leaves and turning to seed is very certainly predictive of a summer to come ; and just as certainly do very many of the circumstances of an old man witness to what is to be his renewal hereafter.

MARHAM.

It is as having a Redeemer, that the old man now is so different from what he was among the heathen. In Latin writings, and, I think very likley, in Greek authors also, there is hardly a thing old age is likened to, but is what is painful to think of. But, indeed, even in our modern, our Christian literature, I know few pleasant emblems of the end of life. It is as though experience and nature yielded none. And yet an old man needs the consolation of seeing his face made glorious in glorious mirrors.

AUBIN.

A good old age is a beautiful sight, and there is nothing earthly that is as noble, — in my eyes, at least. And so I have often thought. A ship is a fine object, when it comes up into a port, with all its sails set, and quite safely, from a long voyage. Many a thousand miles it has come, with the sun for guidance, and the sea for its path, and the winds for its speed. What might have been its grave, a thousand fathoms deep, has yielded it a ready way ; and winds that might have been its wreck, have been its service. It has come from another meridian than ours ; it has come through day and night ; it has come by reefs and banks, that have been avoided, and past rocks, that have been watched for. Not a plank has started, nor one timber in it proved rotten. And now it comes like an answer to the prayers of many hearts, — a delight to the owner, a joy to many a sailor's family, and a pleasure to all ashore, that see it. It has been steered over the ocean, and been piloted through dangers, and now it is safe. But more interesting still than this is a good life, as it approaches its three-score years and ten. It began in the century before the present ; it has lasted on through storms and sunshine, and it has been guarded against many a rock, on which shipwreck of a good conscience might have been made. On the course it has taken, there has been the influence of Providence ; and it has been guided by Christ, that day-star from on high. Yes, old age is even a nobler sight than a ship completing a long, long voyage. On a summer's evening, the setting sun is grand to look at. In his morning beams, the birds awoke and sang, men rose for their work, and the world grew light. In his mid-day heat, wheat-fields grew yellower, and fruits were ripened, and a thousand natural purposes were answered, which we mortals do not know of. And in his light, at setting, all things seem

to grow harmonious and solemn. But what is all
this to the sight of a good life, in those years that
go down into the grave ? In the early days of it,
old events had their happening ; with the light of
it, many a house has been brightened ; and under
the good influence of it, souls have grown better,
some of whom are now on high. And then the
closing period of such a life, — how almost awful
is the beauty of it ! From his setting, the sun
will rise again to-morrow ; and he will shine on
men and their work, and on children's children
and their labors. But once finished, even a
good life has no renewal in this world. It will
begin again, but it will be in a new earth, and
under new heavens. Yes, uncle, nobler than
a ship safely ending a long voyage, and sublimer
than the setting sun, is the old age of a just, and
kind, and useful life.

CHAPTER XL.

With stammering lips and insufficient sound,
I strive and struggle to deliver right
That music of my nature, day and night,
With dream and thought and feeling interwoven,
And inly answering all the senses' round,
With octaves of a mystic depth and height,
Which step out grandly to the infinite,
From the dark edges of the sensual ground.

E. B. BROWNING.

AUBIN.

No doubt, there is in men a love of life, and so
life is eternal with them, I believe. For God is
too good ever to have made us love life, had he
intended to have deprived us of it, ever. So
I think. I have been told that it is because
of my great love of life, that I am so greatly
persuaded of the signs which betoken that there
is a life hereafter, to be entered upon from life
here. But indeed I am not self-deceived, in this
way. For I love life but little, as mere living;
and indeed not at all, I think. Only let me know
that the end of all men is everlasting death, and
any time I would go to my grave like going to
bed for ever. I do not think I have ever known
a moment I would not willingly have had be
my last, might it have been so for ever. All

through my life there has been no book so interesting to me, but I could have laid it down at any
page; no conversation so sweet, but I could have
stopped in it at once ; no pleasure so great, but I
could have turned from it any instant, and been
quite willing to die, if it might have been for ever.
And I say now, that if the coffin-lid were to hide
me from the universe for ever, I could ask to
have it made for me to-morrow. And at once I
would have it made ; for I should like the sight
of it, if under it thought was to torture me no
more, and despair was to cease for ever.

MARHAM.

But now, through our Saviour, Jesus Christ, it
is not despair which comes of loving life, but only
more earnestness of faith. But perhaps, Oliver,
it would be better if I could love this life less, and
life immortal more. I love this life too much, I
am afraid.

AUBIN.

I do not think you do, uncle; and I do not
think any man can, in a wise way. My little love
of life is neither excellence nor merit in me.
Chiefly it results from what my life has been : for
never have my circumstances been what I have
felt at home in. However, as a little child, I was
singularly happy. And yet, at seven or eight
years of age, I used to think of death often, especially in the night. I used to think of it only

as ending life; still I looked towards it quietly and fondly almost. "Vanity of vanities, all is vanity." This was in my mind, at twelve years old, quite as mournfully as it is written in the book of Ecclesiastes. I was very fond of play; unusually so; and yet in the midst of a game, sometimes, something would ask me, as though in scorn and pity, "What worth in this is there?" I do not now yearn for death; but it is not because I am in love with this life, but because I know now that death is not death, — is not so much an ending of life as a beginning of it again.

MARHAM.

But, Oliver, you do not mean to say that you do not like living.

AUBIN.

O, no! But as far as I do love life, it is more as thought than as pleasure. Indeed, for any enjoyment of it, I have never loved life. And so, whatever feeling I have of life as being to be immortal, I can trust to confidently; at least, I can trust to it more reasonably than if I hoped to live again, only out of a mere love of enjoying myself. "It is for immortality thou art made"; this is in me no voice of lust, nor of pride, no cry of my own making, but a voice so awful, at times, that, now and then, almost I could rather not know of it.

MARHAM.

Life, life is so dear! It is to me, at least, and

too much so, at times, I am afraid. Oliver, I
wish I could feel more as you do about it.

AUBIN.

There is no occasion for your wishing that, my
dear uncle. It is no virtue that loves life not at
all. Myself I should have loved it better, if I
had had business to mind, and objects for my affections to lay hold of. I am none the worthier
of the life to come, for never having had a fast
hold of the life that now is ; but quite otherwise.
The oak that reaches nighest heaven with its top
is deepest in the earth with its root.

MARHAM.

So it is ; and firmest in it.

AUBIN.

I know, at least I think I do, that I should have
been now more fit for heaven than I am, if for-
merly I had had more friends to love, more pleasures to be gay and grateful in, and more business to be active in. The more right things a
man loves, the lovelier grows his soul. Neighbours, books, friends, pictures, the country, music,
work, — whatever things are good, let a man love,
and he will himself be the better, and so be the
fitter for what is best. Most persons are persuaded that pains assure us of there being an hereafter ; but that pleasures do the same is what very
few feel. Yet it is to be felt, O, so sweetly and
strangely ! Out of his cup of pleasure, let a man

drink only virtuous delight, and drink of it blessing
God the while ; and it will taste like water of life ;
and easily he will believe in there being a river of
it, somewhere, for him to find.

MARHAM.

That is a right thought, Oliver. At least, I like
it. I like the spiritualism of your philosophy,
because it does not often break away from real-
ities. Whatever it is you are seeing with the
eyes of your imagination, it is out of some window in common life that you look the while.
You are like — like — you are like —

AUBIN.

Some astronomer, that plays with his child one
moment, and the next looks millions of miles
away, to remark on which side of Jupiter some
one moon is shining. Or I am like one that
should gather common apples into a golden basket.
But I will tell you what I think of myself. I am
one that stands by the tree of knowledge, longing
for what fruit is on the topmost boughs. Hours
and hours, and for more hours, perhaps, than I
ought, I watch those high branches ; and now and
then, as I know, an apple falls, which I fancy
sometimes that I find.

MARHAM.

Do thoughts, then, grow for you, like fruit, Oliver ?

AUBIN.

Ah, no, no, uncle! Not so easily. And yet to me it does not feel as though my own best thoughts were of my own devising, but rather as though they were mine simply because my mind somehow had been open for them to come into. The best things I have written do not to me read like my own, nor like any body's else ; but like recollections of some bright dream, or of words heard in another world. But my bad thoughts are my own ; they feel altogether my own. And well they may. For when I am wicked I am so for myself, and while thinking of myself, and while I am intent on some interest of my own, some passion of mine, some wish of mine. After some of my best actions, I have felt as though I had been possessed while doing them, divinely possessed. But when I have been vicious, I have been selfish most for myself, and even most myself, I might say, perhaps. Goodness is godliness, God in us. And wickedness is selfishness, a man's self only. In my best seasons I do not know that I am Oliver Aubin ; I am not any body ; I am thought, I am feeling. But if there is any thing wrong in me, it is I, Oliver Aubin, that think it ; I, Oliver Aubin.

MARHAM.

Just now you were going to say something about some travellers' book somewhere.

AUBIN.

At an inn among the Alps, in Switzerland, some Englishman, ill of consumption, wrote in the travellers' book what his feelings of wonder were at the sight of the glaciers ; how he is one who is going across the Alps to die, and yet

> Here steals a moment from Italian sky,
> And stops and wonders on his way to die.

Dying man as he was, he could not feel himself only mortal, but a man of wonder, and awe, and reverence, — feelings that are akin to immortality.

MARHAM.

I have read the passages I asked you to transcribe for me, from those records of ——

AUBIN.

How my sun went black in the sky at mid-day, and hung there an orb of darkness.

MARHAM.

You have arranged the extracts as I suggested. And I have found a motto for them, as you will see ; for I have prefixed it.

CHAPTER XLI.

Hath he not always treasures, always friends,
The good great man?   Three treasures, — Love, and Light,
And calm Thoughts, regular as infants' breath; —
And three firm friends, more sure than day and night, —
Himself, his Maker, and the angel Death.

COLERIDGE.

SEVEN conclusions from a week of sad evenings : —

Sunday. — About the hardships of life a man cannot murmur, and it not be against God.

Monday. — This breath of mine is God's good giving ; and it is health and life in me, as I draw it : but in breathing it out again, so often I make it into sighs against the Giver of it ! I misuse God's air so ! Such a traitor I am this way !

Tuesday. — Misery, misery, O my misery ! So slowly time goes with it ! To-day has been with me like years, like a thousand years : and to-morrow will pass the same way as to-day ; and so will the day after. And it is well, is it not ? For these long days are making my life the longer, almost ages the longer. But so wretched they are ! Yet they are not too wretched to pray in ! O the feelings I have had the last few days ! This weary, weary season ! Nay ; but it is this

precious, precious time! Because of long days
it is not for a mortal to complain, and of sorrowful ones a Christian will not.

Wednesday. — These long, long - days! Ah,
yes! There may well be to me some feeling of
length in them ; for out of their' hours, myself, I
am growing to be immortal, as I trust.

Thursday. — This trouble of mine is God's
loving chastisement. Do I believe this ? Yes,
I do. Then why am I so wretched ? O, there
is many a man, an angel now, that would take
flesh again eagerly, for the sake of carrying this
cross of mine. But what troubles me most is,
not the weight of the cross, but what men may
think of me for having it to carry. But they are
not all my witnesses, nor indeed the chief of
them : for there are others than they about me, a
great cloud of them, though known of only in
spirit. Courage, then! I have angels looking
on ; and I have my Father watching me : and it
is mine to walk in life abreast with martyrs, for
some few steps, at least.

Friday. — O, how dreary, and friendless, and
helpless, and useless my life is! It is as though
I were out in a wilderness ; so lonely, and so sad
I am ! And indeed it is so ; and there comes the
tempter to me. And one time he will have me
weep, because I have not a friend to understand
me. But I keep my tears for my sins. And

another time he tries to embitter me, and make me say that vanity of vanities, life is vanity. But I answer him, that goodness is not vanity, nor is dying for goodness a vanity ; and that I long for the one, and am ready for the other. Nay, thou tempter ! It is by thy coming to me that I know myself. Yes, like Jesus, I too am a soul, I am a spirit for ever. But I have thee to resist, Devil. Thou art one thing to one man, and another to another ; and to wicked and unbelieving souls, hereafter, thou wilt be strange things, unknown of yet. But to me, just this day, thou art poverty. But I will not be daunted by thee so. I can overcome thee, and I will. For I know of a way, through having nothing to possess all things. Courage, my soul ! Be patient and full of faith. Resist the adversary as poverty, and thou wilt overcome him for this life and for ever. For in a godly way, overcoming him in one shape, thou art conquering him in every other form, as wine, as a harlot, as pride, as a mob, as a tyrant, and as despair.

Saturday. — I am overcoming the world itself, by outgrowing the love of it. As a poor man, if I keep free in spirit, and cheerful, then I am getting gold, and silver, and dignities, and thrones beneath my feet ; and I am growing up to the level of principalities and powers in heaven.

CHAPTER XLII.

Ah, yes! the hour is come
When thou must hasten home,
  Pure soul! to Him who calls.
The God who gave thee breath
Walks by the side of Death,
  And naught that step appalls.

Health has forsaken thee;
Hope says thou soon shalt be
  Where happier spirits dwell,
There where one loving word
Alone is never heard, —
  That loving word, *farewell.*
W. S. LANDOR.

AUBIN.

WATER, uncle! a glass of water! Thank you.

MARHAM.

Are you very much worse, Oliver?

AUBIN.

Only for a minute or two; not for more, perhaps. O pain, pain, pain! O the people I
think of now! What was the sacrament of
blood? Was it not when persons mingled their
blood in one cup, and then drank of it, all of
them? Always, till this moment, it has seemed
to me a fantastical proceeding; but it does not
now; for I think I feel now what the first users
of it meant, though I do not know. O, pain is a

strange brotherhood among men! No, uncle, no! you cannot do any thing for me. But do not leave me. O, it is as though flash after flash of the lightning of God were going through me! Dreadful, dreadful, very dreadful! And it is awful, and it is sublime! For the agonies, as they go, say, " Not in vain have we been through you ; not in vain." And the spirit within cannot but believe. It is as though there were a great mystery growing up between me and God, for explanation some time. Just now, my feeling of endurance is very strange ; it is so strange that I would not but know it, very dreadful as the pain is. It is as though I am being afflicted because God cannot help it. You would think this must be wretched despair ; but it is not. God cannot spare me. Do thy will, do thy divine will, do thy will upon me, O God! God pity me! Yes, I know the Lord does pity me. In the mind of God there is pity for me. Yes, God wishes me to bear, is anxious for it, — he, the Father of spirits. O, then I will! and I am strong to do it triumphantly.

MARHAM.

Think of what Jesus Christ must have suffered on the cross.

AUBIN.

Yes, dear uncle, it is in the spirit of that cruci- fixion that I feel as I do. I know myself to be in no torture-house, but in the latter agonies of an immortal birth.   And this is the faith of my soul, through Him, the buried and the risen, the cruci-fied and the ascended.   Thy spirit, thy spirit, O Christ! is my strength, my hope, my oneness with God.   For in thy mind there was wrestled out the victory of those thoughts that come to me so gloriously.   Glory to thee, who art the light of my light, and the victoriousness of my victory in this world !

MARHAM.

Glory, glory to him !

AUBIN.

It is an odd thing for me to be thinking just now, is not it ?   But I am persuaded that the highest consecration of marriage is in the joint en-durance of suffering by husband and wife.

MARHAM.

Yes, in pain our hearts soften towards one another.

AUBIN.

And more than that, our spirits are sublimed.

MARHAM.

Does not talking weaken you, Oliver ?

AUBIN.

No ; it is a little relief from pain, uncle.   O pain, pain !   I love all men more tenderly for suffering with them.   And Jesus, — he is my Saviour, by the form of God he is in, by his wisdom and power ; but it is by his crown of thorns he is my brother ; and it is by his suffering with me, that I have the feeling of God's being my Father.

MARHAM.

Yes, Oliver, you know that suffering is the will of God ; and that without it even the Captain of our salvation could not have been made perfect. It is what we are all born to ; and some of the best of us to the most of it.

AUBIN.

My thoughts are in hospitals, where men lie in agony ; and at sea, where men drown ; and in Austrian prisons, where patriots rot away their lives ; and in what were the dungeons of the Inquisition ; and in what was the Roman circus ; and by bedsides, where young husbands and wives are parting ; and in places where the tender-hearted are helplessly wronged. And to all this, — to this suffering from one another, and from the elements, and from disease, and from death, — we men have been made subject, though not willingly. O, no ! O God, no ! But thou art thyself the reason of it ; and thou hast done it in hope. And it is bondage that ennobles us by our passing through it ; for so we come to the glorious liberty of thy children.

MARHAM.

You are easier now, I hope, Oliver.

AUBIN.

O, yes ! it is subsiding, the pain is. But I am much better than yesterday, and in a day or two I shall be nearly well again.

MARHAM.

What book is that behind your pillow ? It makes you smile.

AUBIN.

It is Martin Luther's Table-Talk. And I was thinking of what Luther said one August afternoon, when he and his Catharine lay ill of a fever : — " God hath touched me sorely, and I have been impatient. But God knoweth better than we ourselves whereto it serveth. Our Lord God doth like a printer, who setteth the letters backwards : we see and feel well his setting, but we shall see the print yonder, in the life to come. In the mean time we must have patience." It is quaintly but very well said ; is it not ?

MARHAM.

Yes, it is.

AUBIN.

Great sufferers in this world are not very rare, and so are no wonder to us ; but our human miseries are mysteries to the angels, and things they desire to look into. How the more ancient sons of God had their birth, there is no knowing. But some of them, perhaps, grew up to their high estate slowly, and surely, and unerringly, and like the full moon, when she rises from behind a grove, and goes up the sky, in a quiet night. O, to some of them, what a sight, what an awe, must be the growth of a soul in this world! There are some of the sons of God, of an age with the morning stars, and older, perhaps; and their growth was, for the time of it, like the shaping of our earth. But the lifetime of a man is only a small part of the duration of an oak, an olive, or a cedar-tree. And what some spirits have been ages growing up to, man has to achieve in a few years ——

MARHAM.

Yes, but not unhelped; and to begin with, made but little lower than the angels, but still a wonder to them, and a mystery, on account of his different creation.

AUBIN.

And what a strange appearance he must be in their spiritual eyes! — free, most free, and yet, invisibly to himself, hung about with the chains of necessity; with the hand of God always offered him, and yet with the thunder of God bursting upon him from time to time, out of the gathered clouds of adversity; most mortal, and most certainly immortal; a creature of a will, now fleshly, now spiritual, and now at last the same with the will of God. But, O, it is a good man suffering must be the wonder of many a heavenly dweller;

he having himself been formed through another discipline than that of endurance, perhaps. And when he hears of earthly agony, he cannot but learn it calmly and cheerfully, and therefore also with holy wonder, as to why this lower creation has been made to groan and travail in pain together. O, there are heavenly spirits, to whom the knowledge of our righteous sufferers must be more prophetic of creative newness than a voice would be, if heard calling down the depths of infinity, to let new worlds be started. Yes, Paul, yes! Thy Lord and Master, and mine, — if we suffer with him, we shall be also glorified together.

CHAPTER XLIII.

Ah! happy spirits that behold
  The King in love divine,
And see, beneath your floor of gold
  The stars and planets shine;
The dim abysses of the air,
And earth's green orb revolving there.

Each hath his proper meed above
  For actions nobly done;
But love that can another love
  Makes ever that her own;
Each hath his own peculiar good,
But shared by the whole brotherhood.

PETER DAMIANUS.

MARHAM.

THE righteous will differ from one another in glory, as the stars do. This we know. Now may not this imply that they will be in separate places, — in regions, some more and some less happy?

AUBIN.

I do not think it does. To every one the spiritual world will be according to what his spirit is.

MARHAM.

I do not understand you, Oliver.

AUBIN.

Is this earth the same thing to all us earthly

dwellers? Is not it one thing to one man, and another to another, and a third thing to a third man? Is not it thousand-fold and million-fold? To one beholder, the earth is a daily revelation of God; while another man is so mere a merchant, that the earth is to him the wide floor of a place of exchange; and the firmament is only the high roof of it. There are gluttons, to whom the world is only a fish-pond, a poultry-yard, a stall for fattening cattle in, and a kitchen garden; and to these men, the seasons, as they change, suggest only thoughts of what fresh dishes may be had. There are wretched persons in London, to·whom the world is simply a place for street-crossings to be swept in. One man is only a farmer, and only more cunning than one of his oxen; while another is a poet, as well as a farmer; and another is a father, as well as being a poet and a farmer; now these three persons see the world in very different lights. On account of his health, one man as he walks the earth feels it under him like the floor of an everlasting home; and another, because he is ill, stands on it like a gravestone; while another, who is hopeful as well as dying, feels the earth under him like a broad stepping-stone to heaven.

MARHAM.

For the dissatisfied man, all life is unsatisfactory; and for one that is contented, the world is full of comforts.

AUBIN.

Yes, and, for the cheerful man, even the easterly wind is musical in the window-crevices, and it makes solemn anthems for him in the woods.

MARHAM.

So it does. And, to a great extent, life is what we think it.

AUBIN.

Day and night, and every moment, there are voices about us. All the hours speak, as they pass; and in every event there is a message to us; and all our circumstances talk with us; but it is in divine language, that worldliness misunderstands, that selfishness is frightened at, and that only the children of God hear rightly and happily.

MARHAM.

True, Oliver, true!

AUBIN.

It is many things to its many dwellers; this world is. It is a home; it is a workshop; it is a place of amusement; it is a school, with trouble and pain for chief teachers in; and for the devout, it is a church to worship in; and for them that have eyes to see, it is the wisdom, and the beauty, and the love of God.

MARHAM.

So it is.

AUBIN.

So, then, if this world is to us what we think it, the next may be to us just what we are fit for, perhaps. And there may be a thousand of us stand together in heaven, and every one of us with a different degree of glorious feeling.

MARHAM.

But we shall all be in sight of God.

AUBIN.

But not all in the same full sight. For now do we all feel God about us the same? No. And so in heaven, there may be one eternal look of blessing on us all, and we all feel it, but not alike.

MARHAM.

One disciple will be a ruler over ten cities, and another over five. This rule of cities is not to be understood literally, of course; and you think it is figurative, when heaven is spoken of as more than one city.

AUBIN.

Perhaps it is. In the Revelation, heaven is said to be only one city, — the New Jerusalem.

MARHAM.

So it is, and in a passage not incidentally, but purposely, descriptive of heaven.

AUBIN.

There is no reason why we should not expect men more and less rewarded, men of many and few talents, to be together hereafter. According to our worthiness of heaven will be our enjoyment of it. This earth is only an occupancy of some seventy years for us, and the round of it is only some few thousand miles, yet it is a different world to every man of many millions in it ; so that the kingdom of heaven may well be a different place to every one of its gainers, for it is infinite and eternal. It will be, — yes ! heaven will be what we feel it, what we are ready to feel. And our feelings are much in our own making. I cannot will my head to be a storehouse of knowledge ; but my heart I can make the issue of what life I please, — holy, most holy, loving, and hopeful, if I choose.

MARHAM.

Yes, and much wisdom comes of loving ; though a man may know largely, and love nothing.

AUBIN.

For admission into heaven, God asks of us nothing impossible. We have a law to keep, — his law. True, we are creatures of frailty, and yesterday, and the dust, while he is God most high. But it is not knowledge, nor the perfection of service, but it is love, that is the fulfilling of the law, — the love of the law, for what of God's is in it, — the love of God, for his godhead's sake, — and the love of man, for what good is in him, or, if not in him yet, for what will be. We cannot all of us be knowing, nor can any of us know very much, but we can love, and as though infinitely.

MARHAM.

Faith, hope, and love, these three, but the greatest of these is love.

AUBIN.

The greatest! Yes, it is. And in that there is all comfort for them that hope to meet again. Love! why should we doubt but it will have its objects? for that faith will have its, we are sure; and love is greater than faith. O, if there is a heaven for our faith, there are friends in it for our love. I have known those who have grown holy through thoughts of the dead. I have known one who, as he prayed, always felt, as it were, the presence of a spirit about him, — one of the blessed vanished. And it was in her spirit he prayed, and was earnest in prayer. Another person I have known, to whom the meeting of her husband was all of heaven, beside God; for he had been the husband of her soul, as well as her youth, and they had suffered much together, but she much more by herself. We are saved by hope, and some of us by the special hope of being with our friends again. So that if there is salvation by hope, our friends whom we so hope for we shall certainly have again.

MARHAM.

We are not to sorrow for the dead as those

that have no hope; now this implies our knowing our friends hereafter; because our grief is for their having been taken from us, and not for their having been taken into happiness.

AUBIN.

To know our dear friends again is not a fantastical nor an unreasonable wish; it is a hope that is quite rational, and altogether natural to us, as loving and thinking and immortal souls. Our nature is not our own making, but God's. Our souls are made so as to long and hope for sight of the lost; and so naturally do they do so, that it is as though God made them do it. So I cannot doubt our having our friends again.

MARHAM.

Nor I; for that we shall be with them hereafter is often implied in Scripture, though not so often said. But is reunion with our friends so certain as you think, or only as a hope of the soul?

AUBIN.

Yes, uncle, it is, as long as God is God, or till we see creatures falsely made, and in the fields, the woods, and all over the world, thirsting and in agony for a liquid that does not exist, and never will. God would never have let us long for our friends with such a strong and holy love, if they were not waiting for us. They would never be all heaven to so many of us, if their dear faces were not as sure as heaven.

MARHAM.

So one would think, and perhaps not without great reason.

AUBIN.

This universe is no falsehood ; for we have not found it so, but a truth ; so we will not distrust those purer wishes, which, indeed, are promptings of our nature. We long to see and know our dear friends in the next life ; and so we shall have them. And we ought not to fear otherwise ; for we ought to believe better of God than to do that. But suppose it ; the friends I have had, I am never to know again ; so it is God's will, — his blessed will, — the will one prays may be done. That Divine will is better than my wish ; it is many times, a thousand times, an infinity, better. Why, now, as soon as I say heartily, " Thy will be done in this," at once I feel it will be done, the way of my heart. I cannot claim to know my lost friends in the next world, nor can I tell how I am to know them ; but as soon as I trust in God to let me know them, if it be his good will, then I do not doubt, and I am sure of their company. O the peace it is to trust in God ! Sometimes, uncle, I think I will never reason about the future at all, but only pray God his will may be done.

MARHAM.

This is All Souls' Day, Oliver. It is not

much kept now, nor hardly remembered, anywhere, I think. But when I was a boy, the children used to go about repeating two or three
verses at people's doors.

AUBIN.

They are the souls that have been in this world,
and that are now out of it, that are the strength
of our faith in the world to come.

MARHAM.

You mean, it is their waiting us in the next
world that makes it less shadowy, and more real.

AUBIN.

Yes, uncle. And there are some greater souls,
the very thought of whom is an increase of faith.
Men depart this world, many of them having
cheated it, and nearly all of them owing it largely.
But now and then dies one who has made the
world his debtor, and the ages of the world his
witnesses. Such a man, there is no doubting, is
entered into the joy of his Lord, and into a rule
like that over many cities. Joy to him, and
thanks! Ay, many thanks! For his is a high
estate of reward; and by our being kindred to
him in soul, however distantly, we feel certain of
some happiness, though lower than his, much
lower, perhaps. O Pascal! thou wert' pure in
heart in this world, and now thou art in full sight
of God. This I feel; and by this feeling I am
bold to trust that every one, who has lived at all

akin to thy purity, will be purified, so as at last to
be of kin with thee in happiness. O John Milton ! thou art among the angels and the seraphs,
that were once thy glorious song ; and this world
is dear to them, for what thou thyself wert in it.
O, how sublimely dost thou move in heaven, the
love of saints and heroes, and spirits multitudi-
nous ! And I, — I feel as though it were impossible for me to be shut out of heaven for ever and
utterly, even if it were only for the sake of the
dear language common to us both.

MARHAM.

There is right feeling in what you have been
saying. But I am not sure ——

AUBIN.

Of my theology, uncle ? But I am myself certain of its soundness. And what is my certainty ?
The spirit of God. For it testifies within me,
that my love of the good and the great is predestination to their company, earlier or later.

MARHAM.

The love of the best and greatest is.

AUBIN.

You mean God.

MARHAM.

Yes, and I mean also the first-born of us
creatures.

AUBIN.

Who wore our nature among the Jews so

grandly, so like a king and a servant both; and whose heart never changed from what it was in the littleness of childhood, while out of his manly mouth proceeded gracious words to be wondered at, — a son of man in his birth, but in his death the Son of God, — Jesus Christ, through whose life as a man humanity itself has grown divine. Through his spirit in my spirit does my spirit feel itself in God. And so glory to him, over angels and seraphs, and in his exaltation above principalities and powers! Glory to the first-born of us brethren! Glory to him, in the bosom of the Father! And because he is there, and I know it, I am myself strong to trust that I shall see it. " Listen, listen ! " says my heart within me. And, O, like words out of heaven sounds what is wish and promise both, — " Grace be with all them that love our Lord Jesus Christ in sincerity." And it is with them ; and the love of Christ will be the sight of him.

THE END.

Lightning Source UK Ltd.
Milton Keynes UK
UKHW010917050119
334854UK00007B/1293/P